ALSO BY PENN JILLETTE

God, No!: Signs You May Already Be
an Atheist and Other Magical Tales

Sock

BY PENN JILLETTE AND MICKEY D. LYNN

How to Cheat Your Friends at Poker:
The Wisdom of Dickie Richard

BY PENN JILLETTE AND TELLER

Penn & Teller's How to Play in Traffic

Penn & Teller's How to Play with Your Food

Cruel Tricks for Dear Friends

A PLUME BOOK

EVERY DAY IS AN ATHEIST HOLIDAY!

PENN JILLETTE has been one half of the Emmy Award–winning, world-famous magic duo Penn & Teller for more than thirty-five years. He is the author of *God, No!* and the novel *Sock*, as well as several books cowritten with Teller. He has appeared everywhere in the media, from Howard Stern to Piers Morgan to the op-ed pages of *The New York Times*, *The Wall Street Journal*, and the *Los Angeles Times* to *The Celebrity Apprentice*, *Dancing with the Stars*, *Numb3rs*, *MTV Cribs*, and *Chelsea Lately*. As part of Penn & Teller, he has been featured more than twenty times on *Late Show with David Letterman* and on *The Simpsons*, *Friends*, *Top Chef*, *Late Night with Jimmy Fallon*, and more. Jillette is the producer, with director Paul Provenza, of *The Aristocrats*. He cohosted the controversial series *Penn & Teller: Bullshit!*, which was nominated for thirteen Emmy Awards. Jillette lives with his family in Las Vegas.

Praise for *Every Day Is an Atheist Holiday!*

"[Jillette's] words are funny, dignified, and make perfect sense. An outspoken wordsmith offers more intelligent, humorous and against-the-grain perspectives."
—*Kirkus Reviews*

"Jillette, the taller and more verbose half of Penn & Teller, follows up 2011's *God, No!* with this further exploration of his own atheism . . . allowing his intelligence and razor-sharp wit to shine through. . . . [W]ill surely appeal not only to Penn & Teller fans, but also to readers who welcome the opportunity to examine their own deeply held beliefs from a new angle."
—David Pitt, *Booklist*

"His books are where we get the unfiltered Penn. . . . Who wouldn't want advice about April Fools' Day from America's trickster laureate? . . . The best parts [of the book] are random, profane but delicious insider stories that few others can deliver."

—*The Wall Street Journal*

"Readers will enjoy extremely funny stories from a man who loves his family and doesn't let his celebrity go to his head."

—Associated Press

"Penn Jillette is a twenty-first-century Lord of Misrule: big, boisterously anarchic, funny, Rabelaisian, impossible—and unique. There isn't—couldn't be—better not be—anybody like him."

—Richard Dawkins

"Giddily blasphemous . . . Jillette the author sounds like Jillette the performer—sharp and subversive. . . . There is a forceful intelligence at work here."

—*The Washington Post Book World*

"Thoughtful and provocative . . . The man can really tell a story: he is wonderful at finding the right vivid image, the right hilarious detail."

—NPR.org

EVERY DAY IS AN ATHEIST HOLIDAY!

MORE MAGICAL TALES FROM THE BESTSELLING AUTHOR OF *GOD, NO!*

PENN JILLE

WITHDRAWN

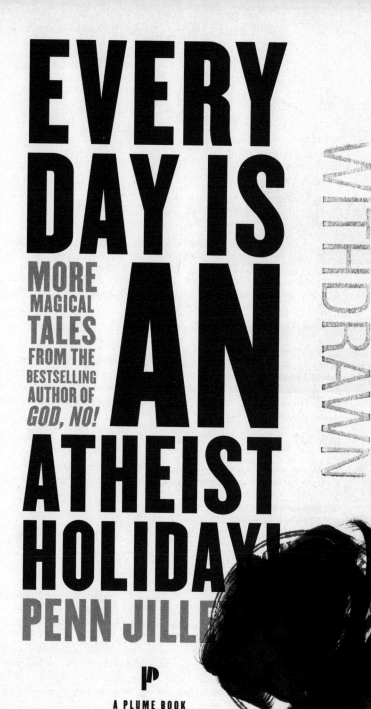

P

A PLUME BOOK

PLUME
Published by the Penguin Group
Penguin Group (USA) LLC
375 Hudson Street,
New York, New York 10014

USA | Canada | UK | Ireland | Australia | New Zealand | India | South Africa | China
penguin.com
A Penguin Random House Company

First published in the United States of America by Blue Rider Press, a member of Penguin Group
(USA) Inc., 2012
First Plume Printing 2013

REGISTERED TRADEMARK—MARCA REGISTRADA

THE LIBRARY OF CONGRESS HAS CATALOGED THE DUTTON EDITION AS FOLLOWS:
Every day is an atheist holiday! : more magical tales from the author of God, no! / Penn Jillette.
p.   cm.
ISBN 978-0-399-16156-8 (hc.)
ISBN 978-0-14-218027-3 (pbk.)
1. Religion—Humor.   2. Atheism—Humor.   3. American wit and humor.   I. Title.
PN6231.R4I546   2012   2012035920

. . . . of America

. . . 3   2   1

. . . . Stephanie Huntwork

DEDICATED TO

FEBRUARY 28, 1966
JUNE 3, 2005
MAY 22, 2006

CONTENTS

EVERY DAY IS AN ATHEIST HOLIDAY!

EVERY DAY IS AN ATHEIST HOLIDAY

Joy to the world, the Lord is come!
Let earth receive her King;
Let every heart prepare Him room,
And heav'n and nature sing,
And heav'n and nature sing,
And heav'n, and heav'n, and
  nature sing.

Joy to the earth, the Savior reigns!
Let men their songs employ;
While fields and floods, rocks, hills,
  and plains
Repeat the sounding joy,
Repeat the sounding joy,
Repeat, repeat, the sounding joy.

No more let sins and sorrows grow,
Nor thorns infest the ground;
He comes to make his Blessings
  flow
Far as the curse is found,
Far as the curse is found,
Far as, far as, the curse is found.

He rules the world with truth
  and grace,
And makes the nations prove
The glories of His righteousness,
And wonders of His love,
And wonders of His love,
And wonders, and wonders,
  of His love.

LYRICS BY ISAAC WATTS

THIS IS NOT A HALF-ASSED XMAS SONG. It's not at all secular Coca-Cola Christmas. This is authentic Christmas jive. The music was either adapted from a song by Handel or ripped off from part of his *Messiah*.

The melody descends right down the major scale on its way to hell but lands firmly on the saved tonic. When the Sex Pistols's music descended directly down the scale, the lyrics were "No future," and those clever boys go back up and start down again a few times until they land on the tonic with "for you." I'm not going to get too programmatic with "Joy to the World." It is a descending scale, but it's major and confident and root landing makes it safe and jubilant. The music is consonant with joy in the world.

But it's not about joy *in* the world. It's about joy *to* the world, and there is a world of difference there. I've read the Bible and I've listened carefully to all of the popular Christmas carols. I enjoy listening to lyrics. I've listened to the "Theme from *Shaft*" a lot and it's an almost perfect song. It's recorded with a full orchestra including two wah-wah guitars. Yes, two wah-wahs. You know that the brown-chicken-brown-chicken-brown-chicken part is wah-wah, but the other guitar is wah-wah too. If Beethoven were writing today, he wouldn't consider an ensemble without two wah-wah guitars to be a proper orchestra.

Isaac Hayes puts that quadruple wah orchestra to use to get the perfect classy, funky, sexy sound. He gives us a few measures of hi-hat for nothing, and the vocal doesn't even start until we're knocking on two minutes. The lyrics start out just right with rhetorical questions that are still answered with "Shaft." It's lush and inspiring and then . . . it turns into an Italian air show as the wings come off with one sloppy line. "He's a complicated man, but no one understands him but his woman." What? "He's a complicated man BUT no one understands him but his woman?" Why is the first "but" in that line? How the fuck does that conjunction introduce something contrasting or contrary to what has already been stated? Huh? Are we to be-

lieve that complicated men are usually understood by most everyone
other than their women? The word should not be "but." "He's a
complicated man, AND no one understands him but his woman" is
not very good either. The only being understood by his woman
doesn't really add information. I guess you could try "He's a complicated man THEREFORE no one understand him but his woman,"
or "He's a complicated man ERGO no one understands him but
his woman," but those seem a little precious and double the sylla-
bles. "Consequently" is way too long—you don't want a four-syllable
word in pop music unless you've got the triple single syllable double
negative of "can't get no" to take the curse off your "satisfaction."
"Consequently" is also not exactly the right word. His complication
doesn't directly cause the lack of understanding; they're really one
and the same. It's just restating the idea to me, which is what's
so wrong with the "but." "Thus," "hence," or even "so" would make
sense if Isaac needed one syllable there, but I don't feel the need. I
would use nothing. "He's a complicated man. No one understands
him but his woman." That's fine, one but, one woman, no woman
no cry—very Bob Marley. Do a full stop after "complicated man" and
it will strengthen the idea; just let it hang there. Then right into "No
one understands him but his woman." Great.

Just when I'm confused by why a complicated man would nor-
mally be understood by people other than his woman, Mr. Hayes
throws me another curve. I would have let this one slide by if the
sandpaper of his "but" hadn't sensitized my song safecracking finger-
tips. For most of the song, the excellent backup singers (one of them
Telma Hopkins from Tony Orlando and Dawn—and Tony isn't a private dick who is a sex machine to all the chicks and that's damn right)
answer Isaac with "Shaft" and then one "shut your mouth" after

Isaac almost says "motherfucker." Hayes explains that he was just talking about Shaft and they affirm that they can dig it, and I'm sure they can, even post–Dawn Telma.

The only other time they depart from just singing the surname "Shaft" is after my hated line with that confusing "but." Right after that line, they add his given name before his surname and sing, "John Shaft" (no one mentions Shaft's middle name, which I've heard is "Troy"). This means the full line with background becomes, "He's a complicated man, but no one understands him but his woman, John Shaft." Once you hear the chorus response of "John Shaft" as an appositive to "his woman," it's hard to ever disconnect it again. It certainly makes sense that a complicated African-American man could have a woman named John. Maybe transgendered, or a butch nickname, or named by the Man as some sort of weird racial commentary. What do I know? To me it would be a fine place for them to sing "Mrs. Shaft," or if that's not what the people want, maybe "Ms. Shaft," although if you're fighting the Man, you might not want to adopt your husband's name at all. That's a different generation's battle and that brings us to my buddy Richie Rich's suggestion that the line be "He's a complicated man—no one understands him but his mother, Mrs. Shaft." The meter fits and it makes sense on every front. If he really is that complicated, it seems like even his woman, John Shaft, might have trouble understanding him, but his mom, Mrs. Shaft, would certainly understand her sex machine son.

I've carried on publicly about Shaft almost as much as I've carried on about "Frosty the Snowman." When the remake or reimagining or re-cashing-in of Shaft came out with the groovy leather coat, I was very excited that Isaac Hayes was redoing the song. I figured that Isaac was going to address my little quibbles and finally perfect the song. I attended the opening night and listened carefully, and there it was: "He's a complicated man, *BUT* no one understands him but his woman, John Shaft." What the f—?

Watch your mouth?

I'm just talking about word usage!

I don't remember anything else from the movie. Right before Isaac died, someone called my radio show and said that Isaac had done a version on some situation comedy where he sang it my way. They played it over the phone, but I can't find it. I don't know how high on Isaac's bucket list pleasing me with his lyrics was, so maybe it was a prank.

Now for "Joy to the World" with a very complicated savior who's an anti-sex machine to all the Catholic chicks: this is a Christmas song that every American Christian I've ever heard about is fine with. They can dig it. Right on! They're protective of this song. When Charlie Sheen sang a parody of it on *Two and a Half Men,* "Joy to the world, I'm getting laid," there was a big hoopla from a couple people calling themselves "leagues" and "associations" but who were really writing with crayons, bitter and alone in their garages. They complained that this was a song about the birth of Jesus, and it was being parodied as a "Joy to Fornication." Well, at least there is some joy in fornication; there sure ain't none in "Joy to the World."

The lyrics are not about the birth of Jesus. This is not "Away in the Manger" or (as children always sing it) "We Three Kings of Orientare." This is not about the birth of Jesus. This is about "Jesus 2, the Return—Electric Boogaloo." It was written by Isaac Watts (See? The same first name as the composer of "Theme from *Shaft,*" and you thought it was a random digression—fuck you), and is based on the 98th Psalm, and is all about Jesus' triumphant return to Earth at the end of times. The big Christian "Told ya so!" So, where is the joy? There really isn't any joy now, here on Earth, not in this world, is there? Not in this song.

> *No more let sins and sorrows grow,*
> *Nor thorns infest the ground*

If you think I love discussing the lyrics of "Theme from *Shaft*," that's nothing compared with how excited I am to segue into the saying "The exception proves the rule." Oh man, feel how hard I am! I know you're reading a book, so we're time traveling, but if you ever bump into me after a show or on the street or something, you just ask me to talk about "The exception proves the rule" and then reach down, grab my crotch, and feel how hard I am. I get as hard about "The exception proves the rule" as I get limp with the misuse of "begs the question" or Phil Collins.

I hope no one reading this book thinks that "The exception proves the rule" means that if you have an exception, it means the rule is true. That's just bugnutty. I had it explained to me as "The exception *tests* the rule." Also not true. The exception does not *test* the rule—it disproves the rule. In its proper use, "The exception proves the rule" is a legal concept, and it's important. If you were to say to me, "No, you can't fuck me in the ass on Saturdays," that implies there's a rule that says I can fuck you in the ass on some other day or days. The example usually given is parking signs. If a parking sign says you can't fuck it in the ass on alternate sides of the street from three to four p.m. on weekdays, it means you can fuck it in the ass all other times. You wouldn't need an exception if there weren't a rule. If you sign a lease that says you're not allowed to have any loud parties on weeknights, that means you can have loud parties on weekends. It doesn't matter—you'll be out in the parking space with that slutty parking sign most nights anyway.

Every good thing in "Joy to the World" is an exception that proves the rule. The joy itself is after the lord is come. Before the lord is come, no joy. Before the lord is come, before the end times, it's all thorns and sorrow. Even when the lord comes, he makes the nations prove his righteousness and what's that going to entail? If the rest of the Bible is any indication, and Jesus never negated anything in the Old Testament, it probably means genocide.

"Joy to the World" is one big exception to the rule of pain and suffering on Earth before our lord and savior comes back. The thing about religious holidays is that they aren't about how good and happy life is. Far from it. Religious holidays are about how bad life was or how good the way distant future or even the afterlife is going to be. The "Joy to the World" is going to come at the end times. Jesus was born in a manger, and his heavenly father forced his horrible tortured death so that anyone who believed in him would experience joy either after they died or right when everyone else was going to die and suffer. It's not joy *in* the world, it's joy *to* the world, and that joy gets here in the future. Way in the future . . . like never is way in the future.

They say this cat, Jesus, is a bad mother . . .

Shut your mouth.

But I'm just talking about Jesus. In his booklet, there's little joy in this life. The Prince of Peace is not a barrel of laughs. I've read the New Testament; there isn't much stop and smell the roses. There isn't much playing with those groovy little Cars toys on the iPad with your son. There isn't much joy in this life at all. There's lots of "forsake your family and come with me." There's a lot about getting your reward in the afterlife.

You don't have to go to the Bible for this POV; just stay with the Christmas carols that flood the ears of Christians, Jews, Muslims, Scientologists, and atheists alike for about a quarter of the year—where is the fucking joy in this life? "O Little Town of Bethlehem" is all "in this world of sin" up in your face. "Silent Night" is full of quaking shepherds reminded that heaven is far away and it's just the dawn of redeeming grace. "Away in a Manger" gives us "Bless all the dear children in Thy tender care and take us to heaven to live with Thee there." You've got to go way back to Lou Reed and the Velvet Underground's "Sweet Jane" to get more dismal than that, but in Lou's case it's some evil mothers (Shut your mouth!) who are saying "Life is just to die." Even the rock-and-roll animal on heroin is tame compared with that buzzkill lord Jesus Christ. "O Holy Night" sings of the thrill of hope, but no joy right now. "O, Come All Ye Faithful" just commands that we fall on our knees and adore him, not that he's going to do jackshit for us. I'm not cherry-picking, or in this case, pit-picking; they're all like this. "The First Noel" talks about how hard the wise men worked to find him and then fell to their knees. "The Dreidel Song" is about playing with a top—it's seasonal—but it's not a religious song. Gaiety is not the backbone of Jewish holidays.

Christmas carols are full of North Korea shit. Our highest incarnation of the revolutionary comradely love must be praised, but where is the joy? It's just around the corner and we're starving.

In *Alice in Wonderland*, Lewis Carroll invents the idea of the un-birthday. If we celebrated those we'd have 365 more (in a leap year) un-birthdays than birthdays. Atheists have always had the corner on un-holidays. Christmas, Easter, Good Friday, Ramadan, Rosh Hashanah, the day Tom Cruise had sex with a woman are all holidays in some religion, but they're never a celebration of life. The joy is the exception that proves the rule. It's the celebration of a joy that we don't have.

The word "holiday" comes from "holy day," and "holy" means "exalted and worthy of complete devotion." By that definition, all days are holy. Life is holy. Atheists have joy every day of the year, every holy day. We have the wonder and glory of life. We have joy in the world before the lord is come. We're not going for the promise of life after death; we're celebrating life before death. The smiles of children. The screaming, the bitching, the horrific whining of one's own children. The glory of giving or receiving a blow job. Sunsets, rock and roll, bebop, Jell-O, stinky cheese, and offensive jokes.

For atheists, everything in the world is enough and every day is holy. Every day is an atheist holiday. It's a day that we're alive.

SOMETIMES A SHEET IS NOT JUST A GHOST

I LIKE THE FEW CHRISTIANS WHO STILL HATE HALLOWEEN because they think it's a pagan holiday. It shows a commitment to history that mirrors my wife's dislike of Xmas. To me both holidays are pretty secular. Halloween in the USA is just a big money day for retailers. It's a chance to sell more superhero shit and let women be slutty and men dress like women and . . . be slutty. It's a slutty fucking holiday.

My wife and I used to go to Halloween fetish balls (why do fetish people have such big balls? Because so many of them like to dance). We never officially decided to not go to them anymore; we just haven't been in a while. We aren't worried, as we should be, about embarrassing our children. We just stopped going because our children wake up early in the morning.

The last fetish ball we went to was on the Halloween right after the only Houdini Halloween séance we ever went to. Every year, Sid Radner, the big Houdini expert, used to honor Houdini's wishes and have a Halloween séance to see if Houdini could come back from the dead. Now Sid is dead, and I guess they still do the séances in hopes that Sid can help Houdini fulfill his promise in case they're both stuck somewhere in the afterlife.

Houdini said repeatedly that if anyone could come back from the dead, he would. No matter what the cost to his everlasting soul, Houdini would come back and bring the proof to the living. Believers took this to mean that Houdini believed in life after death. Atheists, or at least this atheist, took it to mean, "If there's a fucking snowball in hell, I'll be the one to fill it with gravel and throw it at god's ass." I don't know for sure whether Houdini believed in an afterlife, but just to be clear, I don't.

Sid invited Penn & Teller to the séance, and I took Emily along (I could have said I took my wife, but I don't remember whether we were married then). We would get to be part of the jive séance and we were going to have a chance to meet Dorothy Young. Ms. Young was the last living person who toured with Houdini. She was seventeen when she started on the road with him as an assistant. She got the job after she danced a Charleston during the audition. Dorothy died in 2011 at 103 years old. I'm so glad I got to meet her. We also met George Hardeen, Houdini's brother's grandson. The second half of Houdini's career was spent busting phony spiritualists (redundant). He would send his crew in disguise, or if he could get a good enough disguise, he would sneak in himself. They would watch the séance, figure out the tricks, and explain how it was done in his show in the same town that night. Houdini was a motherfucker. Some other folks were at the séance, but none with as much of a direct connection to Houdini. Houdini was very straitlaced and uptight about sex. One of the reasons that some of the spiritualists drove Houdini full-on bugnutty was that they did really sexy stuff. Spiritualists were way beyond Halloween slutty. Some of them would do their séances in see-through robes that were left wide open in the front and the "ectoplasm," gooey manifestations from the other world, came out of their pussies. The sitters would reach in and feel. Yup. No kidding. I certainly could make this shit up, but I'm not. The pure sluttiness of this religion made Harry way uptight. For me, well, it could have made me a believer for a night.

Old Gregor Mendel, the father of modern genetics, may have cheated some of his genetic pea work to make it a little too perfect, but even though we got no evidence of life after death in that séance, we got a lot of anecdotal evidence for genetics. As we milled around, waiting to see if we could contact Harry in the afterworld (much less likely than Godot showing up) and chatted with the other sitters, there was George, the closest living relative to Houdini. George looked a lot like the busts of Great-uncle Houdini that I have all around my home, known as the Slammer.

Why do I have busts of Houdini all over my house? James Randi is my hero. James Randi is the modern Houdini except better. Okay, Houdini was born in Budapest and Randi was born in Canada and Randi never got quite as famous, but Randi does the busting of psychics, faith healers, mind readers and other assholes better than Houdini. Maybe Randi is able to bust a little more bullshit because he's able to smell it from Houdini's giant shoulders. If it weren't for Randi, there would be no Penn & Teller. Randi taught us that you could spend your life studying how to lie and use that to tell the truth. That's our goal. Teller and I were down visiting Randi in Florida at the James Randi Educational Foundation, and as he was giving us a tour of the library he showed us his bust of Houdini, in a sealed case. Randi bragged that this was the only bust in existence. It was a copy of the original bust from the Houdini Museum in Niagara Falls. Randi had sneakily made a copy of it and then the Houdini Museum burned down (Randi's alibi checks out). Randi was so proud of this unique bust that we had to fuck with him. After Randi went home that night, Teller and I went through the Yellow Pages at our hotel (this was a long time ago) and found someone in South Florida who did plaster casting (Cindy, *the* plaster caster of rock star cocks—you can get Hendrix for a couple thousand bucks—was too far north). Later that night (or very, very early the next morning), we broke into the James Randi Educational Foundation, broke into the case and got our hired plaster casters to spend all night making an exact cast of Randi's soon-to-be-not-unique Houdini bust. We were so scared we'd fuck up Randi's priceless artwork by bringing in strangers to handle it, but . . . we *had* to fuck with him. We stayed up all night getting the cast perfect.

Morning broke, we ushered out our hired guns, cleaned up, put the bust back in the case, sealed everything up, and met Randi for breakfast. We mentioned nothing. Randi didn't notice we hadn't slept—we were tired from 1986 through the end of the century anyway. Teller and I got the cast secretly shipped back to Vegas and had copies made. A few years later when Randi visited us, both our houses were filled with exact copies of his unique bust. We had dozens of them all over. We didn't say a word about them, waiting for Randi to notice. Randi never said a word. I couldn't wait for him to ask where we got them so I could say, "Oh, those old things? They're nothing special, you can buy them at any cheap-shit shop." But Randi never asked. He never said a word about the busts. Never. You don't fuck with Shady, 'cause Shady will fucking kill you. I will never beat Randi at anything.

George Hardeen looked just like that bust of Houdini, straitlaced like his great-uncle. George had no date. George was standing alone, wearing a suit and tie. He spoke of the legal work he was doing with his charity for Native Americans. He is a good man. He would have been offended if a spiritualist had stripped naked and shot ectoplasm out of her pussy. Not me. I come from different stock.

Houdini didn't show up at the séance. Emily and I left the Houdini séance and went directly to our last fetish party to date. It seemed that the slutty dead spiritualists were more likely to show up and spew their ectoplasm at the fetish ball than Houdini was to show up at the séance, but neither happened.

Shortly after that, and not directly related to that fetish party, we had children. In the years before children seize the Halloween slutty, the holiday is all about candy, superheroes, kitty cats, and princesses. There's a picture that news stories sometimes use for Penn & Teller where Teller is smiling like a Vegas headliner and I'm wearing kitty-cat ears and painted-on whiskers. It was taken at a red carpet at the opening of Criss Angel's Vegas dance show. I didn't want to go, I wanted to continue trick-or-treating with my family, but my job was to go to this press opening. I kept my kitty-cat outfit on in protest of Criss and to show solidarity with my family. Because of the pictures taken that night, some people think Teller works with the drummer from Kiss.

I liked that our family were all kitty cats. I liked that we just drew on whiskers and had little kitty-ear headbands. I liked that our whole family matched. I love dressing alike. I like it in the Penn & Teller show and I love it in families. Our children are different sexes and eleven months apart. If we had had twins of the same sex, child services would have me in custody, because unless restrained, I would force my twins to dress alike. I want our whole family to dress alike. When I went to London once, I brought back matching hats for my whole family, but I couldn't get us all to wear them at the same time.

Before I was married, after any steady girlfriend had bugged me enough to take a vacation with her, I would fly us to Hawaii, have a big fight, and leave her there while I came home and got back to work. It's a good way to break up—it's over, she's in Hawaii, and I'm working. Everyone is happy. Before I started the fight and got ready to split, I would always buy myself a Hawaiian shirt and my girlfriend a matching sexy muumuu (I've had girlfriends who could look sexy even in a muumuu) and try to get her to wear it out with me so we'd be matching. I love matching Hawaiian tourist clothes on couples. I go to Disneyland and Disney World mostly to watch my children have fun. The only other enjoyment I get is seeing the foreign tourist families all dressed alike. Fuck, I love that.

The kitty-cat year was the only year that I got my way. After that the children wanted different costumes for Halloween. The next year, my daughter, Mox, wanted to be a princess. I was on some stupid anti-commercialization-of-Halloween jag ("Let's put the Christ back in Halloween?" What was I thinking?) and my son, Zz, and I agreed we would be simple ghosts. We would just wear sheets. I had some sort of *Peanuts* cartoon image in mind—just take a sheet, cut holes in it for the eyes, and you had a ghost outfit. Because I'm a rich asshole, I didn't even take old sheets. I bought a new little and a big sheet, and I made us matching Halloween costumes. Even though it was just cutting four holes in two sheets I was really proud. This was going to be a real old-fashioned homemade Halloween for my son and me. I was excited about going trick-or-treating and matching my little boy.

At this time, I had affected the wearing of a kind of straw fedora. In my head, I looked like Sinatra; in the mirror I looked like Junior Samples from *Hee Haw*. (Don't you fucking knock *Hee Haw*. I know for a fact Bob Dylan watched it, and those Hee Haw Honeys had some serious hayracks.) What could be better? I'd just cut holes in a sheet for my eyes, put on my straw fedora, and we'd be handmade ghosts. None of this costume shop commercial jive.

That Halloween morning, I got up stupid early. When you get off work at about midnight, drive home, unwind, read a bit in the bathtub and doze off gently at about four a.m., that seven-thirty a.m. alarm comes quicker than a nineteen-year-old at his first fetish ball. I was tired, but I had promised I would go to the kids' school and read a Halloween story to my daughter's class. I was to be the "Mystery Reader." The idea was that a student's mom or dad would go in costume and read a story, and then there would be the joyous revelation that the Mystery Reader was one of their parents. I was very excited. I was sure my distinctive and street-damaged carny voice would give me away, and I anticipated watching Mox figure it out through the eyeholes of my sheet.

My children go to a bullshit fancy-ass MILF/DILF uniform private school, and I arrived at the desk. "I'm the Mystery Reader today." I was wearing my straw hat, but no costume.

"That's great—do you have a mask?"

"Nope, I have better than that." I was proud. "I made my own costume, and I made one for my son too." I indicated the sheet in my hand.

"Okay, well, put it on before you go into the class. You don't want your little girl to recognize you."

I took off my hat, put the sheet over my head, lined up my eyeholes, and put my hat back on. The idea of a ghost wearing a Sinatra hat thrilled me. I was a ghost with a hat. Work boots, jeans, a sheet and a straw hat. I was ready to go.

The receptionist gasped. She was horrified. I was going to say, *Hey, it's not really a ghost. It's just me, Moxie's dad!* But her reaction wasn't right. She wasn't afraid of a ghost. And it wasn't fear she was feeling; it was shock and disgust. She hated my ghost costume: what was up?

Behind the receptionist's desk was a reflective window. Through the sheet's eyeholes, I could see myself in costume. I had shown up at my child's school dressed as a member of the Ku Klux Klan. Granted, my sheet didn't have the perfectly hateful pointy pope top, but . . . I was wearing my hat. My *straw* hat, so there could have been a point there.

I pulled the sheet off. I had no idea what to say. Just then, my daughter's teacher came out, dressed as a cute little bumblebee. She hadn't chosen any international symbols of hate for her Halloween costume. She was not a bee with a swastika on her chest. The sheet was off by the time she saw me, so she could tell that I was Penn, not a KKK member. The cute bee beckoned me, "You all set? The children are very excited for their Mystery Reader. Mox has no idea it's you. This is going to be great. Do you have your costume?"

"Yes, I'm gonna be a ghost. I'm a ghost. It's a sheet with eyes cut out, I'm a ghost."

"Great. C'mon."

My blood ran cold. I was so embarrassed and guilty. I didn't know what to do. "But . . . When a guy my size puts on a sheet . . . I don't look only like a ghost . . . It's a sheet, I look kind of like . . . Well, I'm wearing a sheet."

"You'll be fine, the children are excited." She didn't get it.

"I look kind of, you know, KKK."

"What do you mean?"

I put on my sheet and hat and looked out the eyeholes.

"Oh my god!" She covered her mouth. The teachers at this fancy-ass school are not supposed to use the lord's name in vain, even though that's the only way one can use any lord's name.

"What do I do?" I thought maybe she'd have a cuddly, non-racist bear costume for a 6'7", 300-pound man in her crafts closet.

"The children are waiting for you. You need to come in . . . But why did you wear that to school? That's not funny."

"I'm a ghost."

"Well, just come in, I guess."

I followed her in. The children saw me and got very excited. I sat down and read some Disney jive about Mickey's not-scary Halloween or something. I had to pull the sheet against my face to see the print through the eyeholes. One of the teachers reluctantly snapped a picture of me reading. I was so embarrassed by looking like a KKK member that I was sweating through the sheet. My stomach was in knots. My breath was heating up my face under the sheet. I was able to feel my blood in my face. I was blushing, which the KKK says is one of the signs of white superiority. In the Bible, Adam is able to show shame by the blood in his face, and white supremacists latch onto that. I sure was feeling shame, but there was no superiority in it.

Then I looked out and saw Moxie. My daughter had started to recognize the husky, scratchy, slightly too-high voice of her daddy. She was beaming. She was thrilled about Mickey and about Halloween and about her daddy, who was never up this early in the morning, reading a story to her whole class. She squealed, "That's my daddy, the Mystery Reader is my daddy."

My blood went back to being evenly distributed. I took off the hat and the sheet and Mox ran into my arms and I held her. I held her and laughed and cried a little. I laughed because I loved her so much and I cried because I loved her so much. I laughed because she didn't know anything about the KKK, so I was okay. I cried with relief and joy because these children and I had an African-American president. Then I laughed a little more because I'm such an asshole, and I cried a little more because I love my daughter so much it hurts and I hope everyone gets to feel that kind of blood in their faces.

In my head while writing this: "Alabama"—Neil Young

CANADIAN THANKSGIVING

CANADIAN THANKSGIVING IS ON A DIFFERENT DAY than Thanksgiving in the United States, so I'll just write a lot of Canadian jokes in this chapter. It's okay for me to make fun of Canadians, because my people are from Newfoundland (rhymes with "understand"), and that means if I make jokes about how stupid Newfies are, it's okay. After she read *Bury My Heart at Wounded Knee*, my mom claimed that we had some aboriginal American relatives, and some TV show recently did some genealogy research in our family background and proved she might have been telling the truth. She wasn't really telling the truth; she was telling a lie that, unbeknownst to her, might be true. So, I can make aboriginal American jokes after the Canadian jokes.

My dad told me that I have at least one African-American ancestor. I'm a pretty direct descendant of Captain Cook, who brought syphilis to Hawaii and gave the English the name "limeys." Statistically, the long line of sailors must have brought in most other nationalities I can think of and some I can't. My dad worked at a Jewish school. Ethnic jokes are a wide-open territory for me.

I had a mom, I have a wife and daughter, and those are only some of the women I really care about. I've been in many situations in my lifetime, and you wouldn't have to be Rick Santorum to consider some of them gay and perverted. Gender and sexually leaning jokes are wide open for me. Insult comics will use the defense that he or she is offensive to everyone and therefore not offensive at all. Equal opportunity offensiveness is the old-fashioned spin. Sam Kinison and Howard Stern often explain they are just saying what others are thinking. They are honest, and that excuses all. Lenny Bruce's genius was carried on by George Carlin, and they both used words considered offensive as just part of their vocabulary. That sure didn't work for Michael Richards, but Dick Gregory talked about getting over African-American slurs, and then another genius, Richard Pryor, used those slurs when he talked about not using those slurs in a casual, fun way.

Paul Provenza and I did a movie called *The Aristocrats* that looked into transgressive humor and let a hundred comics be as funny and shocking as they could, as each of them told the same dirty joke. They all fascinated me, and Provenza's direction really turned it into a study of what offensive comedy could mean—the craft, joy, and intellectual content of that kind of humor. I learned a lot watching all of those brilliant minds explore what "offensive" is.

I was going to start with Canadians and build on the ethnic humor from there, but I've changed my mind. I'm feeling just the opposite. Bob Dylan wrote about a totally different subject (I take Bob out of context the way people take religious writing out of context): "Either I'm too sensitive or else I'm gettin' soft." I believe both are true about me. I cry all the time and everything affects me now.

I read Sarah Silverman's book and was really moved by her discomfort when someone from some eighties band "complimented" her on doing the best race jokes. It's crystal clear with every breath Sarah takes that she is not a racist. Her offensive material is a comment on racism from inside her character. Her character is a stupid bigot; Sarah isn't. It's making fun of racists.

My good friend Emery Emery's favorite joke is about the fellow with a harelip going into a bar. He orders a drink speaking with his speech impediment and the bartender answers with the same speech impediment. The protagonist gets angry, thinking the bartender is making fun of him. The bartender assures the patron that the bartender himself has a harelip, and they chat a bit, sharing that fact. Another fellow walks into the bar and orders a drink and the bartender answers the new guy without any trace of a speech impediment. The fellow with the harelip is angry and calls the bartender out on his cruel mocking of the harelip. The bartender replies, with the impediment in place, that he was making fun of the other guy. That's the world Sarah Silverman lives in. She is constantly making fun of people who might not know they themselves are the brunt of her joke.

I have no doubt that Sarah and all the other comics who explore these areas have their hearts in the right place. I watched Bobcat Goldthwait do a wonderful hunk in his live act years ago. He asked people if they had noticed that there were no offensive words or jokes in his act (we're not talking obscenity here; no one reading this book would consider those words offensive). He explained that he used all those words and made all those jokes with his friends in his private life. With people who knew him, loved him, trusted him and understood him, he would make racial and gender jokes, but he couldn't risk doing it publicly and being misunderstood. What if some bigots were to not know what side he was on and co-opt his jokes for racist purposes? It was too much of a gamble for the Bobcat to take.

The Penn & Teller show hasn't so much as one racial or sexual mention anywhere in the full evening. Not even a double entendre. An alien watching our show would not be able to tell there were any religions, races or sexes on planet Earth. Like Bobcat, I am always worried about being misunderstood. The bad guys can misunderstand the joke, or even worse, the party you're pretending to attack can misunderstand and be really hurt. Those are big dangers.

I remember the rush I used to get when I would joke in a way that could be considered offensive right in the face of the person who might be offended and ultimately got a big laugh. I grew up in Greenfield, Massachusetts, a town where most of us had the same ethnic background. I listened to Lenny Bruce and I read Paul Krassner, Abbie Hoffman and *Screw* magazine. I wanted so much to be Jewish. I wanted to be an atheist from a Jewish background. I also wanted to be gay. I wanted to be part of the New York City pictured in my mind. Lenny said that all people who lived in the city were Jewish and all those who lived in the country were goys, and I wanted to be Jewish. I wanted to be able to make ethnic jokes. As soon as I got out of Greenfield, all my friends were Jewish, gay or both. That was showbiz to me. I remember the thrill the first time I called a gay man that I loved a "faggot." I had never used the word as an insult. I had never used that word to hurt, and when I used it sarcastically to make someone I loved laugh—when I played the part of a homophobic asshole, and my dear friend laughed—I loved the feeling of being in the inner circle. I loved that I could use something that was dangerous and painful in a way that would be understood and accepted by an outsider. It was even a bigger deal for me because of how I look. I'm enormous. I have met people who just assumed I was a bully and a jock when I was young (gone to seed, you know, maybe I wasn't always fat). In my school days, I was the one being beat up for being an outsider, but . . . I sure don't look it. The word "big" goes before "bully" as comfortably as it does before "dumb." And a big dumb bully is what I've always looked like. You should see me without my glasses.

That feeling of using offensive terms with the people those terms were made to hurt and getting away with it was addictive. I never used any of those terms in hate. If you cut me off in traffic, I'm not very likely to notice, but if I do, and I know no one is listening, I'll say, "Oh fuck," or if I'm really upset, I'll say, "Oh, man," like Swiper on *Dora the Explorer* (two words which do *not* rhyme, you stupid little motherfuckers!). My mom and dad never swore and never used any offensive ethnic or sexual putdowns. Not once. Never. The only power those words have to me is a broad cultural power. I'm sure I heard horrible painful words in my hometown, but not often and not in my home either. I learned the slurs against Jews from Lenny Bruce. I learned African-American hate speech from Richard Pryor. All my knowledge of racism was meta. None of those words were part of my formative years. I learned everything about offensive language within the context of the arts. It wasn't real to me.

There were no anti-gay comments from my family either, but the insults were common in my school, and many of them were used against me. I may look like a ex-jock bully now, but back then this embarrassingly dated haircut, a little eye makeup, and a love of the arts got me beat up quite a bit. Word got out that I wouldn't fight back because I was a stupid pacifist, and then it's wicked fun to beat up a big guy. An average guy looks really brave beating up a big guy. I heard those anti-gay slurs, but I never used them outside comedy.

I was raised in a time when feminism was so strong that I still pause before I use the word "girl" referring to my six-year-old daughter. I don't use the word "lady" ever except as part of a compound word with "bug." All the "bitch," "whore," "slut" stuff is either done jokingly or is used in that postmodern, pro-porn feminist way. I'm the exact right age to be very careful about all of that.

When I got out of Greenfield, I loved being around people who looked and sounded like people who were in my books and on my record player. To prove that I was accepted, I would use the hateful words and have my friends look in my eyes. They would know I didn't really feel that way and laugh. I believed it was taking away the power of the words. It was my "Yankee Doodle" moment. I felt I was helping to redefine those words.

The Penn & Teller organization is just maggoty with people from Jewish backgrounds (atheist now), and we've got gays coming out our ass, so to speak. We have people of Irish and Italian descent and, yup, we've had a Canadian or two. People tend to work with us for a long time, so there's not much turnover. Most everyone has worked with us at least ten years, and a bunch have been working with us for more than twenty years. We're a close-knit group that looks a little bit like America, or at least parts of it.

I don't think there is an obscenity that hasn't been said by and to every one of our co-workers. We're all comfortable with one another and we all trust one another. Anything said in anger is said sincerely, honestly and quietly. There's not a lot of yelling around us unless it's a joke.

We do joke. And the jokes are sincerely Sarah Silverman. There isn't one iota of real hate behind any of it—at one point I got sick of it.

Several years ago, I was sitting around with two of my closest friends: Rob pike from Google (then at Bell Labs) and Lawrence O'Donnell from MSNBC (then producer and writer on *The West Wing*). I did a show called *Bullshit!* so y'all know how much I can swear, but unless you know Rob and LOD, you don't think of them as using a lot of obscenity. But back then when we were talking, it was a rare sentence that lacked a "fuck." LOD and I were the worst. The two of us were once in a cab together in New York talking about what kind of picture hanger to use on a wall. There was no anger and no tension, but the New York Fucking City cabdriver said he had never heard people swear as much as us.

The three of us decided to stop swearing. But we weren't going to talk baby talk. We would not turn "shit" into "shoot." We would never do "freaking" or "frigging." We would take out all the religious swears. I used to say "goddamn" in our show all the time; I was proud of how many times I said it in our show. I said it for blasphemy. The idea was to show the words meant nothing to me. I felt it proved I was an atheist. I said "Jesus Christ" all the time too. Then I had children. These were children I wanted to bring up without all the god hate and baggage. So, why would they hear me saying a meaningless name all the time? So that came out of our show and out of my daily life. I'd sometimes catch myself saying "Jiminy Cricket," but I tried not to. "Oh my god" became "my word." That was a powerful one. It seems that many believe that "my word" is "my lord" with one letter change. Or that it stands for "oh my word of god." That etymology bothers me, but only a little. I use it as giving my word. Swearing to god means nothing to me, but I want my word to mean something. I don't know where I come down on "oh my goodness." It seems to me like that's a pretty clear euphemism for "OMG," and it would be better to go with "oh my word," I suppose, but I like "oh my goodness." There's a purity to that. We non-swearing boys found that "ouch" worked pretty well when one dropped a hammer on one's toe: you didn't really need "motherfucker" then. As part of our no-baby-talk rule, we still used "fuck" to talk about fucking and "shit" to talk about shit. We were okay with "dick" for our penises, but not for Kreskin. He is an untalented mentalist. Not knowing which word would be worse to call him, we couldn't talk about him for a while. When you're not talking about the whole person, "asshole" doesn't come up that much. Same with "pussy" and the like. It was fine for sex talk, but no more false metonymy on any of that.

The most surprising result was taking out the word "bullshit." "Bullshit" is good-natured. It's joking around. It has a colloquial playful feeling. Replace "bullshit" with "that's not true" and you've really said something. There was a power to not swearing, especially in light social situations. "Oh my god, what a load of bullshit" becomes "My word, that's simply not true." That sure as fuck means something.

The experiment faded away. I like the way the rhythm of swearing works in sentences and it's one of my social habits. I say "fuck" and "shit" around my children, but they rarely hear a "goddamn" or "Jesus Christ." I don't want them to be confused by any of that from me. The messages from the other children at school get garbled with the home messages, and once when her little brother said, "Oh my god," Mox responded, "You shouldn't say that, because there is no god." Well, she's right, but I'm not sure that's why her Christian classmates don't say it either.

I wanted to take all the power away from the idea of god and Jesus Christ. I wanted to see if I could speak more carefully. I wanted to have the strength to tell people to their faces that I didn't believe what they were saying was true. I wanted more than just the balls to call bullshit.

I'm thinking maybe I'll go back to the no-swearing thing. It worked well for my parents, but whether I do that or not, I'm going to try to phase out all the hateful terms and ideas. I'm sick of racial and sexual stereotypes or even making fun of those stereotypes. I believe people are people. Differences between men and women may exist in the aggregate, but they mean nothing at the street view. I know gay men who are a bit prissy, and I know gay men who are slobs. Gilbert Gottfried is the cheapest motherfucker on the planet, but that has nothing to do with Jews; that's Gilbert.

I'm embarrassed that I wanted to make my African-American, gay, Jewish (background, now atheist) friends (I do have more than one friend who is all of those: African-American, gay and Jewish) prove how much they trusted me every time I felt like making a hack joke.

If I really don't believe in tribalism and I really want all those stereotypes to go away, it's much faster to just stop using them than to teach everyone to understand when I'm kidding. I've made a mistake or two being overheard or typing in a forum online that I thought was private, when someone didn't know my relationship with the person I was writing to, and accused me of being a kind of person I'm really not. It really upset me. Isn't it easier to just not do it than to make it easy for people who are trying to misunderstand?

I appeared on the same episode of *Politically Incorrect* as Jerry Lewis once. I had just done *The Aristocrats* and I was on the show selling it. Jerry was saying that he didn't work blue; that he didn't swear or make dirty jokes (I believe he meant in public). I decided to turn it on him, for the show, and as Bill Maher took the show out, I was saying things like, "Jerry, I think you're good enough to make dirty jokes. I really do. You're good. I bet you could work blue, if you worked on it. You may not be as good as Johnny Carson, Redd Foxx, Lenny Bruce, Richard Pryor, or George Carlin, but I bet you could do a pretty good job if you tried. I think you're good enough to work blue, give it a try."

I thought it was really funny at the time, but maybe it was true. I'm not as good as that list of people. When I make jokes using those hateful terms, am I adding to our culture like Johnny, Redd, Pryor, and

Carlin? When Lenny was swearing and doing all that ethnic stuff, it took a lot of bravery, ideas and talent, but times have changed. It's no longer brave or smart. We've gotten to the place where it's too hard to tell whose side the harelip bartender is on. Even one person's misunderstanding may not be worth the next guy's laugh.

Don't worry about any of that for the rest of this book. I'll still use "fuck," but Canadian Thanksgiving is at a different time than Thanksgiving in the States and that's okay with me.

Listening to: "Don't Call Me Nigger, Whitey"—Sly and the Family Stone

With Ron Jeremy and Paul Provenza, invoking the punch line from The Aristocrats.

HERE COME OUR "CELEBRITIES" —CUE THE FREEZING RAIN

I DID *THE CELEBRITY APPRENTICE* 2012 as kind of a work/study thang. TV networks are dying. The death throes of religion give us jihads. The death throes of television give us reality shows. I blame the writers' strikes. That's not really fair, but I hate a union that forces me to join it. I'd like to be the anti–Pete Seeger on this and stand up against the unions, but they really have Hollywood writing sewed up. Penn & Teller chose a different battle. We stood up to Equity.

Equity is the only live Broadway theater union. Penn & Teller are not members. The first time we played Broadway, Equity tried to get us to join. They said they could get us a better deal. That seemed impossible, because we were producers on the show. How would they help us negotiate with ourselves? They said we had to join. We found a couple loopholes. Equity guarantees understudies, so we said we would join if they could find five or six guys to audition for my part. They had to be 6'7" tall and be able to perform the monologues, eat fire, juggle, play bass and do all the magic. Then they'd need to find someone with Teller's abilities. He's average height, but aside from that, he can do stuff no one else can do. They failed. Then we claimed we weren't actors. (And if you saw me deliver the line "Superman, the others!" in *Lois & Clark*, you saw proof I'm not an actor. We might have been lying about Teller.) Penn & Teller are variety artists, so our Broadway union is the American Guild of Variety Artists. It handles circus performers and Vegas acts. The guild's president was and is Rod McKuen, so don't fuck with us. Equity is a union that boasts ninety percent unemployment at any given time. I hope the plate spinners and Risley acts on Broadway follow our lead and hang tough with AGVA.

Our sucky TV culture is all PBS's fault. In 1971, they put a camera crew into the home of Bill and Pat Loud and their children and, in 1973, put everything the crew filmed on TV. The show was called *An American Family,* and viewers watched the Louds' lives as though it were a TV show. It was a TV show. The Louds went from happy family to D-I-V-O-R-C-E and America watched it happen. Their son Lance became the first totally out gay guy on TV (I guess no one counts the *Hollywood Squares* and *Bewitched*). When Lance died of hep C and complications from HIV years later, there was another TV show.

Before *An American Family,* you would have bet your ass and your colonoscopy video that if you put TV cameras in a room with people, those people would behave better. They'd be kinder, wiser, more measured and more loving than they would be without the cameras. The whole world is watching, so be at your best.

The Hawthorne effect—coined in 1950 in response to factory workers' productivity increasing when they were being observed—manifests in every clinical shrink study of people's motivations. When anyone watches anyone do anything, the watched people do whatever they're being watched doing a little better for the short time while they're being watched. The key is that the behavioral improvements are temporary. If the Hawthorne effect worked for more than a few days with TV cameras, we wouldn't have *The Celebrity Apprentice*.

I noticed the Hawthorne effect for the first few days of my season of *The Celebrity Apprentice*, but it sure didn't last long. We celebrities are desperate pigs. I knew several of my costars prior to working on *TCA* together. I had hung out with them and worked with them in high-pressure situations. None were close friends, but I liked them all and thought I knew them a bit. But sixteen hours a day with TV cameras all around, doing pointless fake corporate tasks outside one's skill set with Clay Aiken (the guy who came in second on *American Idol* years ago), and no one worries about the whole world watching (with the exception of anyone who has a job, someone to talk to, a nice view out the window or a solitaire program). You're happy if you don't swallow your own tongue.

The secret truth of *The Celebrity Apprentice* is that it isn't very hard. The tasks are nothing. Makeup starts just after five a.m. and the show goes to about ten p.m., but you spend most of that time doing nothing. Anyone who isn't in show business could accomplish everything the show called for and have time left over to do their laundry, cook their supper and post pictures of their animal companion on Facebook. *The Celebrity Apprentice* is easy like junior high is easy. All the arithmetic, the creative writing and the history are super simple, but like junior high, you do that easy work surrounded by people who are full-tilt hormone-raging bugnutty. Everyone is panicked, desperate, yelling, swearing, attacking, backstabbing, failing to get laid and acting crazy. With all this drama, any sane person just wants to do

more algebra. *The Celebrity Apprentice* is junior high with a better
brand of acne cover-up.

Like all desperate celebrities, I've been on more than one reality
show. I also did *Dancing with the Stars*. I was amazed to find out that
The Celebrity Apprentice was more honest and straightforward than
DWTS. The idea of *DWTS* is pretty beautiful: half-assed show folk
who aren't dancers are teamed up with great dancers, and cameras
video them while they learn to dance. How well can people learn to
do something outside their ken? It's a beautiful idea. Dance is a joyous celebration of humanity, so it should be an uplifting, inspiring
show to watch and even more beautiful to be on.

Well, I loved being around Kym Johnson, my *DWTS* dancing partner. Kym was a delight. She oozed professional skill and joy. I loved
working on the dancing. I love practicing things I'm not good at, and
it was an easy schedule. But I hated the time that was spent with the
production trying to get young, ambitious Mormon women to cry.
Guys behind the cameras would say mean things at attractive young
men and women and washed-up celebrities about how it would ruin
their lives if they didn't win. The producers were hoping to capture
some "good TV." A young wannabe art filmmaker would take me
into my "confessional" and ask me to talk about how upset I was
going to be if I was the first one voted off—the biggest failure possible in *reality*. I was the most incompetent and I was off the show as
quickly as anyone could be. I found out how I'd feel. The answer was
fine. Others danced better than me, but no one danced with more
joy. And being on that show for one round made me a lot of money
in ticket sales to the Penn & Teller show. If I'd stayed on longer, I
would have made much more money—but I'm paid more than I ever
expected anyway so that failure is pretty easy to take. It didn't take

food out of my children's mouths. A twenty-four-year-old film student with a notebook would ask me (me, a guy who worked in the carny) things like, "Is *Dancing with the Stars* the hardest you've ever worked? Is it the hardest thing you've ever done?" I'd explain that anyone who has a job, any job, or spent any time looking for a job outside show business had worked harder that day than anyone on any celebrity reality show (I specify "celebrity" because it seems those frozen-ass crab fishermen work pretty hard). If you fix cars, sell cars, drive cars, practice medicine, take medicine, sell medicine, give pedicures, give blow jobs or work at a KFC, you worked harder today than any celebrity on any reality show ever has. Every time I was asked the "how hard are you working" question on *Dancing with the Stars*, I gave them that answer. They didn't ever use that answer on the show. They have to pretend it's hard work. It isn't.

The *Celebrity Apprentice* is more honest, in that creepy kind of way that the guy who admits he's a racist is more honest. It doesn't pretend to be about something beautiful like dance. I think business is beautiful, but *The Celebrity Apprentice* has nothing to do with business. No actual business skills are tested. It's not even a real game about fake business. I can tell you the rules of chess (I know the rules well enough to lose to anyone). I can't tell you the rules to *The Celebrity Apprentice*. No one can tell you the rules of *The Celebrity Apprentice*. No one. Donald Trump just does what he wants, which is mostly pontificating to people who are sucking up to him, while the network people try to manipulate him into making the highest-rated show they can. Trump can't be manipulated, so the show isn't even fair in that way. Annie Duke, the poker genius and *TCA* veteran, said to me, "It's a pretend game, about pretend business, where you get pretend fired." Donald Trump couldn't fire me. I work for Penn &

Teller and he's never owned any part of us. Trump tried to book Penn & Teller once in Vegas at one of his casinos, but we were priced out of his budget. He can't fire us from the Rio, because he doesn't own any of Caesars.

TCA pretends to be about raising money for charity. That's true, but only so far. If I had not taken time off from the Penn & Teller show to do The Celebrity Apprentice—if Teller and I had just done our show, gotten usual pay—I could have donated four times the amount of money that Trump had pledged to give my charity if I won the whole damn shooting match. Opportunity Village, "my" charity that helps intellectually disabled adults to enter society, got a lot of attention because I was on The Celebrity Apprentice, and that does count for something. And when I was "fired," my real bosses at Caesars, who own the Rio and the Penn & Teller Theater, said, "Oh, you wanted a quarter million for Opportunity Village? We don't have to do some jive TV show; we'll just write a check." They wrote the full winning amount to Opportunity Village and everyone was happy. But The Celebrity Apprentice people are honest. They don't pretend it's about something beautiful, and they don't pretend it's fair. It's venal people clawing at stupid, soulless shit in front of the modern-day Scrooge McDuck in order to stay famous.

The producers of TCA are a couple of really groovy women whom I grew to know a little and like a lot. They wanted the show to be honest, and they kept it honest. I didn't watch the show, but I didn't hear about any edits that were really disingenuous. They had to tell a story, and stories are never real, but they showed a view of the show that was certainly as accurate as the one you're reading now. I never saw them lie, or push someone to get the reaction they wanted. They just let it happen with integrity and honesty. For one "task," Donald Trump asked us to create a Macy's store display and print ads for his new fragrance. Is there anyone who wants to smell like Donald Trump? Mr. Trump thinks so, so we were asked to create advertising. Instead of the usual twenty grand that the show would give to the winning "team leader's" charity, Donald floated the promise that if he "loved" our promotional material, he would give *one hundred thousand dollars* to his "loved" one's charity. Five times the amount that was arbitrarily assigned to this "task." In other words, if Trump got an ad that he could actually use for his stink-pretty juice, he would pay about twenty percent of what he would have to pay in the free market to hire a professional to do the job properly. Trump was willing to donate one-fifth of what the campaign would be worth to charity. I got fired for coming up with the slogan "You Earned It." They thought that slogan was "pompous." My slogan for a perfume with Donald's picture on it called "Success" was deemed pompous. Wow. The problem was my audience, I think. "You Earned It" isn't good for the Trumps. It should have been "You Inherited It." I would have won. I also helped with some of the parts of the campaign they liked, but the team chose my slogan, so not having a slogan would have been better than having one they don't like. The game theory is to do as little as possible. Not the way I live my life, but it's not my game, it's Trump's.

TCA gets the coin on both sides: they get NBC to pay for the show and they get the corporations to pay for the "challenges."

Trump stays rich in real estate and stays kinda sorta famous for his "brand." Trump is obsessed with his brand and that's all you really need to know. Trump is on a game on TV where my showbiz peers, if they want to play the game, have to suck up to him, and I sucked up to him. I'd sit and smile and listen, because I promised the producers I would do my best. The boardrooms went long and I was there to spend about twenty-two hours over six weeks listening to Trump do his monologues. He'd talk about Occupy Wall Street and global warming while he was deciding whom to pretend to fire from his pretend business. Bill Gates is fighting polio, and polio and I don't suck up to him, but I was on TV with Donald Trump, so I did my job. I wasn't even going to say anything about Trump's hair. I live in a glass house. I've always had ugly, out-of-style hair. Trump's hair is a lot better than mine—but as I sat there for hours half listening to Donald carry on, it struck me exactly what his hair looked like. It looks like cotton candy made of piss. That revelation came to me, and I had to type it here. But my hair is worse.

One day while shooting, Clay Aiken, Arsenio Hall, Lou Ferrigno and I were sneaking out of Trump International Hotel behind a laundry truck, to hide from the imaginary paparazzi. We're all sub-stars, and we'd all been in showbiz for a while, so we were used to being walked in through the kitchen so the paying customers wouldn't see the show folk. There were a few others with us, but I was trying to shock you with that opening foursome. Dee Snider, from Twisted Sister, was with us too. It was November in New York City, but in TV phony-baloney world it was March. I had been up since five a.m. for makeup, and a few days before I'd had a heart-to-heart talk with Clay. I would have preferred waterboarding. I don't like heart-to-heart talks with anyone, but Clay Aiken? Strap me to the board, and put the wet towels over my face. Drowning sounds nice. Clay had put his arm on my shoulder, looked in my eyes and said softly something like, "You know, Penn, I really like you, I do. I think you're really smart, but I have to talk to you about some things that are bothering me." Clay told me, gently and kindly, that I was being condescending by talking over people's heads. He was accusing me of being condescending and he was being . . . condescending. When someone is busting you for being condescending, it takes a bigger asshole than me to say, "Are you sure you know what 'condescending' means? It means to talk down to, not talk over someone's head. So, you see, honey, I'm not condescending, I'm pompous, let me explain . . ."

So, I nodded, yeah, I'm condescending. Greed and clawing for fame got me to the point where I was pretending to care what Clay Aiken thought of me. What have I done? *What have I done?*

Clay spent more than an hour and a half of his time, and wasted much more than that of mine, having a heart-to-heart with me over how he, Clay Aiken, thought I should treat Lou Ferrigno. He wasn't talking about how Clay Aiken thought I should treat Clay Aiken, about which I would have had to work hard to give a flying fuck. Clay was talking to me about how he, Clay Aiken, thought I should treat the guy who played a cartoon character painted green decades ago. He also told me to stop using the word "groovy." This from a man who uses the word "bitch." I like the word "groovy." I don't like the word "bitch." After our talk, I went back to the hotel, called my wife and talked to her about being upset about my talk with Clay Aiken. One's wife could bring home a couple of her sexy MILF friends for a very special sex birthday party and one could be unable to get a hard-on and then pee all over oneself and start crying like a little girl while chewing egg salad on soft bread with one's mouth open, and it would disgust one's wife less than talking about one's heart-to-heart talk with Clay Aiken. She's a very understanding woman.

If you've gotten yourself into a situation when Clay Aiken is going to talk about his feelings with you . . . and if your cock is bigger than a cashew, it's time to kill yourself. If it weren't being documented, you could kill him quickly and bury him in a shallow grave—who's going to notice? You could go on living your happy, normal life, but if there are TV cameras pointed at you while Clay is pretending to soul search, and your wife is going to find out and some of your friends from the carny might watch the show in a bar somewhere, well . . . you should kill yourself.

It is a tribute to having the greatest parents in the world, my wonderful wife and children, and to having character rammed into me by my third-grade teacher that I'm still alive to write this now. Clay was explaining to me how I could live my life in a way that would please him, while we sat on an upper floor of Trump Towers and the door to the balcony was unlocked. I could have jumped. As the cameras shot us, Clay looked directly in my eyes like he was showing compassion for an autistic child while he knew he was on a reality TV show. He was playing compassionate, smart and practical in the face of this big, loud, aggressive guy. Then he used the word "bully" against me (that word was used a lot during that episode), referring to how I dealt with Lou Ferrigno. Lou had called me a "fat motherfucker" and hit me, and hurt me, several times as he pretended to greet me and show me affection but really as he showed me how strong he was. Lou said that his roughness with me was proof that he liked me. I said, "Then don't like me." I sure believed it was affection. He would swear that he never hit me and he wouldn't be lying. What he considering greeting, I consider battery. I'm a pussy. I hate that jock hugging hitting thing. It's why I became a theater guy. Lou explained to me that "no kidding" he was trained in combat and could kill me in three seconds. Clay explained how I should deal with Ferrigno. Clay said that he knew how to deal with Lou because Clay himself had worked for years with intellectually disabled students before he discovered himself on *American Idol*. He thought I should deal with this grown man—who was our peer, who had punched me in friendship—as if I was dealing with an intellectually disabled child, so . . . get this . . . so I wouldn't come off as condescending in front of the non-groovy but very bitchy Clay.

You don't have to be a mind reader to know what I was thinking as Clay's perpetually half-closed, unfocused eyes met mine and he placed his "comforting" hand on my shoulder. I was thinking, *I have made a lot of money. So has Teller. Teller loves me. If I run out to the balcony and jump off, I'm sure my wife and children wouldn't get my huge life insurance policy (I've seen* Double Indemnity*), but Teller would get a big press bump from me being dead, and he'd use that money to make sure that my family are taken care of. And there's a chance, with this conversation on video, they'll get Clay for murder, and my family will get the insurance money after all and can maybe file a civil suit against Clay for more money. I'm bigger than Clay by a lot. I could probably kill him with my bare hands even without Lou's military training, but at this point, I'm thinking my funeral, his trial, instead of the other way around. It's a coin toss.* Condescending. Hand on shoulder. Looking into my eyes and . . . for MORE THAN AN HOUR!

How long is an hour? When my wife and I decided to get married and have children, the conversation took forty-five minutes. On my mother's deathbed, the honest "I love you"s took a half hour. The decision for Teller to quit his tenured classics teaching job and spend the rest of his life working with me took ten minutes. This "good TV" heart-to-heart with the second place winner of a talent show took more than an hour. An hour during which the people I really loved, my mom, my wife and Teller, were being spit and pissed on by my hearing out Clay on camera about something completely unimportant. I should have jumped. At least some of you might have respected that. No one respects me talking to Clay Aiken about feelings. Not even Clay. He was just doing it to win a TV game so he wouldn't have to go back to condescending to mentally disabled children for a career.

What happened? Did I forget how to say "Shut the fuck up"? Or, "I'm sorry, I think I left the bathwater running in Las Vegas, and you know it's the desert, there's a water shortage"? Or, "I'm sorry, I don't speak English. I learned our Vegas shows phonetically"? Or, "Hey, Clay, there are more TV cameras on the other side of the room. Why don't you have a heart-to-heart with Arsenio Hall? That might get you more close-ups"?

I owe my family and Teller my full attention no matter what tripe they want to babble, but those people never babble tripe. I owe Aiken jackshit, and yet I was letting him tell me how I should act. He's not fit to eat shit off Teller's shoes, and I gave him more time than I've ever given Teller? The time didn't mean anything to Clay. He would have a heart-to-heart talk with a salmon if there were a chance it would be broadcast. If you'll listen, he will talk. He's used to having cameras around him all the time, and he knows how to create an improvised soap opera for TV. When he said he wanted me to treat people differently, I said, "Okay," and I changed how I was. Everyone who was on the show or watched the show noticed that I took all his advice and changed how I acted. I did that instantly. I told him I'd do that in the first five minutes of our talk. He got that promise from me and I kept that promise—it's on video. But he wasn't telling me things to have me change. What I was doing didn't matter; it was the talk itself he wanted to have on camera. He was gathering evidence and not actually talking. Crazy world, this showbiz thang.

I try to have an honest relationship with my wife, so that night I called her and told her that I'd had a heart-to-heart with Clay Aiken. I could have told her that aliens had come down and given me intergalactic herpes on my asshole and she would have been more credulous and less disgusted.

So the morning after my heart-to-heart with Clay, I'm sneaking out of Trump International, as part of my quest to have my fake business abilities judged by Trump. I've run a very successful business for almost forty years and have always been in the black. Always. Teller and I never went bankrupt. We've paid all our bills and supported our families and the people who work with us. Before Clay Aiken touched me, I was a fucking artist.

I'm walking beside Dee Snider. We've got our hair and makeup done, and we still look like men in their fifties with long, stupid hair. We get out of the loading dock, and there's freezing rain and wind hitting us in the face. Dee had broken his finger falling off a horse, while dressed in drag, for a medieval dinner theater show in Jersey that I made him do when I was the *Celebrity Apprentice* "team leader." We were both a little damaged, bleary, worse for the wear and tear, and Dee turned to me and said, "I'm getting so paranoid, I'm starting to think that the show's producers made this weather happen just to fuck with us."

Dee had nailed it. His broken finger had not beaten his real-world perspective the way Clay's heart-to-heart had broken mine. He still had some non-*reality* reality left. When Dee said that, I realized that was what I was feeling, without the "I'm getting so paranoid" part. Right before Dee spoke, I was feeling that the freezing rain was some sort of TV producer plot. That they had planned it to see what we would do, that they had done it to make "good TV."

Why people act worse *on* reality than they would *in* reality is a mystery. Other than avarice and desire for empty fame, the main reason I did *TCA* was to feel what it would feel like to be in that situation. I did it to see what made people act like that. Not everyone falls off a motorcycle without a helmet to become Gary Busey. Some people do it just because there are cameras around. When you're in it, it seems like the producers must be making this shit happen, but I don't think they were. I don't think they have to do much to drive people like us crazy. We start with a leg up.

Daniel Kahneman's book *Thinking, Fast and Slow* introduced me to the idea of "ego depletion." I read it after my tour of duty on *The Celebrity Apprentice*, and it explained some of the mysteries I experienced doing that show. Studies have shown that if you make someone very self-conscious about everything they do and say, their self-control just gets tired out. The ego can be exhausted. It's the trying to be one's best on camera that puts one at one's worst on camera. You just can't keep it up that long. You want to be at your best, but pretty soon the internal censors are exhausted, take a break, and pretty soon sweet Arsenio is yelling things like, "I'll tell you what a fucking bitch whore she is!"

The non-sexual question I've been asked the most since *TCA* is "Were those others just faking?" It's a question I can't answer. I know Lisa Lampanelli pretty well. She did our movie *The Aristocrats* and we've been out together socially. We've talked. I sat with her in a room while she was yelling at Dayana Mendoza (who had been Miss Universe). Lisa and others had problems with Dy (she let me call her that), but I had no problems with Lisa or Dy. I just didn't like Clay having a heart-to-heart talk with me. Lisa was really yelling. She was really crying. It was really real. I felt it was sincere. I felt that Lisa was really frustrated and really upset. I sat there. When people are really upset, I sit there. You can find a few ex-girlfriends who will vouch for that and not as a good thing. While she was yelling, she yelled something like, "I've been putting up with this shit for eight weeks." I

don't remember the exact number of weeks she said. But I do remember it was way, way more weeks than we had been there. And I
remember it was the right number of weeks it was going to be when
it aired. It was both of those things. The show is shot with about two
days for every week. We shoot six days a week and during most weeks
we do three tasks and each one of those tasks is a week of broadcast.
The first task was three days and some of the broadcasts used more
or less than one task, but . . . overall, the amount of time we were
there was about a third of the amount of time that it took when
broadcast. Lisa was really upset, but the amount of time she said
she'd been disgusted with Dy was the amount of time the show
would be on the air, not the real amount of time we'd been there. So,
they could use that video and not violate the chronology of the show.
Lisa wasn't lying, she wasn't faking, but she was aware she was on TV.
We were all professionals, we were all aware of the camera, but we
were also living our lives. It makes it very crazy. I spent a lot of time
saying to Paul Sr., whom I love, "It's not real." But that's not true. It's
also not TV. It's really not TV. When I was having my heart-to-heart
with Clay, the full endless horror of it was never broadcast. It was edited down to a minute. When I'm on Piers Morgan and he's ripping
me a new asshole, that's TV, I know that every word he says is going
out. But *The Celebrity Apprentice* is so long that you know the vast majority of stuff will never be seen, but cameras are still on; it could be
seen. It's Schrödinger's showbiz: it's all fake and it's all real at the
same time. The situation itself makes everyone crazy.

The production isn't entirely blameless. There was a lot of alcohol available at any time it could be even slightly justified, but most
of us never drank a drop, and even the drinkers were moderate. But
the producers didn't need anyone drunk; they got their telegenic out-
bursts from ego depletion. And after someone had an ego-depleted

outburst, they'd reward the impropriety. In real reality, there would have been hell to pay for screaming epithets at people, but in *TCA* world, there are no repercussions. No one loves anyone on the set enough to say, "Hey listen, man, take a little break and think about this." No one cares. We're all trying to save our own sorry asses. Then the next day, Trump says something insane like, "I'm glad you showed some backbone. I like passion." He means, of course, he likes passion for his little TV show, but it feels like he's saying the outburst was a good thing. We've chosen to make this whackjob, with the cotton candy piss hair and the birther shit, into someone we want to please.

I made a deal with the producers and myself that I would pretend to care what Donald Trump thought of me. I believe, in the real world, that I care less about what Trump thinks of me than he cares what I think of him. When he was into his free-form rants in front of a captive audience, he would talk about articles written about him and defend himself against charges made, as far as I could tell, by random bloggers with a few hundred hits. Attacks that could have no impact on his life at all. It sounded like this cat was Googling himself, being bugged by what was written, and then defending himself to people who were trying to improve their careers by playing a TV game with him. He sat on this throne and told us he'd made a good business decision by selling a house of his for much less than the asking price and these bloggers should know that. They should know he was a good businessman. The nightmare of Trump is not that he doesn't care what people think; it's that he desperately cares what people think and . . . he's doing the best he can. I don't know Donald Trump. We've crossed paths a few times, but I've never talked to him. He talked to me, but I was on a show where I wasn't supposed to talk back. I still did, but only a little. I disagree with him about a lot, but you know, I disagree with you about a lot, and we still get along. He was wicked wrong about the birther shit, but I'm wicked wrong about a lot, and we both have stupid hair.

So, in order to sell more tickets to my Vegas show, I abandoned my family for weeks, was sequestered in a gaudy hotel, and pretended to care what Donald Trump thought of me. You can't pretend to care about something for more than a day without starting to care about it. Pretending to care and caring over time are the same thing. So, Arsenio blows up, Trump singles him out and shakes his hand, I listen to Clay tell me how I should act, and that's the new norm. Our egos are depleted and we're still on camera. That poor Loud family. At least we knew what we were getting into.

I cracked in a different way. I never raised my voice, except in jest. I'm not a yeller. Yelling in my family was always a joke. Our family pouts. I will never see *TCA*. I don't watch anything that I'm in and it's not the kind of show I watch anyway, but I hope my pouting doesn't look too bad on camera. If it does, I'm sorry, I'm a pouter. From what my wife says, the show depicts me fairly accurately. So there.

I suppose there's a chance that some of you are reading this book because you saw me on *The Celebrity Apprentice*. Collectively, the people who have seen Penn & Teller's *Letterman* and *SNL* appearances, bought my books, seen my movies and acting roles do not add up to the viewers of that one show.

So, thanks, Mr. Trump, and thanks, Clay. Doing the show was a great thing for me and, all things considered, I really like and respect you both.

I should have jumped out the fucking window.

Listening to: "Sweetheart Like You"—Bob Dylan (This REALLY explains all of Celeb App)

Left to right: *Michael Andretti, Dee Snider, Your Humble Reporter, George Takei, Paul Teutul Sr., and Lou Ferrigno.*

NOVEMBER 9, 1909— EVERYTHING IN THE WORLD IS ENOUGH

"I WANTED A MISSION, and for my sins they gave me one."

The first time I went on Piers Morgan's show on CNN, it was right before I started shooting *The Celebrity Apprentice*. Piers had also done *TCA*, and for his considerable sins he had won it. Everyone gets everything he wants. Before we went live on the air, we sat and chatted. Piers was pleasant, but not polite. While we made small talk, he answered texts on his Porsche BlackBerry. You didn't even know they had a designer Porsche BlackBerry. I've given you that information and, in the same breath, told you who would fucking buy and use a Porsche BlackBerry while someone was talking to him. Piers told me that I'd have a blast on *The Celebrity Apprentice* and how much he liked my magic show. He was slamming down Red Bulls like they were going out of style, and indeed they had gone out of style a decade earlier.

The floor manager counted us down from five seconds for the broadcast to go live, and Piers started his interview with a big smile, a quick intro and then got right to a quick and sloppy reading from my book *God, No!* I believe what he read on the air was all he had read of the book. Then he said something to the effect of "I don't like you, and I don't like your book." He hadn't read it, and he didn't know me, but he thought he had a sense of good TV and good TV is sometimes just about being rude and ignorant. He had that in spades. We must always remember that we can never know what's in someone else's heart, but in order to function, we must guess. It sure seemed that as Piers argued with me about religion, he didn't believe a word he was saying. We must go with what he says, and he says he's a religious man and we must believe him, but from a couple yards away, my bullshit detector was pinning the needles. You must trust him and not me, but goddamn, from the guest chair his faith sounded like jive.

It took me until I was fifty-six years old, but for the first time in my life, on Piers's show, I took my parents' advice on how to treat people. I was polite. Completely polite. I sat, as Piers attacked me, and found that simple politeness brought a calm over me that no yogi could match. Under his rudeness, I found nirvana. I didn't once raise my voice and I didn't once say anything like, "Would you please let me finish?" It was his show, and if he wanted me to finish my sentence, I would. If he didn't, it was his show.

Before I went on the show, my buddy Jonathan Ross told me a joke ad-libbed on a British TV show called *I'm Sorry I Haven't a Clue*, hosted by another buddy of mine, Stephen Fry. On that show, Stephen defined the word "countryside" as "The killing of Piers

Morgan." When Jonathan sent it to me in an e-mail, it took me a few moments to get it. In case you have trouble, try spelling "country-side" phonetically. "Cunt-re-cide." Stephen Fry is wicked funny and in my experience is right about everything.

The first Piers Morgan show that I did (yes, it's called show *business*, and now I'm a regular on Piers Morgan, because that's my job and I enjoy doing his show) is perhaps still my favorite interview, because it was the first one I did that I believe my parents would have been proud of. That's a lie. My mom and dad were proud of everything I ever did, that was their default setting, but it might have been the first interview where I was myself. There was no jive from me. I was polite and honest. I can be ashamed that it took me fifty-six years to be polite and honest in the face of an attack, but at least I got there. If you heard me a few times on *Howard Stern*, you may have bet that I'd never ever be able to hit politesse and honesty at the same time.

That first Piers Morgan interview changed the way I acted on TV and in my overall public life. I've always respected honesty in showbiz, but somehow I never considered being polite to be honest. Piers taught me that I could be myself on TV and it would be okay. I could be my mother's son and still be a motherfucker. It's a great feeling.

At one point in the discussion, Piers asked me about fearing death. He hit below the belt and talked about the deaths in my family. He moved it from theoretical and theological to personal and cruel. During that moment, it wasn't my mom and dad going through my head (that would have been self-cruelty), it was the Stones: "All your sickness, I can suck it up, throw it all at me, I can shrug it off." For that moment on live TV, I was rich enough, strong enough, hard enough and, most important, in love enough. It seemed Piers was making the argument that he believed in a life after death because not believing in it scared him. This argument is empty on so many levels. Should I argue that I believe I'm Bob Dylan because being Penn Jillette depresses me? I can argue that I'd like to be Bob Dylan: I'd like to have written the line "It frightens me, the awful truth of how sweet life can be," but I didn't. That is the answer. The frightening sweetness of life is not an argument for life after death. Wanting to believe something is not any reason at all to believe it. If anything, it's a reason to question it.

The other part of that argument or assertion is that death is scary. The loss of life is sad, the wonderful rickety carnival ride being over, but the atheist view of death could not be less scary. The religious view of death, the spook show, is scary. Whether benevolent or not, omniscient, omnipotent, omnipresent creatures up in all your shit is scary. I certainly wouldn't tell my children there is a hell they might go to. Even the idea of purgatory is horrific. I won't go head-to-head with Mark Twain, so read his *Letters from the Earth* to imagine how even the Christian heaven is just real human hell. Add eternal to anything, even eating pussy while listening to Dylan, and you get hell.

After Piers tried to crack me with my mom's death and scare me with my own death, I answered, "1909." That's not true. I don't think I really answered, "1909." If you check it out on the InnerTube you'll hear me say another year. I answered whatever year happened to pop into my head. I didn't have my answer planned. I want to believe I said "1909." My answer confused Piers. He stopped insulting me for a moment and cocked his eyebrow in mock TV wonder. Why would I answer a question about death with a year? He ad-libbed something like, "What?"

I asked if 1909 terrified him. This is the question to ask anyone who is afraid of the atheist view of death. How frightened are you of 1909? How frightened were you in 1909? I've now picked November 9, 1909, because that's the day my mom was born, and I figured, since she would be over 103 years old now, it's pretty safe that if you're reading this book, you weren't alive in 1909. So, 1909 is exactly the same as 2109 for our purposes. You most likely weren't alive in 1909 and you most likely won't be alive in 2109. You won't have any effect on anything then. You won't know anything and no one will know about you. Game over or game hasn't started—there isn't much difference.

I would love to be alive in 2109. I would love to talk to my possible grandchildren, great-grandchildren and great-great-grandchildren. I would love to see what people are wearing. I would love to see if we have flying cars, world peace, and a better song for twelve-year-old boys than "Stairway to Heaven." Will we finally get to wear silver jumpsuits and have big foreheads?

I'm not sure I want November 9, 2109, more than I'd want November 9, 1909. I would love to meet my grandparents and maybe my great-grandparents. I never knew my grandmother, and I knew my grandfather only as an old man. I'd love to meet him when he was young, dumb, and full of cum. I would love to sit and tell my infant mom what her grandchildren would be like when they were her age. I would love to see the horses and buggies and know we would eventually be going to the moon. I would love to put a few bucks in a compound interest account for myself and leave a note to throw some money at the guys from Microsoft, Apple, Google, PayPal and Facebook, and to get credit for coining the term "CamelCase." I'd love to be around for the invention of swing, bebop, and rock and roll. There's so much we miss by being stuck in time. But life is time, and nothing more.

In the twentieth century, we got pretty good at one-way time travel. Since language developed, we have been able to travel to the past, and more and more people since Gutenberg (not Steve, he was off *Dancing with the Stars* almost as fast as I was) have been able to write messages to the future. In the twentieth century, we learned to send pictures to the future and now video. I have a picture of my mom at two years old and another of her at seven, about the same age as my daughter now, and about one hundred years apart.

We have the imagination to imagine our daughters and our mothers playing together at the same age and we have the technology to feed that imagination. I daydream about my mom, seven years old, in her little wool coat and hat, knocking on the door and coming over for a playdate. I see Valda and Moxie being nice to me for a while, and then running up to Mox's room to play princesses. I imagine my mom coming down wearing my little girl's plastic shoes and yellow princess dress. It would take my daughter about two minutes to teach her grandmother to play Plants vs. Zombies, and they would have the unstuck time of their lives. They could be mean to my son, Zolten, together and leave him out of their little girl play and then make him laugh that pure laugh that explodes my world and frees my heart. The daydream of my mom and my daughter at the same age breaks my heart. I want it so badly. I promise you that I want it more than Piers Morgan wants there to be a god and an afterlife. My desire for something impossible does not make it less impossible. My imagination is not bad. My imagined Val/Mox playdate is a real part of me. It informs my love of my daughter and my love of my mom. That love exists. That love is not imaginary. That love is in me. And as far as memories count, and they do count, my mom lives on, and she lives on as that seven-year-old girl in that wool hat from the time-traveling picture. She lives on in a way that I never experienced her for real and never will experience her. It's just a picture, and that's okay.

We do have time travel. Depending on whatever shitty sci-fi story you're following, the rules of time travel change, but they often allow you to go back in time, allow you to know what's happening, even though you can have no effect on the events themselves. I look at the picture of my mom from 1916 and I can see her little wool hat and her smile, the smile I recognize from her deathbed eighty-four years later. By any real definition, we're time traveling. I'm time traveling in any real sense.

New generations will be seeing more and more high-quality video from times they weren't alive. They'll be experiencing part of a time when they did not exist. This is a fairly new thing. I have home movies my brother-in-law and my nephew ripped to computer video that I can watch of myself learning to juggle at age twelve. The sixties and seventies are pretty well documented, and lots of people alive today weren't alive then. My high school girlfriend, Anne, who is some sort of genius scientist now, thinks any theory about the modern world changing human nature is bullshit. Anne points out that what humans do is adapt. It's what we're best at. We got good at going faster than the speed of sound and being able to talk to people all over the world at once. That doesn't fuck with our attention spans. None of that changes our humanity.

But I wonder what all this time travel does to our sadness. I know we've adapted, but how is sadness affected? Just one hundred years ago, the old lady down the street was always and eternally the old lady down the street. You could hear stories about her as a young person, and you could read things she wrote as a young person, and maybe even see a drawing or photograph of her as a younger person, but these were little glimpses. Soon we'll have hi-def 3-D images of our grandmothers sexting.

Davy Jones died in February 2012. We have a lot of pictures of him at age twenty. We have video and shows of him at twenty and now he's dead at sixty-six and it's all laid out there. Mortality is rammed down our throats through our eyes and ears. Paul Newman is the most attractive human being I have ever seen in person. I saw him live and realized the camera was not kind to him. The camera made him uglier. The camera makes David Letterman look better. Off-camera, in person, Julia Roberts is wonderful but looks a bit like a tapeworm. That's a lot of mouth to see up close. We don't have the technology yet to capture the beauty of Paul Newman. But we do have enough technology to watch him get old. Paul never got ugly and that helps my heart, but he got old. Pretty doesn't always hang in there, Mr. Gibson. Things you've felt can show in your face sometimes. Movies can show us aging at its prettiest, and that's Paul Newman, but it's still sad. It's still a bit melancholy to watch *The Left Handed Gun* become *Nobody's Fool*. We live so much longer now than we used to. We are more aware of how time flies and what changes have happened and will happen. I can no longer remember the feeling of holding my daughter in one hand and her being barely bigger than that hand. She's now a little girl. And she will be a young woman, then a woman, then an old woman. I show her pictures of her daddy as a baby. "Did you poop your pants?"

"I sure did."

Piers Morgan was trying to scare me with death. Fuck death. He can't scare me with death. I got death hanging. Death is November 9, 1909—death is nothing. I'm not afraid of nothing. But time passing is something different. I'm terrified of time passing. I tremble at the thought of my little girl growing up. I can't face my son growing stronger than me and helping me up the stairs. I quake at the prospect of looking at my adult children's faces with eyesight worse than I have now.

Motherfucker.

Piers, you have no chance of scaring me with death, because all the fear possible is contained in life. The awful truth of how sweet life can be is enough to crack me every second. That black-and-white picture of my mom, alive and bursting with her future in her little wool hat and matching mittens—that, Piers, is what scares the shit out of me, and your TV religion can't protect any of us from that. I'm not afraid of a hot lead enema followed by some serious ass-to-mouth with Satan—give it your worst. I'm afraid of a life that is so full of joy and love that every second just bursts by and is gone. It's a gorgeous, detailed, 3-D, surround sound, no-flutter-in-the-bass mural done by 10 billion artists, and it's whipping by the car window at the speed of sound, and I'll never come back to it. I can take pictures of it, but in the time I hold those pictures up, I'll have missed another billion images and experiences.

You want to scare me, Piers, try that. But no one claims god can change that. God might promise everlasting life, and the possibility of seeing my loved ones again, but he can't promise that this life that I'm living right now won't go by. I want every time I touch my son's hand to never end, and I want to experience the next time I touch his hand after not touching his hand for a while.

I want the impossible. But I'll settle for what we have. Everything in the world has to be enough. Everything in the world is enough. I'm rejoicing that what scares me and breaks my heart is the beauty of what I have right now.

Are you afraid of death?

November 9, 1909.

I'm making my mom's birthday a holiday. I'm afraid of a life stuck in time, but so what? I'm not afraid of death.

Listening to: "Up to Me"—Bob Dylan

My mom, 6 years old.

Mox, age 6, and me.

I DEFY THE JAILS OF THE WORLD TO HOLD MY SON

WHEN THE FUTURE LOOKS BACK ON American entertainers of the twentieth century, it's all going to come down to Houdini or Elvis. A friend of mine who teaches some bullshit rock-and-roll course at UNLV was asked by a student, one who was "studying" rock and roll, who George Harrison was. A teacher at our child's preschool had never heard of Johnny Carson. There's your legacy—but ask anyone in America to name a magician, and they'll name Houdini as often as anyone who's working today. A few years ago, my buddy Eddie Gorodetsky looked at the figures and predicted that by the year 2053 every man, woman and transgendered child in the USA would be in Vegas impersonating Elvis.

I think Houdini will win. To disappear by "pulling a Houdini" is already a phrase in dictionaries. Houdini was born in Budapest, claimed to be from Appleton, Wisconsin, and stood in front of a nation of immigrants at the sharp turn into the twentieth century and screamed, "I defy the jails of the world to hold me!" My buddy Larry "Ratso" Sloman wrote that Houdini was "America's First Superhero."

Let's forget about Houdini for a second and concentrate on my buddy Ratso. The births of my children were wonderful events, but even that joy has been eclipsed by becoming an adult who has a buddy called Ratso. My cell phone rings, the name "Ratso" pops up, and the voice of pure NYC says, "Hey, Penn. It's Rats." What more could a man accomplish in life than getting that phone call? Well, I'll tell you: Kinky Friedman is a two-Ratso man. When Kinky gets a call from Ratso, he has to ask which one. Hard to beat that, but my caller ID flashes "Kinky" when he calls, so maybe we're even.

Most people go through a Houdini phase. They read a bio in junior high school and get caught up in the escape artist and magician. Even David Copperfield has admitted that Houdini had a great press agent.

I read Kenneth Silverman's book *Houdini!!!: The Career of Ehrich Weiss: American Self-Liberator, Europe's Eclipsing Sensation, World's Handcuff King & Prison Breaker—Nothing on Earth Can Hold Houdini a Prisoner!!!* in the nineties, at a time when I was doing the Howard Stern show a lot. I was on with Gilbert Gottfried, Sam Kinison and other comedy monsters. I struggled those mornings to get a laugh in and plug the show we were doing then on Broadway.

Since my childhood Houdini phase—watching the old Tony Curtis movie on TV and reading encyclopedia entries—I had felt a kinship to Houdini. He worked in magic, I worked in magic. He hated fake psychics, I hated fake psychics. We were both momma's boys. I lied to myself that Houdini was an atheist not a Jew and that we had the same goals in showbiz. But while I was reading Silverman's book, I was disabused of that kinship. Being a magician and skeptic didn't matter to Houdini; he was first and foremost a superstar. After that time, when interviewers would ask me about Houdini, I stopped giving an opinion of my own. I would answer, "If you want to know about Houdini, don't talk to us or Copperfield, talk to Bob Dylan.

Dylan knows what it's like to sum up a generation's dreams and goals. I don't."

By the end of the eighties, Teller and I were far more successful than we had ever expected to be. The Penn & Teller pop-and-pop business plan was to eke out a couple of livings doing shows that we loved. We accomplished that within a few months of working together, and we were pretty satisfied. We kept working, just because we loved working, but every larger accomplishment just amazed us. We figured when we started that a couple hundred creeps a night might want to see our weird-ass shit, and we were off by an order of magnitude. A couple thousand creeps a night wanted to see our weird-ass shit. Creeps wanted to see us on TV. It still shocks us how many fucking creeps there are.

After I read the Silverman book, I realized Houdini was nothing like me. In the nineties, Stern was "The King of All Media." As brilliant as Stern was, as far beyond anyone's expectations that he'd risen, Stern was never satisfied. King of all media wasn't enough. He was disgusted that people listened to anyone on the radio besides him. Similarly, when I talked to Madonna in the eighties, it was clear that she didn't even consider the possibility that she had peaked or ever would—people needed to forget there was ever a Marilyn Monroe or Debbie Harry or Elvis, and she still wouldn't be satisfied.

I finished the Silverman book in the bathtub at about two a.m. and the alarm went off at five a.m. to get in the limo and head uptown to do the Stern show. As I sat in the limo, thinking about Houdini, I realized that if I wanted to know what Houdini was really like, I should not look into my own heart, but I should look into Stern's eyes. Stern and Madonna were driven beyond anything I'd ever imagined. I enjoy working in showbiz, but they need to be fa-

mous and that's all the difference. Houdini could have talked to Stern
and Madonna, and they could have argued about who was more famous. Houdini would have had nothing to say to me, not a word.
Houdini would have said that he heard that the little guy and I did a
cute little show for a few creeps. Hating psychics was not the point;
fame was. It was during that limo ride that I decided that it wasn't
only lack of talent and looks that put the cap on my career. It was
also my own satisfaction with my success. I didn't know it—it didn't
happen until decades later—but it was that morning that I decided to
try to become a good father. I still worked really hard and wrote and
did TV and radio and shows, but I knew I wouldn't ever speak for
anyone but Teller, let alone a whole generation. I would never define
anyone but myself. That shouldn't have been a revelation. Everyone
else knew what league I was in, but I needed to read that book to realize I wasn't in the league with Harry, Howard, and Maddy. They
weren't having fun doing shows; they were walking on the moon.

About a decade later, another Houdini book came out and again I
was reading it at two a.m. in the bathtub and again had an epiphany.
This was Ratso's biography, *The Secret Life of Houdini: The Making of
America's First Superhero*. I wasn't at the end of the book. This time I
was on page eight. I wasn't into the juicy parts where Ratso specu-
lates that Houdini could have been a spy, might have been poisoned,
and could have been banging one of the spiritualists. I was just in the
early nuts and bolts. Ratso and his co-author, Bill Kalush, were writing about Houdini's father. Mayer Samuel Weisz, a lawyer in Budapest who moved his family to Appleton, Wisconsin, and supported
them by pretending to be a rabbi.

Before I started the book, I knew I wouldn't identify with Houdini,
but with a warmth in my heart that heated up the bathwater, I realized I identified with Mayer Samuel Weisz. I'm much less of a rabbi

than Mayer was. Our different philosophies didn't matter. I couldn't even lie to myself that Rabbi Weisz was an atheist. But Mayer was a dad, and as I read in the bathtub, my infant son slept in the next room. I loved thinking that one day I could be fewer than eight pages into my son's 608-page biography. That would be enough for me.

I don't need or even want my son, Zolten Penn Jillette, to have a biography written about him. I don't want him to be in showbiz. I don't want him not to be in showbiz. I don't want him to be driven. I don't want little Zz to grow up to be Houdini, Stern or Ciccone, but I don't want him not to be like them either. I don't really have any plans or dreams for him. If he's an alcoholic pastor who listens to the Grateful Dead, I'll still love him. What I want most for him is for me to love him, and again that goal has also been surpassed. Perhaps the greatest thing about overshooting my goals, being more successful than I deserve or I had planned, is there's nothing I need my children to finish for me. Earl Woods got too late of a start to ever be the golfer he really wanted to be, so he helped Tiger be the greatest golfer of all time (so my wife tells me, I don't even know what end of a golf club to blow into).

My mom and dad didn't push me. They were older when I was born, and they didn't want anything for me except for me to be happy. As far as my children are concerned, I'm not even sure I need them to be happy. We all want happiness for our children, but they don't have to be happy about everything all the time. Life must include sadness, and there's peace and truth to be found in sadness. The best times are not always the happiest times, but the times spent in the flow, the times spent getting things done, the times spent living.

Right around when Zz was born, I took a set of clothes that I wore performing the Penn & Teller show and put them aside for Zz in the future. The Keith Richards belt that I'd worn in every show since the first Off-Broadway run, the Dr. Martens, the pork pie hat that I wore to play pre-show jazz, the gray suit, even my boxer shorts. I had them all vacuum-packed like a wedding dress and put into storage. I don't know what he'll do with them. Maybe he'll keep them for his children, if he has them, and let them throw out the vacuum pack if they don't want it. I like the thought of that generation throwing away my show clothes. But if he wants, Zz will be able to see what his dad wore onstage around the time he was born.

My mom and dad (and most moms and dads) said that I would never understand how much they loved me until I had my own children. I've started saying that often to my children. I want Moxie and Zz to know that they don't understand that yet, so that when they do understand, their hearts will explode in joy. It's the love you don't choose, the animal love that gives the reason to live.

Love for one's children is like a hard-on in a strip club. It's a purer and stronger feeling than the place in my brain where I make decisions. I chose to love my friends. I chose to love my wife. I think I even chose to love my parents as I got older. But I had no say in loving my children. The love for my children is beyond my control. It's animal. It's like hunger. It's more than hunger—there have been times I could control my hunger (although I can't remember any off the top of my head). I love my children like I need to breathe.

One of the things I love about going to strip clubs is getting turned on by women I don't like. I love that I can see a woman naked except for a cross around her neck and feel my cock getting hard. That cross around her neck means I would never want to hang out with her, but my body doesn't know that. My body thinks that I need to be fucking her soon, so we better get the cock ready.

The one thing that every one of our ancestors back to single cell sludge had in common was they reproduced and their offspring reproduced. If an organism failed to reproduce, that organism was a dead end, not an ancestor. The love that I feel for my children is different from the love I have for the cute things they say that get quoted by my wife on Twitter and the fun I have with them. It's different from the hugs and the kisses they give. The real love is a biological urge. Love that is like breathing.

I was the center of my parents' lives. Every one of my accomplishments meant more to them than it did to me, and I was sure the center of my own life. In the bathtub that night, reading Ratso's book, I went from thinking of my own biography to thinking of being a few pages into Zz's biography and that brought me so much joy. I felt a new kind of peace after the Silverman book when I realized I wasn't like Stern, that I could be happy as the center of my own life and I didn't have to be the center of everyone else's.

The next feeling of peace came in the moment when I didn't even want to be the center of my own life anymore. The peace of wanting to be just a few pages in Zz's life.

Zolten Jillette's father was named Penn Fraser Jillette. Zolten's first name was his mother Emily's maiden name. "Zolten" means "King" in Hungarian, and Zolten's father often weakly quipped that they'd named him after Elvis (Elvis was a popular singer in Houdini's century who was also called "The King" of the popular music at the time). Zolten's father was born in 1957, in Turners Falls, New Hampshire [writers never get that shit right]. The older Jillette was not a well-educated man. In his early life, Penn was homeless, worked carnivals and teamed up with Rudy (?) Teller to work as a comedy/magic duo, called Teller & Penn. The Teller & Penn show moved to Las Vegas, Nevada, at the sharp turn into the twenty-first century. Emily Zolten, then a golf producer, met

Penn Jillette after a show. The two were married, and Zolten's sister, Moxie Crimefighter Jillette, was born in 2005. Zolten Penn Jillette was born May 22, 2006. He would, of course, go on to lead the overthrow of the United States government and . . .

It goes on for another 607 pages, but that's the only place I'm mentioned.

Listening to: "Powderfinger"—Neil Young and Crazy Horse

Zz and his dad.

AND SPEAKING OF . . . KEVIN POLLAK NEEDS TO PLAY HOUDINI IN A GREAT MOVIE

IT'S A PAIN IN MY ASS THAT KEVIN POLLAK IS FUNNY. It makes him fun to have supper with, and he was good in *The Aristocrats* telling dirty jokes, but it fucks up my dream. My dream is to have Kevin Pollak play Houdini. Hey, Martin Luther King got his dream—what the fuck am I, chopped liver? Kevin looks like Houdini. Kevin sounds like Houdini (Kevin always sounds really lo-fi recorded on an Edison cylinder). In the world I want to live in, Kevin is playing Houdini in a movie that isn't campy like Tony Curtis's, or jive-ass like that Broadway musical with Hugh Jackman playing Houdini is going to be. I love Hugh Jackman. He's been to our show, and he was fiercely nice and talented when he came backstage. He was more talented backstage than I am onstage. Hugh can sing and dance and everything, and his family is sweet and kind and he's wicked good-looking. So why the fuck is he playing Houdini? Houdini didn't sing or dance, and he wasn't fucking good-looking. This is why Kevin is perfect. Ugly-ass Kevin would be better than piece-of-ass Hugh. Also, Hugh is Australian, and Houdini was so American he was born in Budapest and pretended to be from Appleton, Wisconsin. Did Hugh ever claim to be from Wisconsin? Not that I know of, but what the fuck do I know? I don't stalk Hugh's hot, sexy ass. Kevin could claim to be from Wisconsin, and not Frisco or whatever bullshit city he's from. And if Hugh Jackman were from the USA, like Kevin is from the USA, I bet the assholes in his school would have called him "Huge Jack-off." Assholes do that. Assholes make fun of your name even if it doesn't mean anything. I sure would have called him "Huge Jack-off," and I bet Kevin would have too, because Kevin's funny and Kevin can be an asshole, and you can bet your huge jackman that Houdini was an asshole. Hugh Jackman is a great singer and dancer, and Houdini didn't fucking sing and dance in his show. Hugh is going to play Houdini, and *The New York Times* will write another great blow job on him, because he sings, dances, and eats pussy, and that shocks the *Times*. I can stop Kevin from singing and dancing . . . I'm way bigger than he is. I can't stop Hugh Jackman from dancing and singing because he has big Wolverine claws. Houdini didn't have big Wolverine claws. Kevin doesn't have big Wolverine claws, so why the fuck isn't Kevin playing Houdini? There's an intensity to Kevin that he disguises in his stupid stand-up act. If Kevin weren't funny, we would be more likely to see that focus, playing Houdini. Kevin would be a great Houdini. A non-dancing, non-singing, not funny, not jack-off Houdini. Kevin's name doesn't sound like "jack-off," but don't bring up Polish jokes or short jokes with the little fellow, whose name sounds a lot like "Pollock." I bet assholes called him "Pollock" and I bet Hugh Jackman never called Kevin "Pollock," because Hugh is a gentleman. Houdini was a pure little fireplug of intensity. Who knows, maybe Houdini did the first Shatner that every other two-bit piece-of-shit comic rips off. How would I know? I think Kevin would be great as Houdini, so let's have him star in a serious movie about Houdini, okay? You know, there hasn't been a good Houdini movie. Harvey Keitel sure was good as Houdini (and I bet assholes made fun of the name "Harvey," don't you think? It's kind of a goofy name) in that shitty movie about fairies. But that doesn't count because the movie was shitty. Was Harvey better than Kevin, the Pollock, would be? I don't know, but Harvey didn't ask me to write jackshit for his book like Kevin asked me to write something for his book and Harvey was in *The Piano* and that sure blew. I wonder if Kevin would be naked in his Houdini movie like Harvey was in *The Piano*. Houdini stripped during his escapes, so naked wouldn't be completely gratuitous, but I love gratuitous nudity anyway. I'd like to see Kevin's cock playing Houdini's cock. But I'd probably rather see Huge Jack-off's cock, for lots of obvious reasons. Anyway, Houdini died at fifty-two, and Kevin is fifty-five now, so ticktock, ticktock, people, let's get this movie fucking made. Kevin will be great. Let's all work together and make Penn's dream come true and let Kevin play Houdini! Is that too much to ask? I mean, that and a cure for AIDS with the patent in my name, and an eleven-inch dick like Huge Jack-off—I bet that's why he got the part.

Listening to: "Edison Machine Rehearsal" (1914)—Harry Houdini

THANKSGIVING —IF YOU WON'T PUT YOUR DICK IN IT, I'M NOT GOING TO EAT IT

THE TITLE IS PERFECT. Why put legs on a snake and paint it? I should leave it at that, but I'll tell the story.

I was fairly young when I bought my first house, with showbiz money. I made the money doing street performance, Renaissance festivals, and small theater. Penn & Teller were completely unknown, but we were able to make good, solid livings doing shows in the mid-seventies. We never planned on being famous, so as far as we were concerned, this was going to be it. Teller lived in Hollywood and I lived with my girlfriend in Orange County. My girlfriend worked in a topless bar, and we had enough money to buy her parents' house when they retired. We took over the house she had spent some of her childhood in. I had a nice suburban, cul-de-sac house in Cali that I owned with the woman who inspired me to drop my cock in a blow-dryer.

Teller and I had just done a production of a show that we wrote together called *Mrs. Lonsberry's Séance of Horror*. Teller starred and I directed. It wasn't good. We were two young men who hadn't experienced the death of a loved one, writing about the death of loved ones as an excuse to do magic tricks. We should have written a play about driving around the country eating doughnuts—that was something we had experienced. I'm such a bad director. I hate telling people what to do and I don't have any vision. I haven't directed anything since.

Because of producing and financing that play, we'd lost all our money and didn't have any work, though we still had places to live. There was a few months' lag between booking the gigs and doing them. I went crazy. I wasn't mentally ill. I wasn't a danger to others or myself. Maybe you could say I went eccentric. I stopped wearing clothes. I played croquet by myself in the backyard for hours, naked, with my stereo speakers in the window playing Lou Reed's *Metal Machine Music* over and over. That record is just feedback, and one track is a closed loop, so the same few seconds repeat over and over until the power goes out. Andy Warhol wrote the liner notes to *Metal Machine Music*, but he never listened to it. It's difficult listening. It can make a crazy fellow crazier. I was obsessed with topiary, and we had a big hedge. I let it grow and tried to use a mirror and hedge clippers to do a self-portrait of myself naked, in bush, in the backyard with loud feedback playing and croquet set up for one. I have since found out that many of the "topiaries," especially the ones at Disney, have wire frames underneath and aren't bush all the way down. It bothers me even more than the Legoland Lego structures having frames underneath them. If you're creating something *of* bush or Legos, *use* bush or Legos. (I also don't like the Lego sets that tell my children what the set is supposed to build. That's not creating, that's following directions, and they ask me to help and I fuck it up.) Finding out that there were wire frames under the topiary was harder on me than finding out there was no god. Fuck those wire topiaries. My naked backyard topiary was a failure, but it was bush all the way down.

Penn & Teller were just a pop-and-pop shop at this point. We called ourselves Buggs & Rudy Discount Corporation. Our operation is still called that. Buggs and Rudy were the imaginary business guys who handled Penn & Teller. I answered the phone as "Buggs," and silent Rudy did all the contracts and the graphics. I read one cheesy business book that suggested that while negotiating it was helpful to know something the other party didn't know. I took that to heart on a drive to Tijuana, where I bought a donkey hat. It was a straw cowboy hat with straw donkey ears sticking out and a straw donkey tail down the back. I had painted my office fluorescent orange and green. I figured no one I was negotiating with by phone would know I was naked, save for a donkey hat, in a fluorescent orange and green room. I could drive a hard bargain.

Yup, I went a little bugnutty. I was naked in that hat all the time, playing crazy music and thinking. I would just sit and think. I didn't really talk to anyone. I had a really nice stereo and I played it loud all the time, not just *Metal Machine Music*, but Sun Ra and Tiny Tim. I was afraid the neighborhood suburban teenagers in our cul-de-sac would steal my stereo (but not my music), so one of the few times I put clothes on, I put on a pair of gym shorts, my donkey hat and flip-flops and told the local teenagers stories about "Nam." It worked. They stayed away from the house. I don't know if it was the lies about combat, the donkey hat or the gym shorts, but my stereo was safe.

The silent, loud, naked, brooding phase was coming to an end. Teller and I had to get back on the road and do shows. I can pull it together to be normal enough to do a Penn & Teller show, but that's as far as I go. My girlfriend could now convince me to put on jeans and a shirt, so we decided to have a Thanksgiving celebration at our house.

We invited a creepy elderly sideshow sword swallower, a lighting designer, Teller, a guy who had just quit dealing angel dust in Fresno and was hanging out with us to help him stay clean, and a geologist. It's always important to have a geologist around so that if you end up in space, there's someone to die first. At least that's what happens on *Star Trek*.

I love Thanksgiving. I just love it. My mom would make this great tuna dip and we'd eat it with Bugles. We had cranberry sauce from the can that I could squeeze through my teeth, celery with cream cheese spread on it, turkey, gravy, stuffing that was really just wet bread and goodness and none of that raisin, mushroom, or chestnut hippie shit, and lots of pie. It had no religious overtones for us; we didn't say grace. And no one in our family watched football, so after the Macy's parade, the TV was turned off. It was a pretty great day. We had little pilgrim name tags that I'd made as a young child and my mom still used them to show where we'd sit, even though we'd been sitting in the same places my whole life. My childhood Thanksgivings were Norman Rockwell. Norman Rockwell's stuffing didn't have fucking cornbread and chestnuts in it.

We didn't really have to invite the former angel dust dealer from Fresno to Thanksgiving because he was living with us. We took a liking to him, and he was living with us, until he went to Ringling Bros. and Barnum & Bailey Clown College, my own alma mater. My girlfriend was the only one in the household who worked, and she was going to do the cooking for our Thanksgiving. Right before I went into my naked donkey-hat phase, I had told her that since she was working and I wasn't, she could just name a kind of food that she liked and I would take a continuing education course in cooking at the community college and cook her supper every night at two a.m. when she got off work. She suggested Chinese food. Others in the cooking class seemed to be there to meet people and get laid, but I was there to learn. I took a lot of notes, paid attention, bought a wok and every night after work, we had a home-cooked Chinese meal for two. I made my own fucking dumplings from scratch. The teacher said I was the best student she'd ever had. After three weeks, my girl-friend said, very politely, "I love all your Chinese cooking, but some night could we have something else?" I never cooked again. She was cooking the Thanksgiving turkey. If she needed me, I'd be working on my topiary.

As part of his transition from drug dealer to clown, our friend decided to get a big laugh on Thanksgiving morning. I don't know what got into his head, but he listened to my girlfriend complain about what time she had to get up to start the turkey and then set his alarm for ten minutes earlier. As she groggily walked to the kitchen, she heard a slapping sound and his voice saying in a Spanish accent, "C'mon, baby, you can take all of me." She tentatively walked into the kitchen to see our housemate, with his boxers around his ankles, slapping the turkey and fucking it. I didn't see the event, and it wasn't clear from the story how simulated the sex with the turkey was. At Clown College they teach us to commit completely, but he hadn't been to Clown College yet, so I don't know whether there was an actual erect penis in our turkey or just a limp one bouncing against it, but it was enough to make her scream. She thought it was real, then thought it was a joke, and then settled on it was real and now being passed off as a joke. He had to wait for me to wake up before he got his full laugh. I couldn't stop laughing, and I still can't see a turkey without hearing "C'mon, baby, you can take all of me" in a Spanish accent.

As we sat around our beautiful Thanksgiving dinner table in Orange County, I told the other guests what had happened as we ate the turkey. I spooned the non-hippie stuffing onto my plate and bragged how our friend's dick had been in that cavity. The lighting designer seemed a little put off, so I asked her, not completely rhetorically, "Why would I eat something that he wouldn't put his dick in?"

Since there was no good answer, we all enjoyed our turkey and stuffing, and then it was time for dessert. Our geologist hadn't been killed by giant falling rocks in space, so he proudly displayed a flourless chocolate cake that he'd been working on for a few days. It was perfect and beautiful. I had one question: "Did you put your cock in it?"

"No." He laughed a lot.

"Then I'm not eating it."

"Me neither," a few people chimed in.

He laughed more and then realized we weren't kidding. Well, we were kidding, but we weren't bluffing. He begged us, "C'mon, man, I worked really hard on this, and I want you to enjoy it."

"Not if you won't put your dick in it." I can be like that. Or rather, I'm always like that—she questioned me once, and I never cooked Chinese food again.

There was a long hesitation, and the geologist proved himself. He pulled the flourless chocolate cake over to his place at the table. He stood up, unbuckled his pants, and dragged his cock all over the cake, while saying, "C'mon, baby, you can take all of me" in a Spanish accent. Thanksgiving is a holiday I can get into.

The cake was way good.

Eventually that girlfriend left me. It kind of tells you everything about me: naked in a donkey hat, talking as much as Teller does onstage, my girlfriend stayed with me, but when I started putting on clothes and chatting, she left me and took my donkey hat. She took the house, the car and the donkey hat and all I miss is the donkey hat. A lot of friends have promised they would find me another donkey hat, and they have all failed. One friend even went to Tijuana insisting she would find me a donkey hat, but no soap. Another friend made one. It was lovely, but it wasn't the right hat. If you know what I'm talking about and can find a real donkey hat for me, get in touch. For a perfect donkey hat that fits, I'll pay you a hundred dollars cash money (I can drive a hard bargain even as I sit here in jeans wearing a sandwich hat). I haven't felt right since I lost my donkey hat.

I don't know what got into my head, but I still need that donkey hat. "I don't know what got into my head, but . . ." When guys are sitting around telling stories, or as the carnies say, "cutting up jackpots," those are the words I want to hear. It seems like all great stories have that phrase in them. I was on *Miami Vice* in the eighties because there was no other time to be on it. While we were shooting in NYC and Miami, I was also shooting a feature film with Judge Reinhold and doing eight shows a week Off-Broadway. I went almost three weeks without ever sleeping more than two hours at a time and most of that in limos and mobile homes. It's as hard as you can work without having a job. The hardest work in showbiz is easier than any other job you can have in the world except the job of driving those big billboards on a trailer up and down the Vegas Strip. That job looks easy and fun but doesn't pay as well as showbiz. All that being said, you spend three weeks with Don Johnson and see how much you want to be alive.

One of the security guys on *Miami Vice* was a former professional wrestler. While I was half asleep waiting for someone to apologize to Don so we could get back to shooting, my security guard buddy would tell me wrestling stories. This was years ago and I was sleep-deprived, but the way I remember one of his stories, he was having Thanksgiving with a bunch of professional wrestlers and he didn't know what got into his head, but he bet Captain Lou Albano five hundred bucks that he couldn't get the turkey out of the oven and throw it out the window without the other wrestlers stopping him. It turned their Thanksgiving into a bunch of guys screaming and laughing covered with really bad grease burns and the turkey thrown out a closed window—broken glass and dirty turkey.

I love my life now, but sometimes I'd sure like to be naked with my donkey hat listening to feedback and clipping a hedge to look like me. Maybe that's when I'm at my best.

Listening to: Metal Machine Music—*Lou Reed*

Showing off, kind of, during a B&E at a house in the swamps of Jersey where I didn't know anyone. We kinda broke in. Let's say it was around Thanksgiving time and let's say that I was kidding about the B&E.

THE MAGICIAN STANDS LAZILY HALF NAKED BEFORE THE WORLD

IN MY LAST BOOK, I WROTE ABOUT my friends and fellow Vegas magicians Siegfried & Roy. In describing the purity and honesty of their showbiz glitz, I tried to quote Lenny Bruce as saying, "The purpose of art is to stand naked onstage." I've been quoting that wisdom since I was a child. I was a small-time New England Christian teetering toward atheism and becoming obsessed with the idea of people telling the truth onstage. I was listening to Lenny Bruce and anything else that represented New York City and real art to me. That quote kind of summed up what I was looking for. The problem was that when I checked the Lenny quote for my book, I couldn't find any evidence that Lenny Bruce had said it. I Googled, I listened to all my Lenny recordings, reread the books and I couldn't find the quote anywhere, not by Lenny, nor by anyone else.

So I wrote that I couldn't find the quote and then took credit for the line myself. It was just a joke—I knew it wasn't mine; that's too important an idea for me to get on my own. No one who read the book before its release could place the original quote. The book made the *New York Times* bestseller list for a bunch of weeks, people must have read it, but no one told me where that quote was really from. I said, "The purpose of art is to stand naked onstage," during my book signings and readings, and no one corrected me during the Q&As. I have more than 1.7 million "followers" on Twitter and they love to bust me on anything, but none of them called me an idiot for not knowing who put that idea in my young brain where it would stay, without the correct attribution, for more than forty years. No one seemed to know that quote.

I did a lot of traveling to hawk my book. I was up in Frisco (they love it up there when you call it that, it makes it seem like you're a native) doing interviews and book signings. I had time for lunch before my flight home, and Scotty and Katrine, a couple of juggler friends, took me to a restaurant in North Beach. I was delighted to walk down Broadway, where just up from Carol Doda's Condor Club—which has an official government plaque citing it as the first "topless" and "bottomless" strip club—there is a small Afghan restaurant (what's their special of the day, IED and heroin?), which used to be the Phoenix Theater. Back when the Mabuhay Gardens had Jello Biafra and the other Dead Kennedys making music important again on the stage, Teller and I were across the street in our old performance group, the Asparagus Valley Cultural Society, trying to punk out magic. We did 965 shows over three years, closing on Halloween in 1981. We've done tens of thousands of shows since then, and our old theater has become a little restaurant now, but it made my heart go pitter-pat.

As I strolled with my San Francisco friends from my former theater to the restaurant, we walked past the Beat Museum in North
Beach, nestled among the strip clubs. A storefront museum and gift
shop dedicated to what San Francisco writer Herb Caen called "the
beatniks." They had lots of Kerouac, Cassady, Ginsberg and all the
others. I had recently read the scroll version of *On the Road*, and I
pointed out to everyone that Lowell, Massachusetts, where Kerouac
was from, is just a short patch of holyboy road, madman road, rain-
bow road, guppy road, any nightmare senseless American road, kissing his left front tire fraught with eminent peril and wild wild, mad
to live, mad to talk, desirous of everything, to Greenfield, Massachusetts, where I was born.

The beatnik store had lots of old, sexy *Evergreen* magazines. I
think I saw one issue when I was a child, and it was and still is perfec-
tion to me—black and white naked beat women having sex, smoking
cigarettes, or reading in New York City apartments; dirty stories; and
real literature and culture. The first one I picked up in the Beat store
felt just like the one I saw as a child and got my heart and cock going.
It had a woman on the cover. I swear I'd still give it all up for an ad-
vertisement for Frank Zappa and the Mothers of Invention's first
album, *Freak Out!* I wanted to live in the spirit of that magazine, and
instead I'm featured on Vegas.com. Oh well. They had paperback
translations of *On the Road* in all different languages. They even had
Kerouac's jacket. For a Beat fan, beatnik, peacenik, old hippie capitalist guy like me, this is the only museum that matters. Who needs di-
nosaur bones?

When I picked up *Evergreen* and thumbed through it to see the
model in the flat lighting on her apartment, with slightly crooked
teeth, fat bohemian hair on her head and curly wild hippie un-
trimmed pubic hair, standing there smoking with books all around

her and breasts she was much too comfortable with the hang of, I could feel a sexual flush in my face. You can't get that flush at fifty-six years old; you can get that flush only as a teenager. But these magazines made me time travel. I love naked pictures. There is no one I wouldn't rather see naked (and I've been tested—Ernest Borgnine? Yes!). There on the wall of the museum was a big black-and-white picture of the young poets Allen Ginsberg and Gregory Corso standing side by side, naked, their hands cupped over their genitals. I'm one of those guys who reads all the little description cards at museums, and this one explained . . .

ALLEN GINSBERG AND GREGORY CORSO, 1961

There are many photographs and stories of Allen Ginsberg getting naked in public. Some of the stories are legendary—being heckled by an audience member while onstage at a poetry reading, Ginsberg would proceed to take off his clothes. "The poet stands naked before the world!" he would say, challenging the heckler. "Are you willing to stand naked before the world?"

Allen would sometimes show up at a party and after a certain amount of time step into the restroom, pile all his clothes in a neat pile and step back in to the party completely naked. Legend has it he did this to John Lennon once at a party in New York. John quietly left telling a friend, "I don't want anyone pulling out a camera and taking a picture of me and a naked Allen Ginsberg."

There was my quote. When I was young, I was sucking up everything I could about all these beautiful, mysterious people. To my fourteen-year-old goyishe kop, Lenny Bruce and Allen Ginsberg were the same. To my fifty-six-year-old *epikoros* kop, Lenny Bruce and

Allen Ginsberg are still more alike than they are different. They were both poets. "The poet stands naked before the world!" is way better than "The purpose of art is to stand naked onstage." I'm not Lenny or Allen.

Let's look at how I weakened the quote. I start with "The purpose of art." The word "purpose" is an ugly word in there. Ginsberg doesn't need "purpose," standing naked is not to be a task: it's a state of being. Of course, I would think, "purpose." I was trying to make art, Ginsberg was art. And I end with "onstage." I was trying to be on a stage, Ginsberg was just being.

I thought about my failures as a poet for a while and then called Scotty, Katrine and the curator who was showing us around over to the naked picture. I told them how important this quote was and is to me. I talked about how much better it was than I had remembered. I asked Katrine if she had a camera on her cell phone. I started stripping off my clothes.

I didn't think I deserved to be the same as the poets. I don't deserve to stand symbolically beside them naked before the world. I was too lazy to take my shoes off, I didn't want to crawl around looking for my clothes, and I didn't want to get dressed after the picture was taken. I left my shoes on, I dropped my baggy jeans in a rumpled pile over my shoes. I pulled my boxer-briefs down to my knees, at prostate exam level. I unbuttoned my workshirt to show my fat stomach, but I didn't take it off and throw it. I glanced over at Allen and Gregory's picture, and I tried to match their hands on my penis and testicles.

I wanted to stand naked with the poets in the public museum, but I didn't want to have to lace up my shoes again. So I just pulled down my jeans and underwear and unbuttoned my workshirt. I also felt that to stand completely naked would be to call myself a poet, and I just couldn't do that. If Allen and Gregory had been there, and stripped, I couldn't have put myself in the same category. I aimed for poet and hit Vegas headliner. Billy West, the greatest voice guy in the world (he's done *Futurama*, *Ren & Stimpy* and the best M&M—red), once said there was just one showbiz and we were all in it. Teller says art is anything we do after the chores are done. I agree with them both very much. I believe that Ron Jeremy has the same job as Picasso and Bach. I know that the mall Santa is the same as Bob Dylan and Katharine Hepburn. I know all that and I believe all that. But still, a magician has to be a damn sight lower than a poet. We're above ventriloquists, but not near poets. Imagine if someone said, "A magician stands naked before the world." The answer wouldn't be, "Isn't that brilliant?" but rather, "Isn't that illegal?"

I am one of two magicians who has stood naked, if not before the world, then at least before a paying crowd in a casino showroom in Las Vegas. The other magician is not Houdini, who always had chains in front of his junk and always wore a swimsuit. The other magician is Teller. In the history of Vegas, Teller and I are the disappointing first male full-frontal nudes onstage. Yup, Vegas has male strippers—Chippendales and Thunder From Down Under (which always struck me as an unpleasant name, bringing to mind ripping loud farts instead of sexy ripped Australians). Vegas has had a bunch of shows full of gorgeous, hunky, hung, ripped, sexy men, and yet, the first guys to stand totally naked onstage there were two middle-aged magicians. If that doesn't prove to you that there's no god, I don't know what would. Teller and I ended every show for a few runs at Bally's (the same stage Sinatra and Dino played on, and Dino and Tom Jones were still doing runs there while we were), stripping completely naked. The joke was simple—magicians are always accused of having something up their sleeves, and we wanted to prove we didn't. We would take off our shirts, and then our T-shirts, and then with a few jokes to shoes and socks, and finally down to just boxer shorts. It was a drag, because I wear my microphones in my glasses and the battery packs go in a pouch on my T-shirt, so I had to take all that off and go to a hand mic.

Teller would get a couple of volunteers from the audience, usually an older woman and a young guy, and we'd bring them onstage to examine us. A pair of crew guys would bring out a thin band of translucent plastic and we'd take off our boxers and have the audiences members check out everything. We showed them everything we had, lifting our penises and testicles and letting them check for hidden bunny rabbits. The plastic didn't really cover much and people could always see over, under, and around it. This wasn't a flash—this was a genital tour. The audience members would then examine a couple of long white tank tops and we'd put those on and nothing else. They were short enough that when we lifted our arms, well, on a warm or exciting night, the shirts wouldn't cover the full frontal even during the magic.

Big-band Penn & Teller theme music would play and, out of nowhere, we would produce a few liters of stage blood each and cover ourselves from head to toe with it while doing a little dance routine, soaking the T-shirts. That would be the end of the show, and we'd appear afterward in the lobby to meet people and sign autographs wearing Carrie-like, blood-soaked T-shirts with our little Houdinis hanging out. It was pretty great, because instead of having to sign autographs, we could just slap our chests and give them a bloody handprint on their souvenir programs.

In Atlantic City once, a professionally beautiful woman came up to me, wearing a white minidress without undergarments just like me, and gave me a big hug. The blood left her dress slightly transparent and imprinted all of the private parts of my body onto hers. So sexy. It was a great moment. I felt I should invite her backstage to shower with me, help her pack up her souvenir minidress, give her a P&T T-shirt, but the girlfriend at the time wouldn't have been cool with that. I'm such a loser. But it's a great memory. Wow. I should have gotten her e-mail address and I could see that great tit/cock blood live gravestone rubbing. Shoot.

I've stripped naked in public other times too, maybe not as much as Ginsberg, but a lot of times and I learned a few tricks and tips. I stripped in Zero-G on the Vomit Comet, and I stripped a couple of times in business meetings (I once stripped naked for all the Disney execs and served them doughnuts to show I didn't think a certain deal with us was going to happen) and on radio shows.

Once while cohosting radio with Alex Bennett in Florida, we had some Hooters waitresses on who served everyone chicken wings, including the whole live audience. Alex always had a live audience of about thirty people, and the women had brought enough buffalo wings for everyone. They got to talking about how they themselves weren't bad people like the topless dancers we'd had serving doughnuts on the air the morning before. Alex and I argued that the name Hooters was a joke about breasts, and it just wasn't a classy organization. Alex asked the self-righteous servers if they would go topless if Hooters changed their policy and offered them more money. One of the women said, "Would you take your clothes off for a million dollars?" She thought that was a rock-solid argument. She didn't know whom she was saying it to.

I took off all my clothes as fast as I could and threw them into the audience. I stood naked, not in front of the world, but in front of a Florida radio-station audience. I was standing on top of the engineering board. My friend's elderly parents were in the audience to see me, and there was their son's buddy naked. A few nights later the same couple came to see our show, and Teller accidentally picked my friend's mom to come onstage for the stripping bit. My buddy called me up and said, "What is it with you exposing yourself to my mom?" He had a point: she had seen my penis twice in one week. That's not right.

I learned that day at the radio station why professional strippers don't throw their clothes into the audience. When Alex threw to commercial and I wanted to get dressed, I had to walk naked among the audience trying to find all my clothes to get dressed again. No matter how humiliating the scene standing on the radio desk had been, bending over naked to pick up your boxer shorts from under an elderly woman's chair is worse. "Please excuse me" doesn't help much.

The poets stand naked before the world. The magician is always just left clutching his naked penis, wearing half a shirt and a proud, satisfied smile.

Listening to: "Take Your Clothes Off When You Dance"—The Mothers of Invention

Allen Ginsberg and Gregory Co

There are many photographs and stories of Allen Ginsberg getting naked
stories are legendary—being heckled by an audience member while onsta
Ginsberg would proceed to take off his clothes. "The poet stands naked b
say, challenging the heckler. "Are you willing to stand naked before the wo

Allen would sometimes show up at a party and after a certain amount of ti
room, pile all his clothes in a neat pile and step back in to the party comple
he did this to John Lennon once at a party in New York. John quietly left te
want anyone pulling out a camera and taking a picture of me and a naked A

A TELEPHONE CONVERSATION WITH GILBERT GOTTFRIED ON JANUARY 13, 2002

PENN: Are you the Aflac duck? Is that your voice?

GILBERT: Yeah.

PENN: Is it just saying "Aflac"?

GILBERT: Yeah, and a few other sounds.

PENN: But no words, right?

GILBERT: No, just kinda quacking.

PENN: I can't bring it to mind. Just do the voice for me once—just do "Aflac."

GILBERT: I'm not going to do a voice for you.

PENN: C'mon, I want to hear it.

GILBERT: "Do the parrot." "Do Comedy Central." I'm not doing a voice for you. I'm not performing for you.

PENN: Listen, you little fucking bastard, do the fucking duck or I'll slap you. I'm not kidding.

GILBERT: Is that technologically possible over the phone?

PENN: I'm coming to New York tomorrow, asshole.

GILBERT: . . . . . . Aflac.

"Little White Duck"—Burl Ives

NEW YEAR'S DAY, GYMS, WHORE- HOUSES, AND MOURNING WITH PROSTITUTES

NEW YEAR'S DAY IS A BIG, HAIRY DEAL DAY FOR ME. On New Year's Day 2000, my mom died after spending the last few days of 1999 relaxing in a coma. January 1 of every year our family releases balloons into the sky in memory of all the people we've loved and lost. My mom's final conscious days were spent watching some helium balloons that dear Teller got for her, tied outside her bleak Massachusetts winter window, dance around in the wind. Mom asked if I would let her balloons go free right after she died.

New Year's isn't the only day I show our children pictures of the grandparents they never knew and tell them family stories that now are theirs, but I always do that then. We give the children a ton of presents that day, one week to the day after Christmas, to make up for all their Christian friends who taunt them about not having pres-

ents from Santa and Jesus. I believe in this arena the theological debate can be won with more toys. Penn & Teller don't do a show on
New Year's Eve, so it's a rare evening at home, hanging with friends,
watching movies, and eating ice cream. I like to start the New Year
with friends and family, not selling people our show with a glass of
champagne added for three times the price. If the gift battle for the
hearts and minds of our non-Christian children continues to esca-
late, Penn & Teller may have to go back to New Year's Eve shows so
I can afford to buy my children a dozen ponies with Richard
Dawkins's picture stenciled on their sides in Sour Patch Kids, but
until that time, we'll take it as a day of rest.

The private Jillette New Year's Day is spent at home with the family. But public New Year's for sub-star celebrities means writing up
our jive-ass New Year's resolutions beforehand to sell tickets. These
are unabashed advertisements for our show: "I resolve to try to go
another year without blowing Teller's brains out on the Penn &
Teller Theater Stage at the Rio All-Suites Hotel and Casino in Las
Vegas, Nevada, during our world-famous bullet catch—featured as
the #1 Best Magic Trick of All Time by *TV's Fifty Greatest Magic
Tricks*." We're always trying to put asses in the seats, but I've never
made a genuine New Year's resolution.

I'm the essence of a sixteen-year-old Midwest mall girl in the
body of the three-hundred-pound, fifty-six-year-old Las Vegas man. I
don't watch any sporting events. I've never seen any whole game of
anything live or on TV. Paul Simon and Lorne Michaels took me to
one Yankees game. We arrived late, talked, ate hot dogs, and left
early. I once escorted a woman who worked in our Penn & Teller office to a local Vegas hockey team. She was trying to explain "icing" to
me when the guy in the Thunderbird mascot suit recognized me
through the face mesh of his sweaty heavy suit and decided that we

would do improvisation together while the hockey game was going on. I stood up and waved when he beckoned me to do so. I did a little dance in the aisle with him. Then he sat on my lap. Then we stood up again. He left and came back a bit later and we did all of our bits again. When he left again, I snuck out. I was out of material. My repertoire for interacting with a guy dressed in a blue suit is waving, laughing, dancing and receiving an ever-so-slightly too-sexual-for-public smelly lap dance. Once I've run through that whole show twice, I think it's time to tag it and bag it. I believe I could have been there for days without any Thunderbird character distractions and still wouldn't have understood icing.

When I was a kid, my mom and dad took me on a yearly trip to the numismatics convention in Houston, and my mom took me to a baseball game at the Astrodome. She was doing her best to make me act like a normal boy. Mama Tried. I loved the tour of the Astrodome, but I insisted on leaving before the first game of the doubleheader was over. I don't know who was playing, but I do know that the inside space of the Astrodome is so big they have their own weather system, but it's not as big in terms of open cubic space as the Vehicle Assembly Building at Cape Canaveral. A buddy of mine was almost fencing in the Olympics, so I saw half of one event there. He taught me to fence in my apartment. As soon as our first practice match started, I said, "Watch out for the TV." He turned; I stabbed him and retired. A few weeks later, I tried that with a smarter friend who was teaching me boxing out in the alley behind our house. "Watch out for the car!" I said, and he punched me hard in the face. I retired from boxing after one round too.

I can explain what bugs me about sports and games in general. For some Caesars Palace PR thing, they invited Penn & Teller to a real boxing match. It wasn't heavyweights, but it was heavy. There were billboards and building and bus ads with the fighters' faces all over Vegas. This was real boxing, and Penn & Teller were right up front in our sub-star position, waving and waiting to dance with any bird-suited boxing mascot who happened to show up. I thought I was going to get all acoustic-guitar-I'll-get-laid-by-being-a-pussy-peacenik about the whole thing. I thought that the real blood would freak me. I love the artistic depiction of violence, but I don't like the real thing. Hillary Clinton gets all high and mighty about video games and how violent they are. Fuck her—they aren't violent at all. Video games depict fantasy violence and someone in her position should know the difference. Real violence is what her boss does with the real drone planes really killing real people really spilling real blood. Drones may also be run by joystick, but there's no fantasy and no joy. People who love artistic depictions of violence are celebrating being alive with art. Art is life. Drones mean death. Even though the people bleeding in a boxing match are choosing to take the chance to bleed, I thought the real violence of boxing would freak me out and I'd get all emo about it. But my problem was the opposite. I was driven crazy by how little the guys got hit. Most every punch was blocked. One guy is trying to get a punch in and the other guy is stopping him. The frustration of all these little plans being foiled was nerve-racking. "Get your arms out of the way and let that guy hit you in the face." Later I read a great quote from Mike Tyson: "Everyone has a plan until they get hit." That's what really bugged me. I hated that every one of these guys had a Rocky story and a coach and a plan and the plans never worked because the other guy knew how not to get hit. I hated the frustration.

I spent most of my childhood juggling. Hours and hours and days and days and weeks and weeks and years. I juggled and I masturbated and once I tried them at the same time. I didn't have video equipment then; otherwise I hope you would be watching it on the Web right now. I practiced all the time (juggling, that is; I was a natural at masturbation). I did shows (juggling, not masturbation; supply and demand). And I practiced some more. And I'd do a show with cheerleaders and masturbate a little more and then do more shows, then practice more, and as I got a little older, fucking and unicycling were added to my activities. I had a high school girlfriend who I'm sure was small enough for me to fuck on the unicycle, and although we fucked everywhere else, we never did it while riding. I bet the Web would have inspired us to go the extra mile—well, I was sixteen then, so it would have been only the extra fifty feet, but we should have done it. There must be video of someone getting fucked on a unicycle but I haven't found it yet. It would crush the guy's balls something wicked, but it would be so worth it.

When Teller and I are promoting our act, we're in a competition—people decide every night in Vegas whether to see us or guys on skateboards wearing featureless face masks and Beatles wigs. We compete for the attention of the ticket buyers. But it's different from sports. No one is fucking us up. There isn't anyone who tries to guess our dreams and plans and then fucks them up on purpose. I take that back—there's one magician in Vegas who I think has gone out of his or her way (I put that "her" in to throw you off the scent, but the fact that there are very few women in the stupid magic boy's club makes my attempt not very successful) just to fuck Penn & Teller up. This gal or guy wouldn't sign a deal at one of the hotels we worked at before the Rio until we were fired from that hotel. S(he) wouldn't let us work there when he/she wasn't. (S)he did that only a couple times that we know of, and it didn't really bug us. There are other places for us to work. Sports are somebody fucking you up all the time. One team has a plan to run down a field with a football and the other team has a plan to fuck them up. Everyone has a plan until they get hit. I don't mind working against my own incompetence, random chance and the whole universe, but I hate there being a guy or gal who's trying to fuck me up. I don't like games. Trying to get your chess pieces around the board, and the other guy takes them away. Even the game Trouble bums my shit, but my children like it and sometimes I cheat so I don't fuck them up (I tell myself that's why I lose).

Couple my lack of interest in sports with my lack of drug or alcohol use, and my lack of masculinity is ridiculous. We were doing *Penn & Teller's Sin City Spectacular*, an hour-long show with a big song-and-dance number every week, and we were wicked overworked. I had been diagnosed with a cholesteatoma in my left ear, which is one of the reasons I'm deaf as a post. They said it was "benign," but that if they didn't get it out, it would grow into my brain and kill me. I have a different definition of "benign." They had to take off my ear and drill into my skull. I couldn't take that much time off from shooting the TV show without getting something out of it. Teller suggested that we do a trick with a signed penny. Teller would make it vanish and then when the doctor opened up my skull and saw my brain, he'd find the penny—ta-da! We'd video the whole thing and we'd get a great bit out of my required surgery. The surgeon was very Hollywood and had no trouble with all the cameras as long as the crew scrubbed up and wore scrubs and masks. The penny had to be put into an autoclave and Teller had to learn the sleight of hand with surgical gloves on.

The big problem was that I had to be conscious to do the bit. This is an operation they do under general anesthetic, but I would be the first to do it conscious, just so I could sign the penny, watch it vanish and then say, "That's my penny!" when it came out of my brain. Funny, right? When it got to the day, I told the anesthesiologist that because of my long hair, my age, my size, my job and the number of times I say "fuck," he was going to be tempted to give me a lot of drugs to calm me down and cut down the pain (I wasn't going all the way unconscious, but I wasn't going full straight-edge either). At the end of the operation, as I came to, he told me, "I gave you enough Valium to make a ninety-eight-pound sixteen-year-old mall girl a little tipsy and almost lost you—wow, you are a cheap date." It was really hard being able to hear and feel them drilling into my head. Teller was trying to get me to do my lines into the camera, and I was crying and saying, "Please help me, Teller. It hurts. Get me out of here. Please help me. Help me!" Teller was in my face, yelling, saying, "Stop crying! Focus! Just do the fucking line! Look at me and say, 'That's my penny' with a smile. C'mon, do it. Do it now. C'mon, Penn, focus. *Do it!*"

After they got the video, Teller said, "Okay, knock him out!" and they put me under and I was gone for the rest of the operation. Humans don't really remember pain, but I remember the screaming and I remember them drilling into my head. It's the loudest sound a mammal can hear. I know the decibel scale is logarithmic so you have to pick your numbers carefully. I know that 19 decibels is twice as loud as 18. A jet taking off in the sixties or Black Sabbath playing in the seventies is about 120 decibels. I'm saying when they drilled into my head it was like a gazillionmotherbuttfuckinggoogol decibels. I don't remember it, but I was told after that when the electric drill pierced my skull I yelled, "Ramones!"

Teller left the operating room and took off his mask, gloves, hood and bunny suit. One of the other writers came over and said, "Man, you were so cruel to Penn. He was really suffering and you were screaming in his face. Man, there was no compassion." Teller said, "That was nothing but compassion. He went in for that operation conscious so we could do our bit. When he comes to, crying in pain, do you want to be the one to tell him that we didn't get what we needed, so he did it without drugs all for nothing? Is that your job? Because I'm afraid it would be my job. Penn did his part, so we sure as fuck better do our parts."

As it turned out we all did our parts perfectly . . . except for the concept. The concept sucked. The editors cut it together and it was so fucking intense, no one could watch it. It looked like just what it was: a man in a huge amount of pain having a penny appear inside his skull. Teller did the magic; it was competent. I did the lines; they were clear. My acting was passable, but the whole thing was unwatchable. We had to fight with the network even to show a small amount of it, and then we had to show it on a TV on the stage with me leaning in and narrating to show I was okay. It didn't show I was okay; it showed I was Charlie-Manson-bug-fucking-nutty. It didn't look like the health channel; it looked like a snuff film. My mom saw the broadcast and couldn't stop crying about her little boy in pain. That's comedy.

I have no manly love of recreational drugs or sports. I like to put my hair up in a Judy Jetson ponytail on top of my head (I'm aware that a real sixteen-year-old mall girl wouldn't have heard of Judy Jetson, but we're talking heart not memory), talk on the phone in a bath full of scented bath oils, get manicures and write obsessively in my diary. I don't write "Dear diary" to start every entry, but I do often write, "I got up." I don't watch sports; I keep a diary. I'm not a man's man or a woman's man.

The image would have been more perfectly mall girl if I'd said "bubble bath" instead of scented bath oils. But I don't like bubbles in my tub. They're distracting. I didn't used to like bath oils either, until I got bathtub syphilis. In 1979, Teller and I were part of a show called the Asparagus Valley Cultural Society, which we ran for three years in Frisco. The AVCS, or Asparagus, as it was shortened to, was kind of like Penn & Teller with a third guy, named Wier Chrisemer, who did some verbal comedy bits with me, a monologue about the history of music, and played classical music in odd and comical arrangements. Teller wore all-black dance clothes, I wore white cutoff shorts and a T-shirt, and Wier wore a three-piece suit. He split and we kept the suit idea. Some of the bits from Asparagus are still part of the P&T repertoire. I was twenty-four years old, and although it was a small theater, it was still a show that I had written, and I was making my living, and a good living, just doing shows. I was making less money than I made street performing, but still more money than anyone I knew. This was before I met Steve Jobs and Bill Gates, but I made more than they did at the time—I made coin early. During this period, I took baths a lot. I took baths all the time. There were days when I was in the bathtub more than eight hours a day. I started out reading and talking on the phone in the bathtub, then I added eating in the bathtub, and finally I would work with Teller in the bathtub. It was just me in the bathtub, and he'd sit in the bathroom with me. We were writing *Mrs. Lonsberry's Séance of Horror* that Teller would costar in, along with a really, really old woman (about ten years younger than I am now), and I would direct. Teller would pull a chair and a notebook into the bathroom, and we would talk while I lay in the tub.

I've talked to Adam Carolla about my bath obsession. Adam knows that I don't fit in a bathtub, not because he's seen me in a bathtub but because he's a carpenter and has a trained eye for how things fit together. I now have a stupid-big bathtub in our home, but in the past, and in hotels on the road still, I use a regular bathtub. They're all kind of sitz baths for me, but I love the hot water on my

ass and back. I don't know why I spent hours and hours in the bathtub during 1979, but I liked it and Teller indulged me. We wrote a
failed play while I soaked.

Penn & Teller have always greeted people after the show, and one
night in 1979 a woman came up to me and asked if she could talk to
me privately. Hell yes! When the rest of the people left, we went over
to a side of the theater and she started with, "I'm a nurse." This was
getting good. Then it got bad, "I'm a nurse. Can I see that rash on
your arm?" Sure. I did the show with short sleeves and I showed her
this weird rash that I had all the time. "It doesn't hurt," I said confi-
dently. She said, "It's secondary syphilis. It's all I could think about
during your show. Go see a doctor soon." It didn't seem like the right
time to hit on her.

I went backstage and everyone figured I'd be meeting her after I
got out of wardrobe. "Nope, she wanted to tell me I have syphilis."
No one but me was surprised.

I made a doctor's appointment. I walked in, rolled up my sleeves
and said, "Someone last night saw this rash—"

"Secondary syphilis."

"No, I don't think it is."

He started into his doctor speech about nice girls and boys having
syphilis and he was sure that my sex partners all had sex only with
me but there were toilet seats and so on, so let's just get me a shot
and be done with it. I explained that, yes, I did have a few sex partners, but I used condoms and I was a blood donor.

"Well, they sure didn't let you give blood with secondary syphilis
sores on your arm."

"I didn't have them then, but—"

We argued a bit, and I got him to agree to a blood test before
treating me. He called back a couple days later and told me I didn't

have syphilis. He had no idea what I had; I had to come back to his office. He examined me again and said it sure looked like syphilis, but the blood test was negative. He said, "Okay, we have to talk hygiene."

"Okay."

"Do you keep clean?"

"Fuck yeah, I spend four to eight hours a day in the bathtub." I was proud.

"What? What do you do in there?"

"Everything, read, type, talk on the phone, have meetings, sleep, eat. . . ."

"You also ruin your skin and give yourself syphilis sores."

"I gave myself syphilis in the bathtub? I have bathtub syphilis?"

"Yes. Stop taking baths. Pay on the way out."

"I can't stop taking baths. I find them . . . comforting. It's the way I live."

"Stop it."

"How about two hours a day?" I was negotiating.

"How about a couple baths a week, less than an hour, and use bath oil, something to stop it from ruining your skin."

I cut down to a couple hours a day with bath oil and my bathtub syphilis went away. I still take baths and read, but I try not to do more than two hours a day. Even without the sores on my arm, baths disgust Adam Carolla. He's a man.

The bathtub syphilis doctor thought I was an idiot. He's not the only doctor with that professional opinion. Teller and I did our first big network TV special for NBC called *Don't Try This at Home*. It wasn't a bad show; I drove an eighteen-wheeler over Teller's chest and that looked okay, and some of the other tricks were fine. Our craziest trick involved us producing more than three-quarters of a million bees out of nowhere. We thought it was really funny to parody Siegfried & Roy producing tigers, by producing many, many more dangerous animals. Not huge wild majestic dangerous animals, but rather tiny domesticated stinging dangerous animals. The idea really made us laugh. We looked into how to do the trick and talked to a few entomologists. We were looking for animals that looked just like bees but didn't sting. There had to be close-ups, and nothing looked enough like bees at close range. We knew from county fairs and my love of beekeeping that people do "bee beards" and move comfortably among them. If they're not protecting the hive and they're not in danger, the little stinging sisters stay cool. We would just be in the cage made of very fine mosquito netting with the real bees. We went to our doctors and got a lot of allergy tests, but more than ten stings for anyone and all bets are off. The camera people would be in full protective beekeeping fashion and there would be triple air locks to protect our live audience. Teller and I would be in the regular gray suits and we would just do it. We rehearsed without bees and did a few very scary practices in a room full of bees. It was scary, but we could do it. The way one dies from bee stings is ana-phylactic shock, so we had EpiPens on necklaces and we were told to look for symptoms in each other. We hired EMTs and there was an ambulance standing by. A nurse gave us some speed before we started, because that was supposed to help. It sure made our timing more like the Ramones doing a Starbucks ad.

We did the bit. We started in an empty cage, and Teller produced one bee bare-handed. It looked great. Then he produced about a dozen from a tube and then it escalated. As usual, I didn't do much besides talk and Teller just kept producing bees and dropping them on me. Teller got stung a couple times, because he was paying atten-tion to the bees and dropping them on me. I lost count after my twenty-fifth sting, because as I did the bit and moved my arms and talked, bees would get trapped in my sleeves or collar, feel threatened and sting the shit out of me. There was the sickening sweet smell of fear pheromones and bee shit and I was being stung every several seconds. One bee got trapped in my mouth, and if you watch the YouTube video, you can see it happen on a close-up and watch me flick the stinger with my tongue and spit it out. Everyone thought I was a real tough guy and not a sixteen-year-old mall girl at all, but the truth is, if I fucked up or screamed or stopped, I would have to do it again, and I was too much of a coward for that.

We finished the bit and stripped naked in the cage with the live audience watching, but the TV audience was watching the much more attractive commercials. Stripped naked with bees all around us, we moved into an airlock where the bees were vacuumed off us by our prop guys. When there were no bees left on us, we went into another air lock and then out into the theater proper. Not one bee escaped into the audience. I stood naked in front of the audience (thank you, Allen Ginsberg) while the nurse and entomologist picked stingers out of me, put on salve, and checked my pupils and vital signs. I was a-okay. We got dressed and went on to the next trick.

Naked isn't a big deal for us. I believe if you haven't been naked onstage, you're not really in showbiz. It's what we do. When we were doing our *Bullshit!* show, we would hire people to be naked on the set. We were doing a science show on cable and to do that we needed obscenity and nudity to make it worth paying extra for. We would hire nude models. It pissed me off how many of the models got to the set and then were uncomfortable being nude. They would wear robes and get all shy. It would be like I was supposed to seduce them into taking off their clothes. In my personal life, I hate seduction. Why would I want to talk someone into being naked with me if they didn't really want to? But in my professional life, it's just people not doing their jobs. These aren't people I wanted to see naked. I didn't care at all. It was their job to be naked. If they didn't want to be naked, they should have a different job. It's like you hire a plumber and she comes in and says, "I hate getting my hands wet." Well, then don't put "plumber" on the side of your Econoline! If you want to keep your clothes on and have any dignity at all, don't be in showbiz.

In my last book, people seemed to like the story of me dropping my cock in a blow dryer, so it seems that my stupidity plus my genitals is my ticket to the *New York Times* bestseller list. So here we go again. After shooting the bee bit, we did a bunch more tricks for the audience that day and then went into production meetings and planned for the next day of shooting on our special. I was bee-stung and exhausted and worried about how the show was going. I also knew something was wrong between my legs but didn't want to look at it, talk about it or even think about it.

I went home late that night, with an early-morning call the next day. At the time, I was dating a beautiful New York City model. She was so sweet and caring and just gorgeous with her figuratively bee-stung lips. I was exhausted, and when we were finally alone in my apartment, she was in the bathroom, naked, washing her face and brushing her teeth, and I was standing in the doorway to the bathroom watching her and digging her. She was telling me the show was going to be great and I had done a good job. I was barely awake. As I watched her and listened to her, I took off my shirt and dropped my pants, but as I went to take off my boxers, something was very wrong. Oh, so very wrong. The skin of my scrotum was attached to my boxers and my boxers had blood all over the front of them. When I peeled off my boxers, the skin of my scrotum came with them, and I was standing there with bloody balls. I was horrified, but when I looked back to my girlfriend, she was more horrified. "What the fuck?" she asked. All the kindness was gone.

"I never told you. I have an exoskeleton, so to get bigger, I have to molt. Your ass looks great."

"What the fuck is wrong with you?"

"I don't know."

"I'm calling 911."

"It really doesn't hurt. It's disgusting and it burns a little, but it's not bad. It's like a bad sunburn on my balls."

"Your balls are bleeding. You have a bloody sack. We're going to the hospital."

"I'm too tired. I have to work in the morning. I'm going to bed."

"You can't do this. This is disgusting."

"Okay, so don't blow me. Good night."

I woke up the next morning in sheets that could be displayed and confuse an entire Jewish neighborhood. I could peel off all the skin of my scrotum in one very thin sheet. Just like a sunburn, if you went on the tanning bed in a completely opaque body suit with your balls cut out and hanging (is that sexy? I think so). My girlfriend wisely insisted that I call my doctor. I had become friendly with my doctor: "Hey man, my ball sack is bleeding. It started last night."

"Cool. I want to see it."

"It'll cost you a quarter."

"No, seriously, come to my office."

"I can't, man, I have to be on set. We're shooting our TV show."

"Nope, you have to come in. I'll call the board of health and shut down the whole shoot if you don't. Jump in a town car and get over here, I'll get you back on set ASAP."

"Okay."

I went to his office, pulled down my pants, and showed him my bloody sack. He got really serious, a nutty kind of serious. "We have to talk."

"Okay."

"Listen, the lie is over as of today."

"What?"

"We'll get you help."

"Yes, for my bloody balls."

"No, for your drug addiction. It's not secret anymore."

"What?"

"This is an allergic reaction to shooting up street drugs. Let me see the tracks on your arms."

"I don't have tracks, because I'm not doing drugs." I rolled up my sleeves. Luckily I didn't have bathtub syphilis at this point.

"Where are you shooting up?"

"I'm not shooting up."

"I know you do the whole no-drugs-and-alcohol pose, but that's over. You're a junkie. Admit it and let's get you help."

We went on like this for a while. I finally got him open to the possibility that it could be something else, "An allergy? Did you eat anything unusual?"

"Cheeseburger and pizza."

"No shellfish?"

"Nope."

"Nothing unusual happened yesterday at all?"

"Nope, just shooting the TV show, tired, overworked—lots of pressure—could it be pressure?"

"No. Just shooting TV?"

"Yup."

"When are you doing the bee thing we checked you for? How is that going?"

"We shot it yesterday."

Long pause. Then another long pause. Then another long pause. Then eyes rolling. He asked, "Did you get stung?"

"Yeah, some."

"How many times?"

"Lots. Like, more than twenty-five times."

"You were shot up more than twenty-five times with dirty little hypodermic needles full of poison and shit and you didn't mention that?"

"Oh, is that it? But I didn't get stung in the balls."

"It's an allergic reaction, you idiot. It's not right on the area. It's systemic. Fuck, you are stupid. If you'd have said that on the phone, you'd be on the set working now and not wasting my time."

"That could do it? What do I do?"

"Yes, that did do it. I don't give a fuck what you do—put some cream on it and toughen up. Oh, and the skin will probably peel off the tops of your feet too. Man, you're stupid. Get out of my office."

Once my girlfriend knew that it wasn't life threatening and, more important, wasn't going to spread to her girly parts, she thought it was hysterical. She was running around the set telling everyone, "You know how Penn's balls usually look pretty good and tight? Well, now they look like Ernest Borgnine's balls and they're bloody—show them, Penn." And I did. It's the least I could do after freaking her out the night before. But how did she know about Ernest's balls? She was a model.

CNN was there doing a piece on our TV special, and when I was done doing the hype, I said to the camera guy, "Want something for your Christmas reel? Shoot this." I pulled down my pants and pulled out my balls. He was freaked. Sometimes I'm more of a nut than I realize. The skin on the top of my feet did peel off too, but that was so much less entertaining.

That kind of stupid can't be fixed with a resolution, so I don't try. I read an article in the *Times* that said that New Year's resolutions really do help people. I was surprised by that. I thought they helped only health clubs. People make a promise to work out and get in shape, they join a health club and then they stop going. Health clubs, like insurance, are businesses based on people paying for but not using the business. They count on people not showing up. They count on people not knowing themselves.

I have a friend who runs a legal whorehouse. He told me his whole business model is based on having a guy pay for what he wants before he knows what he can really use. Have a guy pay for three sex partners for six hours, and when he uses one and a third partner for fifteen minutes, the men and women supplying the service get to sell that same time slot again to another guy who thinks he's going to fuck for six hours. If you can do six hours of work in fifteen minutes, you start to turn a profit.

I played Reno the New Year's Day that my mom died. It was her dying request that I miss no shows for her sake, so I didn't. I don't remember anything from the sound check or the show. I just know that I got through it. My friend who runs the brothel came to the show, with a couple of his coworkers in tow. They were scantily clad and they were there to enjoy the show and say hi afterward. I had offered my friend my complimentary tickets for the show a few months before, so they were all set up, and with my mom's death, I'd forgotten all about them, but there he was with a couple/three coworkers to help him reciprocate. They were ushered back to my dressing room after the show.

I don't know a lot of etiquette, but I approve of those rules that tell us how to act when we don't know how to act. When someone experiences the death of a loved one, one says, "I'm sorry for your loss." If you say something other than that, you may cause even more discomfort. You don't want to say "I know how you feel" because you just fucking don't. You don't want to say, "They're in a better place" because they're fucking not. You don't want to say, "Things happen for a reason" because they fucking don't. "I'm sorry for your loss" is safe and kind. They are magic words. There is no etiquette for how you tell an attractive person who is not wearing any underwear that your mother died that day. I'm not saying it's wrong to fuck or be fucked on the day a loved one dies. It's very good to throw raw life in the face of death. I understand the point of view that it's good to be human when you've lost a human that you love. I understand all of that, but it hasn't been the way I've felt. I didn't want to be crying with a prostitute in Reno in the middle of the night. I know I wouldn't be the first, but I didn't want to do it. Go ahead, call me a pussy.

That was the scene in my dressing room the night my mom died. A pimp, three prostitutes, a friend of mine who'd driven up from L.A. separately, and me. The prostitutes had seen the show, and they were guessing I was a fun guy. No etiquette. I said, "Um, yeah. Thanks for coming to the show. Thanks for coming backstage. It's nice to meet you. Um. My mom died today and I'm in kind of a weird mood. Not a weird mood for my mom having died—I think my mood is appropriate for my mom having just died—but a weird mood for the way you're dressed." They were dressed very appropriately for a performer's dressing room backstage, but inappropriately for a wake. They put their legs together and crossed their arms. "So, thanks a lot. Nice to meet you. Hope you come see the show again. Good night." My friend showed them to the door, and I got to the work of mourning and crying.

New Year's Day is a complicated holiday for me. Everyone in showbiz works on New Year's Eve. I don't. People drink. I don't. People watch sports. I don't. It's a day of resolutions that I don't make.

It's an important day for me. It's a real holiday for me. On New Year's, I think about death and remember my losses fondly, and I celebrate life by bribing my children with toys.

Listening to: Bach's Sonata #2, BWV 1028, Andante—Gary Karr

MARTIN LUTHER KING JR. DAY— YOU CAN BE IN MY DREAM, IF I CAN BE IN YOURS (BOB DYLAN SAID THAT)

OKAY, HOLD YOUR HORSES. JUST CALM THE FUCK DOWN. I'm NOT going to write about race. I'm not going to write about racism. I'm not going to take a quote from someone on Twitter, credit it to Martin Luther King Jr. and send it around the world. Not again. I'm going to try not to write anything stupid. Most of the time I'm trying not to write anything stupid, but maybe I'll get lucky this time.

In my little dead-factory hometown of Greenfield, we had only a few African-American families. The few African-American students in my little school were cousins, and they would dance with one another at school dances. It's a small town and maybe a lot of cousins were dancing together; I just didn't notice the others. I didn't go to many school dances. I'm not the one to write about racism in Greenfield, Massachusetts. I just don't know anything about it. I never heard overt racism until I left Greenfield, but that doesn't mean it wasn't there. The cousins dancing together certainly showed we weren't living in utopia. Utopia would have everyone dancing and fucking with everyone else.

My buddy Karen Russell, the daughter of Bill Russell, was in Massachusetts when her superstar dad was playing basketball for the Boston team. I know nothing about sports, so the few times I met Bill Russell we talked about magic and comedy. Mr. Russell knows more about magic and comedy than I know about basketball. It's likely Mr. Russell knows more about magic and comedy than I know about magic and comedy. He's a smart cat. The best thing about having Bill come backstage was how much it pisses off my buddy Arsenio Hall that I've spent more time with Bill Russell than Arsenio has. Maybe the secret to Bill Russell's attention is not talking about basketball. Or maybe it's because he loves his daughter. I bet both help. Bill Russell being a superstar could not protect his family from subtle, overt, and criminal racism. Karen tells me stories and I listen, but those are her stories. It's not my place to write down those stories. I'm not qualified to comment.

I am welcome to write about Martin Luther King's "I Have a Dream" speech, because Dr. King included me in that speech. I'm one of the ones he wrote it for. I just watched it and read it again while thinking about Martin Luther King Day. We can ignore everything else Dr. King did, and I'd be okay with celebrating Martin Luther King Day based just on that one delivery of that one speech.

The being-on-a-Monday thing instead of his birthday pisses me off, but I like observance. He was the best of us.

Before I reread the "Dream" speech, I listened to Dr. King's "The Drum Major Instinct" speech. That was the last speech he gave before he was assassinated. "I Have a Dream" is way different. "The Drum Major Instinct" speech was given in a church. It's a sermon. He was speaking to believers about religious issues. The "Dream" speech was given during a secular March on Washington. That difference matters. The difference mattered to Martin Luther King. He knew I wasn't going to be at church, but he knew I was going to listen to the speech he gave from in front of the Lincoln Memorial, and he wanted to make sure I was included. He was a preacher, a religious man, and a real no-kidding minister. I don't doubt his faith, but he constructed that speech to make sure I knew his faith shouldn't exclude people who didn't share his faith.

I'm going to write about this speech from my tunnel-vision perspective. What I'm about to do with the "Dream" speech is the equivalent of writing about Bob Dylan's life work by critiquing his three-ball juggling cascade in the "Blood in My Eyes" video. *(Bob does almost five throws of a three-ball cascade before we cut away. Those throws qualify him, barely, as a juggler. Mr. Dylan never really has this pattern under control. Every throw is too late. Instead of throwing at the apex of the subsequent ball, he throws when the next ball is already on the way down. This gives his juggle a precarious feel. The audience never relaxes in the knowledge that Bob is in control of his props. Juggling should be carefree at least until the final trick. Mr. Dylan's throws don't stay in the same plane; they aren't straight up and down. Bob throws every throw a bit in front of the last. This reviewer would humbly suggest more practice with his knees pressed against his couch. I would also humbly suggest that he think more musically and less visually about the throws. Each throw must be connected to the pattern and not a separate event. You can't do that if you're waiting to see when to throw; you have to feel the beat of the next throw independent from the visual. Bob gives us a new thought with every toss, and we never really feel the security of an established pattern. Bob Dylan's juggling is a tentative series of throws, a very long way from a professional juggling routine. It's acceptable juggling for his grandchildren, but Bob Dylan doesn't seem prepared for juggling clubs or rings outdoors where his props might be blowing in the idiot wind.)* I want to write about Martin Luther King's "Dream" speech from the POV of separation of church and state, about how religious folk can include the non-religious folk without distorting their messages or their philosophies.

I will attempt to do this without distorting Dr. King's message or philosophy. After the 1962 U.S. Supreme Court decision prohibiting state-supported prayer in public schools, Dr. King said it was "sound and good, reaffirming something basic in the Nation's life: separation of church and state." I'm using that quote as my defense for thinking about Dr. King's speech from a secular point of view.

That March on Washington had no shortage of religious speakers talking religion. There were a lot of Christian ministers in the civil rights movement. There were also plenty of Muslims and Jews and, as Christopher Hitchens pointed out, Martin Luther King's inner circle was maggoty with atheists. Many of the ministers were very open in mentioning god and religion and the singers sang bunches of gospel music. Many of the individuals holding the lectern before MLK wore their religion on their sleeves and I'm fine with that. I'm also glad their speeches are less remembered. Bill Russell was at that speech. Next time Karen brings her dad backstage, that's something else we can talk about that he knows way more than I do.

Bob Dylan isn't just remembered for his juggling. He was at the March on Washington with Martin Luther King, and Dylan sang "Only a Pawn in Their Game," spreading the guilt from the active racists to our whole culture. He brought Joan Baez out to sing "When the Ship Comes In," about how the bad guys will go down, and we're all still waiting for all that to come true. I love that Bob brought Joan out after he started singing. Didn't they plan this? There weren't any jugglers or magicians asked to perform on that historic day. I guess I don't know that for sure, but I'm guessing that if any were asked, they would have shown up. We don't get asked to work historic days very often; we work children's birthday parties.

I pulled up the "I Have a Dream" speech on my computer and did some searching. I typed in "Jesus." "'Jesus' is not found." Well, that's the joyous story of my life.

I typed in "Religion."

"'Religion' is not found." Yup.

"'Churches' is not found." Probably should be *"are* not found," but I'm looking forward to that day when we don't need churches.

"Pray" is found once in the speech. It's in a list of things people should be able to do together. I'm okay with that, as long as it isn't a list of things we have to do together. The list includes being able to work together and stand up for freedom together. I'm all for those. It also includes struggling together and going to jail together. A lot of people did those things together to get us to where we are now.

"Faith" is found five times. Once, it's faith that "unearned suffering is redemptive." I'm not sure if this is afterlife redemption, redemption in this life, or both. I'm betting King meant in the afterlife, but I can spin that to this life and be content. The other mentions of "faith" are faith in himself and his dream and, finally, faith in the people of the United States of America, and indeed in the world, to share that dream. I'm way more than just okay with all that.

"Lord" is mentioned once in the context of the "Glory of the Lord" being revealed.

"God" is found four times—three times under "all God's children," and once, at the end, quoting the spiritual: "Free at last! Free at last! Thank God almighty, we are free at last!"

Dr. King doesn't avoid the Bible in this speech. He uses biblical images, including quotes from Psalms, Amos, and Isaiah. There isn't a day that goes by that I don't use many images from the Bible, so why isn't there a day named after me? Just kidding. King is just using poetic imagery from the Bible, using the Bible for its images and rhythms, not justification for any action. He holds the truths to be self-evident. He doesn't go to a higher power. Bible imagery is part of our culture, like Shakespeare, which Dr. King alludes to in the exact same way with his reference to "this sweltering summer of the Negro's legitimate discontent will not pass until there is an invigorating autumn."

I must mention the fact that the Bible condones slavery and tribalism, but I won't dwell on it. Martin Luther King's speech has more wisdom, bravery, humanity, compassion and love than the whole Bible and that is damning it with faint praise. Gilbert Gottfried's act also contains more wisdom, bravery, humanity, compassion and love than the Bible, and Gilbert is doing dick jokes. The Bible sets a low bar for compassion.

I'm not trying to paint Martin Luther King as an atheist. I do not doubt his religious faith in any way. I'm showing that when he made the most important speech of his life, one of the most important speeches in American and world history, he backs off the god shit. He chooses to include instead of exclude.

The word most conspicuous in its absence in that speech to our twenty-first-century ears is "Christian." "'Christian' is not found."

The word "Christian" has become a magic word in my lifetime. It means something different now than when I was born. It used to be a throwaway word. People didn't used to use it much. Martin Luther King was a Baptist—Progressive National Baptist Convention—but not even the word "Baptist" appears in the speech. People just started self-labeling or getting labeled "Christian" in the last part of the twentieth century. A little before my time, in the nineteenth century, people weren't even using the general term "Protestant" very much. They were Baptists or Southern Baptists or Dave's Specific Southern Mississippi Snakes, but no Poison Pentecostal Church of our Unique Christ. Every religious cult was afraid of every other religious cult. The bugnutty Pentecostals didn't want the bugnutty Methodists to have too much power. There was no "Christian Nation"—the Christians were all afraid of one another. America was founded on Christians not trusting one another. Robert Ingersoll, "The Great Agnostic," was also an atheist and was courted by many politicians. He spoke on atheism (three of the top speakers of that time were atheists speaking about atheism: Ingersoll, Mark Twain, and Darwin's Bulldog, Thomas Huxley, who used the weasel word "agnostic" but he doesn't fool me). Contemporary candidates wanted Ingersoll on board to show they were open to free thought. It was a rhetorical trick to show that they weren't going to use their political position to give their own specific flavor of Baptist too much power. Ingersoll on board showed they'd let the other cults flourish. I'm no

Ingersoll, but I'm an atheist who speaks on atheism and no politicians ever courted me.

Even in my lifetime, when I was a child, John F. Kennedy could have never talked much about his religion, except to alibi it. He was Catholic, and that scared all the Protestants. He just ducked and covered. If he could have used the word "Christian," he would have and been able to go hog wild on the Jesus stuff. As it was, he spoke of the separation of church and state and made Rick Santorum vomit.

Freethinkers, a great book by Susan Jacoby, explained that the modern use of the word "Christian" was pushed to fight *Roe v. Wade*, and that was almost a full decade after Dr. King inspired his country talking real inclusion. The anti-choice people wanted a big tent word for the religious objection to abortion, they had to bring all the Protestants and Catholics together, and "Christian" did that. It was their magic word.

Jimmy Carter was "born again" and that phrase and the magic word started to be used more and more. I heard on NPR (yup, I'm an atheist who reads the Bible every day and a libertarian who reads *The New York Times* and listens to NPR every day) that if religion is measured as references to god and appearing in churches, our most religious president was Bill Clinton. Slick Willy really rammed home the idea of "Christian" as a church slut, not caring what church he appeared in, as long as he was seen at a church.

I've had friends argue that Clinton was not our most religious president, but he sucked up to churches because he was our least religious president and wanted to stay president. That argument is a bit cynical for my tastes, but that doesn't mean it's not true.

Now we have TV political talking heads who are disgusted by Bachmann, Perry, Santorum, and Gingrich, and the TV announcers use that magic word that gives those whackjobs their power. They don't say "Southern Baptist"; they say "Christian." I've sat around with my atheist friends and tried to be as blasphemous as possible. I've used pornographic images, obscenity and poetry to try to make even the most doubtful blush, but I've never touched Michele Bachmann's insult to the gentle, honest faithful by saying the suffering and casualties of natural disasters are her god's message to wayward politicians. It's hard to imagine Martin Luther King even thinking that. What she said was disgusting and not a general "Christian" belief at all, but her blasphemous religious message was delivered on the news clips as a message from a Christian. Imagine if that had been positioned as a message from Michele Bachmann of the Salem Lutheran Church, a specific cult that had stated that the pope is the antichrist. Michele denied they believe that, but all the same, how are the non–Salem Lutherans (and that group includes all the Catholics, most of the Protestants, Martin Luther King, Mitt Romney and me) going to react to that bugnutty stuff coming from a Salem Lutheran? Even in the broad, broad definition of Lutheran, you have only about 13.5 million and that's not enough to be president. Now Michele has moved to the Eagle Brook Church, but without the alibi term "Christian," that gives her only 26.3 percent of the American people. With that percentage, you need to shut up about religion. You need me on board to show that you won't sell out all the others.

John F. Kennedy had to alibi his Catholicism; Rick Santorum just uses the magic word "Christian," and it goes away. Rick Santorum brings his religion into everything. I think he's deeply wrong, but I have no problem with him being a believer running for public office. All his talk of god will get his core followers fully hard and wet (and we can hope dripping some santorum out of their assholes), and with the word "Christian" it doesn't lose as many people as "Catholic" alone would. Now let's watch Mitt Romney as he works on trying to get the magic-underwear-wearing, the-Garden-of-Eden-was-in-North-America Mormons considered part of that "Christian" magic word.

If I make all my deadlines, our president might still be Barack Obama. If you search on the Web for Obama's religion (and ignore the stupid Muslim shit), you'll find he is Christian. He goes right to the magic word, and stays there. He names no specific cult ever. He no longer belongs to Trinity United Church of Christ, but our magic word saved him there. Trinity Church describes itself, on its website like this: "We are a congregation which is Unashamedly Black and Unapologetically Christian . . . Our roots in the Black religious experience and tradition are deep, lasting and permanent. We are an African people, and remain 'true to our native land,' the mother continent, the cradle of civilization. God has superintended our pilgrimage through the days of slavery, the days of segregation, and the long night of racism. It is God who gives us the strength and courage to continuously address injustice as a people, and as a congregation. We constantly affirm our trust in God through cultural expression of a Black worship service and ministries which address the Black Community." If Obama had run as a Trinity Church believer, he would have had a lot of explaining to do, but being "Christian" solved everything.

Again we have the Clinton cynic problem. If we see Obama as a Trinity Church believer, he's as bugnutty as Sarah Palin, but my friends don't see him as a believer, not even as a Christian. They see him belonging to a church and saying he's Christian so he could get elected. Many people have said to me that Obama claims religion because otherwise an African-American liberal would never have a chance of being elected. If he didn't call himself a Christian and talk about praying in the White House, he would be painted as a Muslim and have no defense. You and I know, as the condescending argument goes, that an atheist is further from being Muslim than a Christian, but Americans don't know that. The argument says that Americans could never understand that not believing in god means not believing in a Muslim god. Yeah, fuck you, if Americans can program in machine code and understand icing in hockey, they can understand this. I've had many liberal friends (are they really friends?) defend Obama by calling him a liar. They have made this unilateral secret deal with Obama that Obama will say he's Christian to get elected and then he will govern as an atheist. Obama doesn't have to wink when he says he's Christian; these liberals just know. It's supernatural. These people might be right, but it doesn't make Obama a hero to me. I'm way more against lying than I am against Christians.

It's not hard to picture Obama in that kind of cynical deal. When he won his Nobel Peace Prize, he felt he had to address the fact that he had sent more soldiers overseas to kill and die than all the other Peace Prize winners put together. Alfred Nobel wrote that the person who won the Peace Prize "shall have done the most or the best work for fraternity between nations, the abolition or reduction of standing armies and for the holding and promotion of peace congresses." I don't know who that would be, but it's demonstratively not Obama.

Obama's speech got a laugh at the top referring to this controversy. He worked a laugh out of the crowd by pointing out that a guy running a couple of wars had won the prize. I believe that anything can be funny—there are funny AIDS jokes—but this one rubbed me the wrong way. He then addresses Martin Luther King's winning of the same prize:

"We must begin by acknowledging the hard truth: We will not eradicate violent conflict in our lifetimes. There will be times when nations—acting individually or in concert—will find the use of force not only necessary but morally justified.

"I make this statement mindful of what Martin Luther King Jr. said in this same ceremony years ago: 'Violence never brings permanent peace. It solves no social problem: It merely creates new and more complicated ones.' As someone who stands here as a direct consequence of Dr. King's life work, I am living testimony to the moral force of non-violence. I know there's nothing weak—nothing passive—nothing naïve—in the creed and lives of Gandhi and King."

Man, that's some great speechwriting and Obama sure can deliver, but then I wanted him to say ". . . so I will be bringing all our troops home and we will stop dying and killing people for ideas we don't understand." But he didn't say that.

He said, "But as a head of state sworn to protect and defend my nation, I cannot be guided by their examples alone. I face the world as it is, and cannot stand idle in the face of threats to the American people. For make no mistake: Evil does exist in the world. A non-violent movement could not have halted Hitler's armies. Negotiations cannot convince al Qaeda's leaders to lay down their arms. To say that force may sometimes be necessary is not a call to cynicism—it is a recognition of history; the imperfections of man and the limits of reason."

Evil is strictly a religious concept. That word does not appear in the "I Have a Dream" speech. Not once. It's not found. You would think that Martin Luther King Jr. had seen some evil in his day, but in his speech, he doesn't use the word. He keeps it secular. People can be wrong, cruel, ignorant, and horrible, but there's no separate evil driving some of us. We are all people and our mistakes are our own.

Obama finishes up his sweet spin with this: "The non-violence practiced by men like Gandhi and King may not have been practical or possible in every circumstance, but the love that they preached—their fundamental faith in human progress—that must always be the North Star that guides us on our journey." I guess it's good that he doesn't dismiss them, but that sure feels like a pat on the head to a couple of sweet nutjobs, and not real respect. I don't question that Obama has real and pure respect for Gandhi and King (and the other men like them who are, um, give me a moment, um . . .), but I wouldn't be that quick to say that I had all their thinking covered and I was ready to move on to using violence.

Similar to the secret deal that some of my friends have with Obama—that they'll know he's really atheist when he says he's religious—is the deal that peaceniks have with presidents they like. Bush was killing people overseas because he was evil and wanted to; Obama is doing it because he's good but he has to. That's the thinking: when a president is sworn into office, the military shows him shit that they keep secret and that changes his whole worldview. There's heavy, secret shit that justifies war that the public could never handle. If this were true, there would be no reason to ever vote on an issue. There's no reason to ever have a public debate. We want our benevolent despot. We vote for the best-looking president who we trust and then let him do what he wants because we can't handle the truth.

I don't buy any of this. I think King did a pretty fucking good job of speaking truth to power and he did it non-violently without lying and secret deals. I think he was a real hero. He was not just a Christian, but a Baptist, yet he trusted me, an atheist, to care about his cause and join together with him. I didn't actually join with him at the time, but I like to think that's because I was eight years old.

Atheists are growing way, way fast. The end of the twentieth century, atheists were under 2 percent, probably lower when King gave his speech. That number got to 8 percent in the twenty-first century, after the faith-based initiative of September 11, 2001. If you throw in self-labeled "agnostics" and "not religious," some people have gotten the atheist/agnostic/humanist/secularist/freethinking cult numbers up to around 20 percent. Evangelicals are about 26 percent, Catholics about 23 percent, Jewish, 1.7 percent, Mormons also 1.7 percent—if you start breaking up these "Christians" into their smaller groups, non-believers get close to being the dominant "religion" if you can call no religion a religion like not collecting stamps is a hobby.

The March on Washington was important and MLK needed everyone. He ends the speech by saying that "*all* of God's children, black men and white men, Jews and Gentiles, Protestants and Catholics" should join in singing "Free at last!" I guess my argument breaks down here. Dr. King doesn't mention atheists, and you could argue that he didn't mean to include atheists. I guess if there's one thing we're not, it's god's children. But I'm not sure Martin Luther King would see it that way. I feel, listening to and reading this speech, that he would have included me in the list of god's children even though I'm not. I can't argue that it's not exclusive, but it doesn't feel that way.

I hope that our politicians will learn from Dr. Martin Luther King and keep expanding the group of people they want to serve until we move the next little step from "Christian" being the magic word to the real magic political word: "American." Then let's go a step further and make the magic word "humanity."

Free at last, free at last, thank god almighty we are free at last.

Let freedom ring in the human heart.

Listening to: "Free at Last"—Al Green

GROUNDHOG DAY

THE MOVIE *GROUNDHOG DAY* POSTULATES perhaps thousands of years' worth of a single day, when Bill Murray's character learns to live that one day the right way, and by extension his entire life. Bill's character has to learn to get his heart right and learn to love. I don't care much about that; I care that he learned to play piano and speak French and read a lot of books. I like time to get good at real things; the heart stuff is easy. And in reality, Murray, Harold Ramis, and the rest of the cast and crew making the movie had only a bunch of rewrites and a few takes to accomplish that idea.

Teller has been doing one trick called "Shadows" in our show for his entire professional career. We did a version at our first indoor stage show together, he did it in our Asparagus Valley Cultural Society show, and it's been in most our live shows ever since. When Teller was a child, he had a dream where the cutting of an object's shadow had the same effect on the real object. Teller used magic tricks to make others share that dream. On one level it's a celebration of magical thinking: that the shadow, the idea, can affect the real thing. It's voodoo. Teller is a magician who fights against magical thinking, but onstage, in fantasy, magical thinking is a beautiful dream. To the non-magical thinker, to the atheist, "Shadows" can be seen as being about art. Art is the representation of ideas that can change the real things, the shadows on the back of the cave wall that teach us about the real world. As writers and performers, we're always trying to make others see our ideas, the images inside our heads. We're trying to make others see our dreams, our hopes, and our fears. Maybe if we can all see more points of view, we can all learn. Art is the real magic.

It's good, in this anthropic world where "good" is defined as anything we've found a way to live with, that magical thinking doesn't work. We don't have to be careful what we wish for, only what we work for. One of the big reliefs for the atheist is not having to worry about what to hope, wish, and pray for. Did I want to pray for my mother's suffering to end? Did I want to hope for her death? I didn't have to worry about that. I could hope one day that she'd live longer so I could talk to her and wish the next day that she would die and not have to suffer her paralysis and physical loss any longer. My wishing and hoping were inert; I could let them run wild. I could use them as pure solace.

"Shadows" addresses this pretty idea directly in just a couple of minutes. Teller uses a stemmed rose in a vase with a light in front of it, casting a shadow on a screen. He cuts the shadow on the screen and the petals of the actual rose fall as though they had been cut. It's probably the defining trick of our Penn & Teller career. I'm not onstage for it. Fuck you. I didn't think it up, and . . . I don't know how the trick is done.

I don't know how a lot of the tricks in our show are done. We did one of our non-performance shows called *35 Years of Bullshit* (the number of years changes, but the Bullshit stays the same) with, I think, Stephen Fry, interviewing us onstage in London. For these appearances Teller talks and answers the questions. Teller is an engaging and articulate conversationalist, and when we do a "Teller will talk" show, I really don't have much to do. People have heard me enough. They all want to hear Teller for a change. But during this appearance, I went off on a jag, talking about how the tricks are done. I was explaining a moment in the first trick we did on *Letterman*. In it, Teller tries to do a classic of magic, a card stab, and as part of the act I'm being such a dick that my hand gets in the way and the knife goes through my hand. Teller has the correct card impaled stigmata-like to my palm as the blood flows. We named the bit "Handstab" and that name stuck with us and our crew before we realized that naming the tricks mattered. Now we try to name tricks with names that don't give away the big surprise endings. We learn slowly.

In London that evening, I was explaining how Teller switches the real knife for the fake knife and I load the blood into my palm with the right card. I had explained my part and I was explaining Teller's part—the real knife has a hook on it and Teller hangs it on the back on his pants as his hand was coming up to meet mine with the fake knife. Teller spoke up and corrected me. We hadn't done it with a hooked knife in years and years; we now used a magnet setup in his back pocket. I didn't know. No one had mentioned to me that it changed, I never checked, I never noticed, and I never asked.

My lack of concern for how tricks are done is partly why Teller chose me as his performing partner in 1975. I had just gotten out of high school. I don't like to use the word "graduated," because my exit from high school was messy, but I got out. The teachers told me in high school that these school years were the best years of my life and I'd look back on them with fondness and regret that I didn't enjoy them more. I never have. For the first few years that I was out of high school, while I was hitchhiking around, living on the streets and juggling for food, I used to take some of my scarce money and send a postcard to my principal and guidance counselor, with a picture of some exotic location and a message saying something about the road being way better than high school. They needed to teach the children that the real world is wonderful. What's the use of teaching preparation for regret?

After a few months of bumming around, I went to Ringling Bros. and Barnum & Bailey Clown College in Florida. That was a couple of months. Clown College was the first time in my life that I worked hard. I was already a great juggler and I could ride a unicycle, but I learned tightwire walking, and back flips, and falls, and I was in remedial makeup. *Makeup* makeup. It was the first time I met really funny people. It was the first time I'd exercised and trained. It was the first time anyone had ever taught me something that I was interested in. It was the first time I'd ever seen people take comedy seriously.

I met Teller while I was in high school, but he was still teaching high school (different schools). I went into a stereo store in my hometown. I'd saved up my money from juggling and doing odd jobs, and I was going to buy a good stereo. The salesman was Wier Chrisemer. In a few years, I would form the Asparagus Valley Cultural Society with Wier and Teller. Teller is seven years older than me, and he'd graduated college while I was still in high school. I got to talking with Wier that day in the audio store. I told him I was a juggler and demonstrated in the shop with whatever was around. It's not hard to get me to do tricks. He said maybe he could use me in his college classical music parody group called the Othmar Schoeck Memorial Society for the Preservation of Unusual and Disgusting Music. Wier asked if I could read music well enough to play bass drum on Beethoven's Ninth Symphony while juggling, hitting the drum with the clubs. He had written comedy words to the symphony about eating and was going to have the vocalists served supper by the chorus, but he thought a little juggling would make it more absurd. I said I could read music well enough while juggling to do that. We started brainstorming on other ideas and he asked if I could juggle plungers and I said I could juggle anything I could hold that wasn't attached. I told him I also rode a unicycle. He asked if I could ride in on a unicycle, juggling the plumbers' helpers while he played Aram Khachaturian's *Sabre Dance* on xylophone. Easy. Could he then stand against a board and have me throw the plungers around him and have them stick in a parody of a knife-throwing act? I said I had never done that, but I loved to practice and I would learn it for him. It took a stupid lot of practice, Vaseline on the plumbers' helpers and a very smooth board, but I learned it. He was skeptical of bringing a high school student into his fancy tight-ass college comedy, so he assigned me *Watt* by Samuel Beckett (still one of my favorite books) to read. He told me to come back in a week when I picked up my turntable and tell him what was funny about the book to show I understood it, and if I impressed him, I could work for free at a time when I was already getting paid to do juggling shows. I had never met anyone with that advanced a sense of humor and I was thrilled. I worked and did the show. His friend from college, Teller, drove back up to Amherst College for the show and pretended to be blind and sold pencils out front while reciting poetry he'd written in Latin about the conception of Othmar Schoeck in the womb. After that show, Teller and I got to talking. We've never stopped. Bob Dylan talked, wrote and sang about hitchhiking and hopping trains, so I did it to be like him. But while he mostly talked, wrote and sang about it, I really did hop trains and hitchhike around. All over the country. I was homeless, with $500 sewn into my knapsack and a loving home I could go back to any time I chose. I called my mom and dad collect every day I was gone. I talked to my mom and dad every day that our lives overlapped. Either in person or on the phone. They supported me while I hitchhiked, hopped trains, and got all Woody Guthrie on America's

One of the fucking clowns in my class in Florida, Jeff Siegel, still a good friend, started booking acts for the Minnesota Renaissance Festival. His idea was to bring in people who had a lot of experience street performing, and figured it was easier to put those people in tights than to teach a guy already in tights to be funny. I was hired to do my juggling street show with wooden balls and striped tights. I threw in a few "ye oldes" and we were done.

With a full stomach, I started to listen and I got excited about Teller's ideas. When Jeff called a year later about the Minnesota Renaissance Festival, I asked him if I could bring a magician along. Jeff drove a hard bargain: I would have to take a big cut in my pay that Jeff could pay Teller. I said okay. I owed Teller some suppers.

Teller had been preoccupied with magic since he was a child. He put himself through Amherst College by doing magic shows at frat parties (and the diamond miners in Zimbabwe think they got it tough). When we first met, I watched Teller in a New Jersey library basement performing for about thirty people. He wasn't doing "Shadows" then, but I watched him silently pluck one hundred needles out of an apple and swallow them with an audience member this close to him. He swallowed some thread and after that audience member gave him a full mouth examination with a dentist's mirror and flashlight, Teller brought the shimmering needles back up all threaded. It was creepy, beautiful, classy, amazing, and all silent. It's a trick he still does today.

I called up Teller and told him I had a magician gig for him. I asked him if he wanted to put together a street show and do it with me in Minnesota. We could get a car and drive out there together.

"When?"

"It starts in August."

"Perfect!"

"And it goes through October."

"Oh, I have to be back to teaching by then."

I said, "Okay, I thought you were a magician, not a schoolteacher," and I hung up. It probably wasn't really that precise a conversation, but that's the way it's become over the years of telling it.

He called back a few hours later and said he'd take a leave of absence from teaching and do the gig. This was a really hard decision for Teller. He had just gotten tenure, and he was a great teacher. I can't imagine a better teacher. While I was still in high school, I went to visit him and sat in on one of his high school Latin classes. He was getting New Jersey public school students excited about Latin. Beat that.

It was a conspiracy between the Viet Cong and the American military industrial complex that made Teller a teacher. He was the right age for Apocalypse Then. In the draft lottery he was number 3. Penn & Teller are very different from each other, but neither of us would do well in the military. "Bombs bursting in air, man, not my thing," as Tony Bennett allegedly said. I was too tall to go in and too young to be drafted, but Teller with his number 3 was on his way to Saigon, shit. He got a school deferment to go to college and then a teaching deferment. My aboriginal American name for Teller is "Terrier-with-a-Slipper." All our pluses are our minuses and Teller does not give up. His tenacity is infuriating, and I've built a very good life on it. He doesn't give up. Was it hard for a guy with a classics degree to get a teaching job in a public school in the late sixties? Sure enough. Would you have bet against Teller doing it? You would have lost.

Without the best and the brightest forcing us into an immoral, undeclared and unconstitutional war, Teller might have gone right crazy—but we were going to do some stuff onstage that we loved. We weren't going to be greasy guys in tuxes with birds, torturing women in front of Mylar to bad small-dick rip-off Motown music. We were going to speak our hearts while doing tricks. Some of the specific ideas talked about on those drives weren't realized until thirty-five years later, and we're still working on others. The results of those theoretical conversations can be found in all the Penn & Teller shows. Our career is just an appendix to those conversations.

When we got to Minnesota, we didn't do an act together. We each did our separate shows and then would meet back in the employee area in the hay behind the trees to reset our props, count our money and roll our quarters. My show was a very long crowd gathering. I would explain to a few passersby that I was going to do "absolutely nothing" and when I signaled them, they were going to scream, yell and applaud. When other strangers heard this and ran over to see what was happening, the original "crowd" could all turn and laugh at them for rushing over to see nothing. We'd do it again and again until there were a couple hundred people watching me do nothing. It got funny. With my audience in place, I would juggle balls, while commenting in a disparaging way about the routine, explaining, in different ways, that I bothered to do all this practicing, so they could at least bother to watch it. I moved from balls to very big and really sharp knives (I was a juggler, not a magician—I didn't fake much). First I would juggle the knives with an apple. I would eat the apple while juggling and spit all over myself (slightly less of a hackneyed trick at that time, and much more interesting when juggling knives along with the apple). I went to all knives, and then got a "volunteer" from the audience, put an opaque bag over her head, stood behind her, and juggled the knives around her. I'd return her to the crowd and then put the same hood over my head and juggle the knives blindfolded. That was the big finish and then I would do my money pitch. I said I'd do a magic trick and change the executioner's hood into a change purse, snap my fingers and claim it was done. I then said to prove I had been successful, I would need money from all of them. I then did a list of reasons they should give me money and excuses that I would not accept. There was lots of talk about my size, and my aggression, so it was mostly threats. The money speech was the longest (and most important) part of my act. I had forgotten it, but just this week, I mentioned to Teller I was writing this, and he performed my whole speech from memory. It's his favorite thing I've ever written.

After all this loud, insane aggression, I ended my show with a very quiet "thank you" and then moved into the crowd to collect my pay. The ball and knife juggling were part of the Penn & Teller show even into the first Broadway show, but the crowd and money gathering fell away. Resetting my props meant dumping money out of my blindfold/bag and grabbing a new apple. Teller had all this niggling magic shit to do, so I just watched him. I don't want to give the impression of starving artists here, but we were working hard for showbiz. I always have to add "for showbiz," because no one in showbiz works as hard as anyone with a real job.

Springsteen does a three-hour concert with people cheering for him, while people work at a desk for eight hours just taking shit from assholes. We were doing eight shows a day, and that's a ten-hour day with a lot of time to talk and roll quarters and it was only weekends. Even when we were "working," we were getting paid for doing what we would have done for free. We were doing what we had to do. If writing or going into showbiz is a choice, you shouldn't choose it. Morally and politically I'm a capitalist, but money was not my motivation for getting into showbiz. I didn't really think I had a chance of making my living in showbiz, and when that started to happen, I was shocked. I still can't believe it.

I have a commie friend, a good friend, a famous friend, a political friend, who, when he admitted to me privately, after he'd admitted on TV publicly, that he was a socialist, explained to me the real reason. He believed that big salaries paid to hard workers were just society wasting money. "Hardworking assholes like Bill Gates are going to work no matter what you pay them. They like to work. Look at you, you're not anything compared with Bill Gates and yet you'd do your little shows even if you were being paid 1/100th of what you get paid. You'd do the same quality show and work just as hard for a sub-sistence wage. It's bullshit that money is the motivator for people who really work hard. Hardworking people have a mental illness that helps all of us, and we should exploit that. They don't really work for the money, so let's give them a lot less. Take that money and give it to the lazy fucks like me who don't really want to work. Then take the rest of the money and use it to motivate the people in the mid-dle, who do need incentive." It's the best argument for socialism I've ever heard. I would do our show for next to nothing.

In Minnesota, Teller and I were trying to get better, and how much money we made was a good measure of how well our shows had gone. Somewhere we have the booklet in which we kept track of every penny we made. If you're with the IRS, that booklet might be hard for us to find. There we were in leather tops, tights and dance belts resetting our shows and counting our money. I was sitting across from Teller, both of us sitting on the ground, while Teller reset all his magic tricks. After a few weeks working, Teller asked me to take a look at his brilliant "Needles" routine. He wanted my eye and some pointers on how to make the trick better. How he could be a little more deceptive. I said, "Sure, but it's already deceiving me, so you'll have to tell me how it's done before I can help you conceal how it's done." Teller was stunned. I had sat and watched him set up all his tricks and I still didn't know how they were done? I never paid any attention. I didn't care. I liked the way it looked onstage, and I wasn't interested in the mechanics.

I think it was that moment. The moment that Teller realized he had found someone who really deeply didn't care about how the tricks were done was the moment that he decided to work on a magic show with me. We did the Minnesota Renaissance Festival a few years, added Texas, Maryland, Canada, California, and North Carolina, and during the drives back and forth to New Jersey, we wrote bits and shows and talked over the theories that we're still carrying out. Nothing is more fun than taking one's work seriously, and we always have.

I did very well street performing and it was mostly a cash-only enterprise. I did a show that was shorter than fifteen minutes and most of that was crowd gathering and collection. Not a lot of juggling in my juggling show. I didn't study anyone else who was street performing, and with the exception of the Renaissance festivals, I performed mostly where it was illegal. Most street performers get people to give them money because they look like they need it. People gave me money because I looked like I deserved it. Offstage I'm a slob. I've never dressed well. I sit around in gym shorts and a work shirt. I don't look in mirrors. I don't shave or get dressed unless I have a show. I have to be paid to brush my hair. "Who's looking at you?" my mom would ask when I made any comment about the clothes she chose for me to wear. But when I was street performing, I always dressed very nicely and made sure that everything I wore looked expensive. I didn't play poverty. I tried to work places where people were upscale.

Teller and I were partners, and while we were getting our stage show together we needed to make money, and I always hit the streets. Teller had put his Renaissance act together but there weren't always festivals, so I dragged him back to my old way of making money. Teller and I staked out the area of Philadelphia where we wanted to do our street shows. Before we did any shows, we sniffed around. We went to all the local merchants and spent money and talked to them. We went to them, bought their shit, and said we were going to be doing street shows, and if we hurt their traffic flow at all, could they please let us know right away. We wanted to help their business.

We found out the area we'd chosen didn't have other performers because there were a bunch of young men around who considered themselves a gang and made it impossible to work there. Maybe they were a gang. I don't know how gangs work, but these were young men with a median age of about fourteen. I guess they were scary, but we didn't think they really hurt people. Maybe they did really hurt people. I didn't know and I don't know. We did know that other people who had tried street performing had their props and money stolen and blamed these guys, and we knew they disrupted acts. Teller and I decided to try something bold with them. I decided to gamble about a grand to see what would happen if I tried trusting them. I had one of the first really fancy digital watches. I loved it. It would be worth nothing now, but then it was almost a grand. In our age of iSleek it would be just clunky and ugly, but back then I thought it was really sexy and groovy.

I arrived to do my first street show in that area. I had my juggling balls and my wooden log with my big juggling knives stuck into it. I had a suitcase with my blindfold, apples for juggling, and my bank bags for money and quarter rolls and hundred-dollar paper bill-bands. While I was juggling balls at the beginning of my show, all that other stuff was easy to swipe and run away with. One of the "gang" guys was watching me closely as I set up. I said to him, "I'm going to do a show here in a little bit." He nodded. He had seen other street performers come and go on his turf. Maybe he was the one who forced them out.

I said to him, "I have trouble juggling with this watch on, and I'm afraid to leave it in my suitcase. I'm afraid someone might steal it. It's a wicked expensive watch." I took off the watch. "Would you hold on to it while I do my show so it'll be safe?" I threw the watch to him. It was a gamble, but it felt right. The story is better if you see this guy as the main potential thief, but I have no evidence of that. He was just a tough-looking child with a different complexion than mine. He caught the watch and said, "No problem."

I did that whole first show without ever looking back once to see if my props were okay. I never checked on my watch. I gathered a crowd of a couple hundred people and juggled my ass off and blew my voice out. I used to put Chloraseptic in a Coke can and use it to stop my throat from hurting so much. I had no vocal training, I just yelled. The voice I have now is not just my age; it's a lot of stupid screaming. Some people have told me very kindly that I have a sexy voice. It's just damage. I guess damage is sexy. Bob Dylan has the blood of the lamb in his voice; I have the blood of screaming for hundreds of people in my voice. It was a really good show. Teller might be right—that street show might be the best thing I've done in my life. My crowd gathering was ripped off and is now part of many, many street shows. I asked a guy doing it on the street where he got it, and he said it went back hundreds of years. Some of the lines in my money collection are also used as standards. I'm pretty proud of all that. It was a good show.

After I had gotten the last penny from the crowd, I turned around and there was my newest friend still guarding my watch. He was beaming. He liked my show and he liked holding my watch for me. I asked him if he wanted to help me out and he said yes. His name was Jose, and I threw him the whole moneybag. I asked Jose to separate the bills out, sort them, and count them. At the end of every night, Jose would reach into my moneybag and take a handful of the unsorted money from the last show and that was his pay for helping and protecting me. Some nights he got a twenty-dollar bill in the handful, maybe one or two nights two twenties, and some nights just ones and quarters. He never complained and neither did I. I would arrive at my corner, Jose would run over, take my watch, take my suitcase, set things up, and I would do shows. At the end of every collection, I would throw all the money to Jose and he kept everything safe. He cleaned and organized my props and bought apples for me and made sure I had a fresh one for every show. He said he was part of a gang, and he told me one night about a fight that he got in and I let him "hide" at our house out of the city for a few days. I never knew anything about it. I never asked him about his "gang." We talked about juggling and how much money we'd made. Maybe he just wanted to see my house. I know he didn't steal my watch, but maybe he lied about other stuff. I knew Jose for a couple of years. He was a good friend.

Jose and his gang also watched over Teller, and they made it very difficult for any other performers to take over our corner. We had to give our imprimatur for anyone else to work. We shared our area with a harmonica player, an old sailor named Big Al. Occasionally a magician named Chris Capehart shared our space. Chris was one of the finest performers I've ever seen. Chris is still working, doing all sorts of shows and he's great, but his street act was really something else. Chris is African-American and back then looked really tough. He dressed for his street act in these weird jumpsuits with bat-wing arms. I don't know if his mom made those outfits for him or a girlfriend or a friend or if he sewed them himself. I never asked him. He didn't talk during his act, but he wasn't silent like Teller. Chris whistled. He whistled for the whole show. He was a whistling, scary guy dressed like James Brown in the "hot pants give you con-fi-dance" period.

Chris did the "Miser's Dream," a standard magic trick where you pull coins out of all sorts of places and drop them in a champagne bucket. Teller uses a fishbowl instead of a bucket and then turns the coins into goldfish in the P&T show. Some magicians use a beautiful classy bucket and some use a beat-up bucket more like a spittoon (as though I've ever seen a spittoon). Al Flosso, one of the best ever at the "Miser's Dream" would bring up a child and do the routine with him, pulling coins out of the child's ears and nose and armpits. Flosso was the best. Very much a "Go away, son, you bother me," W. C. Fields type.

Chris, with balls much too big to fit in his beat-up champagne bucket, would walk around with his wings flapping, whistling and gathering a crowd. With all the people standing around him, he would pick the biggest, strongest, meanest Caucasian man in his front row and get in that man's space. Then he would get in his face. He would stand too close to him, whistling and making eye contact. He had done no magic yet. It was just uncomfortable. He would hang there a little too long and then reach up and slap the guy lightly in the face, not a painful slap, no one was hurt—but it was a real violation of personal space and a racially charged gesture. It was a heavy moment. This is on the street. This isn't a theater. There's no one around to make it okay. His mark always had friends standing nearby, and Chris was always alone. The reaction was strong, and as his audience member recoiled and considered how he was going to kick Chris's ass, a magic coin fell from where the man was slapped and jangled into Chris's bucket. It was a magic trick. The slap had produced a coin from nowhere. There was a pause and then the crowd would react huge. This was a coin that meant something. The guy would give Chris a dismissive, relieved laugh. The guy thought it was over, but it wasn't over. Chris kept eye contact and kept whistling. It was unbelievable. He'd reach up again, but this time he wouldn't slap—he just flick the same guy's nose, and another magic coin would fall. "Fine, that's funny, magic boy, now quit it." Chris wouldn't. He would continue to pull coins from all over the guy, until everyone was laughing. The guy's only way out of this uncomfortable position was to let it all go and be the child in the magic act. He had to trust Chris. He had to like Chris. He had to laugh. There was no other choice. He had to be the little boy, to this whistling, jumpsuited, batwinged, crazy African-American authority figure. There was subtext and there was tension and then it was all okay. When we achieve world peace, Chris's act will deserve some of the credit. Chris's act identified the problem and then solved it. I watched him do it a lot, and every time my stomach tightened up and every time it worked. He and I had long talks at Burger King after our shows. Chris is very successful now. He works cruise ships, clubs, and even children's parties, and every time I see him, my heart goes back to those days on the street. What a genius.

Chris, Big Al, Teller, and I would talk to the police on that beat and do little tricks for them and make jokes. Our shows would have been illegal if we were panhandling, but there was no law against entertaining for money. The police liked our acts. Once I got a few policemen to line up behind me for the whole show. During my threatening money collection speech, that show I ended by gesturing to the line of policemen, saying, "And they're on my side." On my cue, all the police pulled out their billy clubs and brandished them. It would have been a lot funnier if they hadn't been laughing. Amateurs.

I made a shit-ton of money working the streets. Teller and I bought all the equipment for our theater shows with that money. My parents bought me a sound system with the money they had saved for my college tuition, but most of the rest we made there on the streets. We had spotlights and dimmer packs and all the stuff we needed for our theater show. We could produce our shows ourselves with our own money.

When I was twenty, I went to an accountant and asked what I should do about paying taxes (all taxes are theft!) on the money that I made street juggling. He asked me how much I made and I told him. He said, "If you say you made that much money street performing, they will arrest you as a drug dealer." Even he thought I was a drug dealer and wouldn't work for me. So Teller and I bought a van with bundles of tax-free singles.

Some of the tricks we're doing in our Vegas show now, we've been doing since those street days. We've done them tens of thousands of times. Our Vegas show is made up of bits we've been doing for more than thirty years right alongside bits we've been doing for a few weeks. People ask how we can stand doing the same show every night. Do we put the new bits in just for ourselves, to keep it fresh? Nope. There is no need to keep it fresh. It is fresh. It's *Groundhog Day*.

There is a myth that improvisational comics are in tune with the audience and really reading what the audience is doing and reacting to that. Bullshit. I've done appearances that are improvised and I have no knowledge of the audience except an occasional laugh. I'm just trying to save my ass any way I can. The focus is on survival, not the audience. I'm trying to keep it moving and get laughs. When I'm doing a bit I know how to do, I can tell you everything about the audience. I know who is smiling and where the big laughers are. I know every word I'm going to say and when I'm going to scratch my nose, so I can really feel the audience and go with them. The first time I do a bit, I do big gestures to make sure everyone gets the joke. After a thousand times, I've made everything smaller. As small as I can, so the audience can't even tell how they know what I'm thinking. Repetition in front of different audiences gives me the information about how subtle I can make things. We've lost a lot with vaudeville gone. There were people who wrote a twelve-minute act when they were sixteen years old and performed it multiple times a day until they died. They learned things about how people learn things that no one else will ever know. They knew about language and pronunciation and breathing. I tried to see as many of those acts as I could. There aren't many people around today who can do a real twelve minutes of *Groundhog Day.*

We have a bit we call "Water Tank." The gist is that Teller holds his breath completely submerged in a tank of water, which is locked from the outside, until I find the right freely selected card. I find the wrong card and he drowns. After he's dead, the right card appears on his dead face underwater. It's a great bit and one that was responsible for one of my stupidest showbiz decisions. We were asked to appear on *The Tonight Show Starring Johnny Carson.* I'm talking the real fucking *Tonight Show.* We were going to be on with Johnny. I was going to sit on the couch next to Johnny. The couch that meant showbiz.

This was going to be it. We wanted to do the "Water Tank." Johnny's people said that after we showed the card was right, before we went to commercial, Teller would have to pop out of the tank and wave to show the audience he was okay, and then we'd go to commercial—just a quick wave on the pull back. We said that we wanted to leave Teller dead going to commercial. They said wave. We said that everyone knew Teller wasn't really dead and we'd go to commercial with him lifeless floating in the tank; that was the respectful way to do it. They said theirs was a happy show, and waving made everyone happy. We pretended to have integrity about something where integrity doesn't matter and we hung tough. They said that they wouldn't hang tough. They wanted us on the *Tonight Show*, and they wanted us on our terms . . . okay—but we couldn't do it with Johnny. We could do our bit, as we wanted, but we'd do it when *The Tonight Show Starring Johnny Carson* was guest-hosted by Jay Leno. We won. And then because we're loser assholes, we changed to another bit for some reason I can't even remember and went on with Jay, without doing the "Water Tank" at all. No waving, no not waving, no "Water Tank." We love Jay and he's been great to us, but it meant although we were on *The Tonight Show Starring Johnny Carson* we were never on *The Tonight Show Starring Johnny Carson* with Johnny Carson.

I never met Johnny Carson face-to-face. But we did e-mail and talk on the phone a lot. I take about one real day off a year, but one year I took more than a week off, in Newfoundland with my bride-to-be. Everyone was told that I was not to be contacted. Not for any reason. I was with my love and the moose and that was it. We got to our hotel room in St. John's and the phone rang. "Sorry to bother you, Mr. Jillette, but this is Johnny Carson." I froze. The voice was perfect. This was after he'd retired, and my heart flew, my heart banged, my heart stopped. "Is this a bad time?"

have met Johnny Carson, but we talked on the phone and we wrote e-mails, and maybe that's okay. It'll have to be okay.

The first time we did "Water Tank" was on *Saturday Night Live* with Madonna hosting. There are a few moments in it where the audience has to know that I'm worried I won't be able to find the right card. If you watch the *SNL* performance, I play it big. Wicked big. Stupid big. I don't trust myself or the audience. I make sure I get the laughs.

Ten years later, we had done the bit thousands of times, and we were playing much bigger places. I was able to get the back row of a 5,000-seat theater to understand with less than I used to get a close-up on TV to be clear. With my style and my movement, one little move of the head could get a bigger reaction from the back row than a full body turn. And those people wouldn't even know how they'd figured out what I was thinking. Thousands of times had taught me how to really communicate. It takes so little, but it takes time to get that little.

Electronic media had forced a lot of novelty down our throats at the expense of skill. Novelty at the expense of nuance. I thought Andy Warhol said something like if they were going to do pretty much the same situation comedies every week on TV, why didn't they do the exact same situation comedy every week on TV and get good at it? Since electronic mass media, there's this sense of "new" that really bugs me. *Saturday Night Live* is a scripted show that's more a sitcom, with returning stars and premises, than it is improvisation. Imagine if the brilliant men and women who did the first *Saturday Night Live* shows had done that same first George Carlin show every night for ten years. Imagine if all their tension had gone away. Imagine if they knew how big every laugh was going to be and exactly where to stand. Imagine no cue cards. Imagine no unneeded pauses and no mugging. The situation comedies don't explore the depth of plot or those characters in a situation with all the depth that learning can bring; instead they get good at using those same characters in slightly different situations. I guess that's why it's called situation comedy. People get good at forms and not ideas. It's fun to do and it's fun to watch, but I love watching things that have been done just that way a thousand times before. I think the performers learn stuff that no one would have ever thought of.

Lance Burton, Master Magician, has a dove routine in Vegas. He's magically pulling birds out of his jacket. Everyone knows he's pulling them out of his jacket; there's no other way to do the trick. He comes out onstage looking twenty pounds heavier than he looks when all the birds have flown magnificently to the back of the theater. Lance did that show seven nights a week, two shows a night, for decades. Other stuff in his show changed, but that dove opener was the same every night. Exactly the same. Every move. Every smile. How could he stand that? Well, he could stand that because he was living Groundhog Day, and he loved it. Lance had a chance to get good at something.

John Belushi had that one chance to nail that *Star Trek* sketch and he had to make sure everyone got it. Lance had thousands of shows to get that bird out right and every single night it got a little better. The magic was not in hiding the birds in his jacket. The magic was in doing it over and over again.

I can go out onstage and just try breathing in a different place to see if a line is smoother. I'm living my thousand years of Groundhog Day. That's a rare thing in life, where you have something you want to say from your heart and you get to say it over and over again and get it better. Get it right. There are conversations with my wife I would like to have a thousand times so she understood me perfectly. These audiences get to hear me say for their first time something I've said a thousand times. I should be able to get them to feel what I want. There is the art. The art is Groundhog Day.

Listening to: "Like a Rolling Stone"—Bob Dylan (a live performance from last year of a song written in 1965 and performed thousands of times since)

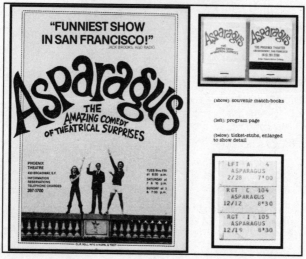

(above): souvenir match-books

(left): program page

(below): ticket-stubs, enlarged to show detail

SICK DAYS

HOW MUCH WOULD YOU SPEND, right now, cash money, for five photographs of me getting a blow job? There are a lot of sex pictures in my collection, but only five of them are clearly me. It's my fifty-year-old, 6'7", 300-pound body standing there with an attractive, redheaded woman, a good friend of mine, and she has my proportionate-but-no-more penis in her mouth. I'm enjoying myself. She's enjoying herself. She's wearing a blindfold, so one of my personal sextortionists billboarded it as "Hardcore S&M." At the time the pictures were taken, both of us were single, and so was the person taking the picture. I don't remember her birthday, but she was just under thirty. There might have been a twenty-year age difference, but I'm so wicked old that she was still double the legal age in some farm states. Someone who used to work for me sold a laptop without wiping it really clean. Someone else got hold of it and went to a lawyer who specializes in extortion. That asshole lawyer got in touch with my groovy lawyer, who specializes, at least with me, in death threats against me for being an atheist. The asshole wondered whether I might be interested in keeping these pictures from going public. This is known as extortion. Or blackmail. The only unusual thing about it is that it was happening to me.

How can blackmail happen to me? What's to blackmail me on? I wrote a bestselling book that included a chapter on my visit to a gay bathhouse, possibly with "Patient Zero" and trying to have gay sex. In the same book I wrote about group sex and having a fat Elvis impersonator piss on me in public. I've written about dropping my cock in a blow dryer and fucking a famous model underwater. I once had a CNN cameraman shoot my poisoned bleeding balls. There are pictures and stories of me wrestling naked with a little person, a man, both of us naked, in wet cornstarch. To use incorrect terms, there are pictures of me butt-naked wrestling a butt-assed-naked dwarf. We got rough, he was choking and he almost died. I came close to being the perp in naked homosexual dwarf murder. Isn't that a little kinky? Even in the twenty-first century, that's a little kinky, right? I've been to the Fetish and Fantasy Halloween Ball dressed as a leather daddy. I did a show called *Penn & Teller: Bullshit!*—available on iTunes, YouTube, and Netflix—where I've been naked and surrounded by naked people and have talked about and cheered for all kinds of sex. I also used every obscenity you've ever heard and I may have been the first to say "cunt pickle" publicly. I did a movie called *The Aristocrats* that was banned by a whole chain of theaters just for the graphic verbal descriptions of perverse sex acts. You can go to YouTube right now and watch me dance naked in Zero-G on the Vomit Comet with my cock flapping around. I have a United States patent on a female masturbation device that I demonstrated with nude models for *Playboy*. Bill Maher listed a bunch of "perversions" on his show and I said, seriously and honestly, "I've done all those." Howard Stern talked to me about my sex dungeon in my home being used as a nursery when our children were young. I've attended the AVN Awards and felt Nina Hartley's and Carrie Fisher's breasts almost at the same time in public. At that same convention, I slipped behind a curtain with a porn star for an embarrassingly short time. I dropped my pants at a TSA checkpoint and was detained for indecent exposure. I've never done a drug in my life, never had sex with anyone who is underage (since I was underage myself), never committed an act of bestiality (mostly because I just don't like animals), never coerced anyone into sex and I have no secrets from my wife. She sees every picture and she knows every woman who walks by in Starbucks who I find attractive and that's most of them. I don't lie to her. Unless there's a surprise party coming up (that might include wrestling a naked dwarf), we have no secrets. How can blackmail scare me? But it made me sick for weeks. It fucked up my life.

What was your number for the five pictures of me getting my cock sucked? The extortionists started at "six figures." When bad douche bags are stealing money, and they say "six figures," that doesn't mean $1,000.29. They don't put the decimal point in. Their jive-ass six figures start at $100,000.00. Let me tell you right now, if you'll pay six figures even with the decimal point for a picture of me getting a blow job, my wife and I are happy to oblige and you can run the camera yourself. Hell, you're welcome to join in. My wife and I sometimes have sex just for fun, sometimes for no figures, and not for procreation and not to sell on the Internet.

When the sleazy extortionist lawyer got in touch with my super-expensive honest lawyer and laid out the threat, I had the odd feeling of being innocent and guilty at the same time. I knew I had done nothing wrong. If there were something I would feel guilty about, I wouldn't do it. I believe very much in privacy, but I don't keep much private. I get interviewed and I answer questions that others just say "no comment" to. I try to be a little cagey about what I think of Criss Angel, but people see right through me on that, and I don't even try to be cagey about sex. I should be blackmail-proof, but when my lawyer called and explained that someone had my private pictures and were threatening to make them public, I almost threw up. Later, I did throw up. I got real, no kidding, sick. I ended up in the hospital and I'm sure stress was part of it. I don't want to make comparisons with other sex crimes that are much more serious, but it is true that something that one gives up happily and for free can feel awful when it's taken without permission. I felt awful.

I asked Teller, "Who the fuck would want pictures of a fifty-year-old fat guy getting his cock sucked?" He answered, "Apparently you do, and that's the mystery." Teller always has the right answer. As funny as that is, it's also true. It was his way of saying "no one," but why the fuck did I have those pictures on my computer? Why the fuck did I want those pictures? What was I thinking? I understand why I have thousands of pictures of women (and a few men) that I took or had sent to me, I love naked pictures, but why pictures of me? I don't even look in mirrors. I don't brush my hair. I hate photo sessions. Why was I posing with my cock out? Well, I was thinking it was no big deal. We were playing around, there were three of us, one had a camera and the pictures were hot to us. They weren't hot compared with SpankWire and xHamster or any of those professional porno sites, but they were hot to us because they were us. They wouldn't mean shit to you. I'm not a sex symbol. I'm not attractive, but the wonderful thing about humans is that we can find people who find us sexy, and I've been very lucky. We had a really fun evening and took a few pictures so we could remember it and maybe rub a few more out to those same memories. It was efficiency as much as anything. It saved energy. We did it for the planet. I think others do this too. My politics and theology are certainly weirder than my sex life. I think I'm pretty much in the American sex pocket. I'm not a big deal. I'm not blackmail material.

If I were a piece of ass, like Tom Cruise, or I was anti-ass like Rick Santorum, it seems a lot of people would want to see these pictures, and you could probably get six figures without the decimal point, but Penn Jillette? Who cares? No one cares, and I was still vomiting.

If I were the person I'd like to be, I would have told my lawyer to throw away the letter. No answer is the answer that was deserved, or I should have told my lawyer to just quote Shakespeare: "There is no terror, Cassius, in your threats: For I am arm'd so strong in honesty That they pass me by as the idle wind, Which I respect not." That's the person I'd like to be. The person I am threw up.

There was a sickening fear. Maybe it's the sickening fear I feel every night when Teller points a gun that can't hurt me at my face. A blackmail letter is scary. Was it possible there were pictures I didn't know about? When the first e-mail came in, they didn't say they had all my pictures. I thought they might have someone else's pictures. I don't know of anyone else's pictures, but what if there were some? What difference does that make? It's the same fat guy. The same cock. I'm used to my cock. I've accepted my cock. I've used my cock. What's the difference who took the fucking picture? But I wasn't strong enough. I threw up and I chattered in fear to my lawyer while her clock was running.

My lawyer and manager met with the extortionist lawyer. I didn't want to feel like prey—I'd rather feel like the predator—so I engaged the lawyer who helped out David Letterman with his blackmail case. You may remember, Dave was embarrassed and the bad guy was incarcerated. Dave won. My new big-cheese blackmail lawyer told my manager and my regular super-lawyer to push hard when they met with the asshole lawyer. They were told to say pretty much what I said in the first paragraph of this article: Penn lives his sex life in public already, we know he fucks and fucks hard and has pictures of it all—now shock us. You better have him fucking a dog or a young boy. My guy is a fucking badass. Shock us. Make us sick.

This is a goofy situation. It's like the thief inviting my manager and lawyer to his house to see the Ferrari he stole from me. As soon as he shows my pictures, he's admitting to a crime. It's bugnutty. The dickwad led with a picture of me and Liberace. Sadly, both of us fully clothed and not even kissing. He followed that with a picture of Gilbert Gottfried and me with a stripper on my lap. I think the stripper had claimed that she was Dolly Parton's cousin and fronted that claim with a couple of similarities. My manager said, "That picture hung in our office for sixteen years." Then my manager was shown the pictures of me getting a blow job from a woman in a comfortable blindfold and the extortionist pointed out that that woman was married (she was married five years *after* the pictures were taken, but why quibble) and she had a job she might worry about losing. Wouldn't it be more embarrassing to have a homeless woman blowing me? He then showed them some video of my wife fucking and having sex, and yes, my wife knew the camera was running. I was running the camera and I told her that the red light was on. It would embarrass my wife in front of her mom and dad, but even if it was on SpankWire, her mom and dad would at least fast-forward through the good parts. So what?

The lawyer tried to argue that this was pretty shocking for someone who was on *The Celebrity Apprentice*. *What?* Do we believe that Donald Trump doesn't get blow jobs from his wife? She might *need* a blindfold. Aubrey O'Day was on *The Celebrity Apprentice* and so was Miss Universe, and I found both of them naked on the Web the night I got back to my room after meeting them. People want to see them naked more than they want to see me, and they want to see me more than Donald Trump—I mean, I hope they do. So what?

So then the pissant lawyer got stupider. He showed my lawyer and manager some financial reports. Oops. This changes the crime. This would get the FBI agents hard enough to blow each other on camera. Then he made it clear he had my whole hard drive, which would help me figure out who his secret "client" was. It also meant

that he had my files from Teller that show me how some Penn &
Teller magic tricks are done. Some of our tricks are so complex, and
Teller does most of the work on them, that sometimes I'll perform
my part in a trick for years not knowing how the whole thing is done.
At magic conventions, I have explained our magic tricks wrong—I
just didn't know. But Teller has sent me diagrams. These are trade
secrets—oops. Now the FBI is hard enough to cum in their pants
without blindfolds on.

The fuckhead extortionist lawyer, from Hollywood, then told an
implausible story of how his client got this information: the client
had bought the laptop from a Craigslist ad the year before and saw
some files on it. He waited a few months to look at the files (a few
months to see what the fifty gigs were? Not likely), saw it belonged
to me and took another couple months (until the premiere of *The
Celebrity Apprentice*) to engage a scumbag and extort me. Oh, and
the lawyer said his client bought this alleged laptop in Las Vegas,
Nevada—ooooooops. That's not California. Now it's interstate;
now the FBI can fuck him hard every way they want. The FBI really
loves to hate-fuck extortionists and they take pictures.

Most people who go to the FBI have already made blackmail payments and are scared to death of the blackmailer. I had paid nothing
(let's not count the thousands to the good lawyers), and I wasn't really very worried about the stuff coming out. There was nothing
even close to illegal. I knew the women in the pictures wouldn't be
happy with these out there, but I own the copyright and where
would they go? Who would post them? I didn't fuck movie stars or
politicians. I fucked businesswomen and scientists. I fuck citizens. I
find real people sexier than showbiz people, and that's fortunate for
me, because movie stars seem to have no desire to fuck me.

TMZ won't pay for any sex pictures. The sites that put up sex tapes of Paris Hilton and Kim Kevorkian (is that right?) aren't going to put up stills of my wife having sex. Who cares? Blackmail is just stock options; they are worth nothing unless I happen to believe they're worth something. They are worth my fear and shame. I'm not without fear and shame, but I'm not overflowing with it either. I don't have six figures worth of fear and shame.

Before I called in the FBI, my lawyers said, "You want to think about this, because you'll be turning your whole hard drive over to the FBI. They will have everything. You're the victim, they're not looking to bust you, but they might see letters to your pot dealer or offshore accounts or something like that." I don't have anything like that. I don't even drink, and I don't understand hiding money. "Also, what about your wife?" I told her about all this and she said, "So what, let them put it all up. I wish they had pictures of me younger, but I look okay. Fuck them." Some people have asked why this woman is the woman who became my wife. Have we answered that? She is perfect and so much stronger than me. If this was going to be a scandal, I supposed it could hurt Teller's career too. I talked to him about it, but he just laughed at me. The whole thing tickled Teller pink. Anyone wondering why he's my business and artistic partner for life?

So I turned the case over to the FBI and they got all FBI about it. They started wiring people and setting up installment payments with FBI money and handcuffs and shit. My lawyer said, "I don't think you want to play cops and robbers." And I said, "What the fuck are you talking about? I absolutely want to play cops and robbers—I want to be wired by Sam Waterston." But I didn't get to do anything. All the e-mails were written by the FBI and sent by my lawyers. All the meetings were done by lawyers. My lawyer made phone calls while she was wired. She wrote leading questions in e-mail like, "If Penn doesn't pay, what will you do with these pictures?" And the scumbag answered all the questions by the extortion handbook. Oh, that six-figure price? What the scumbag lawyer thought five pictures of Penn Jillette getting a blow job were worth? Do you have a figure in your head? Get ready. His figure was $900,000.00 cash money. Give me a list of people to whom you'd pay that much money for five blow job pictures. I'm not on it, right? If I am on it, give my manager a call—you'll get the deal of your life.

What would happen if I didn't pay? Would the headline in *The New York Times* be: "Old Fat Sub-Star Gets a Blow Job from More Attractive Woman with Blindfold—His Career Is Over!"? I guess that could happen. If I had just been the human being that Shakespeare wanted me to be and sent the *Julius Caesar* quote, most likely the pictures and the story would never come out. The article you're reading now is all you would have ever heard of it if I had done nothing. When this book comes out, I might get disgusted and set up "Penn's Blackmail Page" and put up the pictures myself and be twelve feet tall and bulletproof for the rest of my life. Fuck blackmail.

My children were five and six years old at the time. If they had been fifteen and sixteen, this would be a whole different issue. They could be embarrassed in school, but I still can't imagine giving those scumbags even six figures of dimes. It would just be some gossip with the MILFs and the teachers and it wouldn't filter down to my children. By the time they'll care, my blow job will have blown over. They have much more to be embarrassed about by me. Look at my haircut, for Christ's sake—who wants to be dropped off at school by an elderly hippie magician dad?

As it turned out, after all the phone recording and cat and mouse, the FBI just showed up at the scumbag lawyer's office (in his home, what a fucking loser) and said that they were conducting an investigation into stolen material and they were watching him. The lawyer said he didn't know that and he was dropping his client right away. He wasn't going to even call him. A few weeks later, I got the laptop FedEx'ed back to me, and the whole thing was over. Maybe the fuckwad kept a copy in case I do end up running for mayor, but after the FBI said it was stolen, he might just want to not have any blow job pictures of me anywhere around him. My legal fees were five figures, and that sure seems a stupid amount to pay for nothing, but they did a good job. So, some asshole cost me tens of thousands of dollars because I had some pictures of myself getting a blow job. If you want to hear the sound of Teller's voice, listen carefully; you can probably hear him laughing from where you are now.

All this waving my cock around makes it sound like I didn't care at all, but the truth is I did care. No matter how much I try to pretend I don't care about this, I do care. I can write here about everything I've done, but I don't like someone else threatening to tell people. My whole system shut down. I got physically sick. I cried. I cried to my wife. I left my office to get hugs from her. I didn't feel sexy. I did nothing wrong. Nothing. I wasn't even in danger. I suppose if it had all come out in the worst way possible on a slow news day, it could have hurt ticket sales at the Rio's Penn & Teller Theater, or hurt book sales, or TV deals, but it was just as likely to help those, right? There's no such thing as bad press. I think Lee Harvey Oswald said that. So, I was an innocent man who was not in danger, and I was attacked by an impotent dick, and I got sick. It's amazing. Even being right can't make me as strong as I'd like to be. I'm no Julius Caesar.

I don't have the self-control to say, "I'm in the right and I'm out of danger—fuck them." I could tell someone else to do that, but I can't tell myself. And that makes me feel weak. Everything conflates—I had an ear operation, I was on *The Celebrity Apprentice*, we were putting a new trick in the show—and everything just ran together. I didn't know what I was feeling. I couldn't tell if I was depressed about the blow jobs, Clay Aiken, or an ear infection and those are way, way different things, you know, except for the last two.

I didn't want the FBI to put the asshole in jail. I don't want to spend the rest of my life dealing with the fact that someone was in jail because of me. I just wanted them to stop bugging me and they did. I knew when I took those pictures that anything on your computer can go public, and I found out what that feels like. I'm stronger now. If there's any advice I can pass along from this experience, it would be that if someone tries to blackmail you, go right to the FBI. They're smart, they're tough, and they're fun to talk to. You know when your mom told you to go to the police if you were in trouble? She was right.

I was flying to Burbank just before this book went to press. Porn superstar Ron Jeremy was on my flight. I got close to him and tried to change my voice a little, which is stupid, I always sound like me, and I said, "Hey, show me your dick." I thought it was the kind of thing a stranger would say to Ron and the kind of thing I wish strangers would say to me. He looked up, saw it was me, smiled, and we chatted a bit.

Before I got to asking him who he'd been fucking lately, Ron said, "Hey, this porno press agent asked me for your number a while ago. He wanted to get in touch with you. He told me why. I thought it was bullshit, so I didn't give him your number." (Do you love that Ron has my number?)

"Good thinking."

"Yeah, he said it was some preemptive thing. He said he had

pictures or videos or something that you might not want out there. Like sex shit. I told him that you didn't give a fuck, as long as your dick looked big enough, right? You don't fucking care. Right?"

"Right."

"Hey, you want the asshole's name? I have his name, I can give it to you. He's a bottom-feeder." A guy who got famous blowing himself has met some bottom-feeders. I got the name from him and we did a Web search, and that name shows up with the name of a dirtbag lawyer who was able to get my number through my lawyer. Ron's analysis of the situation was perfect, instantaneous, and completely free. So, let me change my advice some: If you're ever blackmailed, either go right to the FBI, or ask Ron Jeremy what to do.

Similar weird bad shit has happened to me once before. In one other instance I've been totally innocent and was ripped apart with guilt. I had a radio show and I made some jokes about Mother Teresa. They weren't good-natured jokes. Not at all. They were mean-spirited. I said that Paris Hilton was too moral to play Mother Teresa and that Mother Teresa's "kink" was suffering. Previously when I talked about Mother Teresa on *Bullshit*, I called her "Motherfucking Teresa" but this was CBS so I couldn't. I didn't know anything about it, but some local DJs (I don't even know how many or where), commented on my show and offered money to have me killed and said they'd pay more if I suffered. I didn't even know about it until my boss called up right before my show and said, "We want you to know we take death threats very seriously." I said, "Good thinking, but why are you telling me this?" He said, "Oh shit, you didn't know." He explained and I went directly on the air and did a radio show. It's shocking, but the DJ worked for the same company I worked for. We had the same boss. The next day the DJ and his crew were fired.

I didn't want him fired; I just wanted him to shut up. My daughter was a year old at the time, and I didn't want headlines saying, "DJ Fired for Offering Money to Kill Penn Jillette." I didn't want "Kill Penn Jillette" to be the first thing that popped up on a Google search when you typed "Penn J—" This time I didn't call in the FBI. I just wanted it to go away. My father-in-law called me and asked me what the fuck I was doing getting death threats when I was supposed to be caring for his daughter and granddaughter. He was right. I had armed guards at our house around the clock and Rio security walked me from the Penn & Teller Theater to my unmarked Penn & Teller car after every show. What the fuck? We managed to keep it pretty quiet and none of the death threats (and there were a few like this) hit the national media, and we finally got rid of the guards, but we still have a pretty good security system at our home. If this gives you ideas, I believe the guy's withdrawn his offer. And he's flat fucking broke anyway, so don't bother.

But this story gets weirder. The DJ who was fired sued me for getting him fired. Here's the position I was in. It seems like I had a right to ask to have him fired, since he threatened on the air to have someone kill me, but I didn't. Right after my show, I called the big cheese and asked him *not* to fire the guy. I thought if they kept him on payroll, they could keep him under control. Tell him he was no longer allowed even to say "pen" or "Gillette" again, let alone my name. I thought if they fired him, they would have nothing to hold over his head. My strategy was to keep him working and shut him the fuck up. The DJ found out about my phone call, but not the content, and claimed that I had called to have him fired and sued me for that. He also thought that I'd have more money than CBS Radio. I sure wish I had the money that people who want to attack me think I have.

I ended up having sixteen hours of depositions where an elderly

Christian lawyer asked me questions about Mother Teresa and how much money I had. I was supposed to follow rules and never help him at all, but after he asked me if I was familiar with Dave Carlin's "ten words you shouldn't say on TV" or something that far off, I finally said, "You mean GEORGE CARLIN'S SEVEN WORDS YOU CAN'T SAY ON TV?" My lawyer said that was wrong—I should have made him work for it. Jesus Christ. He also didn't believe that I'd never heard his client's comments about me and that I didn't want his client to be fired. Everyone in the office heard the MP3 of the DJ threatening me, but I didn't want to. And I didn't want my wife to hear it. Would you want to hear someone offering money to have you killed?

I had nothing at risk. I was completely innocent. CBS was paying all the legal fees and they were signed to pay any damages. I was facing nothing at all. But I was in the system with people attacking me and I felt sick and depressed. There's a line by Sly Stone in "Family Affair": "You can't cry 'cause you'll look broke down, but you're crying anyway, 'cause you're all broke down." That's how I feel at these times.

In both of these cases, I had no reason to be worried. But the system is set up to make a person feel danger. It's impossible to feel safe and innocent, at least for me. I've heard that really bad people thrive in this situation, but I don't. I way don't. I'm happier when I'm completely separate from the United States Justice System. I don't want to sue anyone. I don't want to be a victim or a perp. I just want to stay away.

I was talking to my senior adviser, Lawrence O'Donnell Jr. LOD and I were talking on the phone about how safe and innocent I was and how shitty I felt. This is what came to me. This is the self-help portion of the book.

I think you just have to take sick days. I always tell people when they're going through a romantic breakup that "It's just the flu—give it a week to ten days and you'll be better. There will be some diarrhea and vomiting, but you'll be fine. Just accept that you're going to be sick and get through it. Don't fight it. Don't try to be happy and well. Go with the sickness—just get through it."

I guess that's what to do with blackmail and death threats too. Just take some sick days. Throw up, bundle up, drink plenty of liquids, take an analgesic for relief of pain and fever, and wait for time to pass. You'll be fine. That's my advice.

Now, wanna see some pictures of me getting my cock sucked? I'll make you a deal.

Listening to: "Family Affair"—Sly and the Family Stone

What would this picture be worth to you?

APRIL FOOLS' DAY

OUR MOVIE, *Penn & Teller Get Killed*, is about two guys, named Penn and Teller, played by Penn Jillette and Teller, who play practical jokes all the time and—this isn't more of a spoiler than the fucking title—those practical jokes end up killing Penn & Teller, and depending on how you read the ambiguous ending, maybe those jokes end up killing everyone in the world. Our movie was not the first movie starring people using their own names as characters who die in the movie. The Monkees' movie, *Head*, stars Peter Tork, Micky Dolenz, Davy Jones and Mike Nesmith playing characters of the same names and they all die at the end (also not a spoiler, the end is shown at the beginning).

Penn & Teller Get Killed was directed by one of the greatest directors of all time, Arthur Penn, and he made exactly the movie we wanted. The movie we wanted was not the exact movie the audience wanted, and now it's called a "cult film." I'm pretty proud of it. I'm happy we did something that nutty for our movie. Nutty made me proud and ended our movie career.

The movie would have been better art if it had been popular. I'm fascinated by the difference between characters and real people in entertainment. I've spent most of my life playing a character that has my real name and many of my real-life personality traits. I try to make that character as close to my real self as possible, but that's still quite a distance. The Penn who lives with his family doesn't always feel like doing those tricks onstage every night in Vegas at nine p.m. But the Penn who works at the Rio wants to put on his suit and walk onstage every night at the same time, in the same mood, and perform those same miracles. The real me, the I, always feels like being onstage when the other Penn is supposed to be, but if I were totally myself, I might not leave my children to drive into the theater and put on a suit. Once we're onstage, doing those tricks, we're pretty much the same guy.

I try not to say anything in character that I wouldn't say myself. People ask me if I believe everything I said on *Penn & Teller: Bullshit!* and I did and I still do believe almost all of it. There has been some information that's changed my mind on a few things, and I'm also a different person now, so some of my opinions have changed a little, but when I said it, I meant it.

I've done a few TV dramas where I played myself and then it gets tricky. I did a detective show called *Numb3rs* and I was playing myself. Someone else wrote the script, but I was pretty much myself. The Penn in *Numb3rs* was proud of having known Richard Feynman, and the real Penn is even prouder.

I know the audience makes very sophisticated separations between fantasy and reality, but some reactions still confuse me. Lawrence Konner, one of my friends, was a writer on *The Sopranos*. He gave me a call once and asked my permission to write a scene in which one of the women on the show, Adriana La Cerva, confesses to having sucked my cock in a men's room in Atlantic City. He was inspired to write that after an evening he and I spent hanging out in Vegas—you know what I mean. I was flattered. Even more flattered when a morning DJ told me that Mick Jagger had called Steve McQueen to ask if it was okay for Mick to sing about someone sucking Steve's cock in the song "Starfucker" (it's copyrighted as "Star Star"). Steve said yes to Mick and I said yes to Larry. Steve and I are that same kind of guy. After it was shot, Lawrence called me to apologize. I guess in his script she blew me in the men's room, but they changed it on set to her blowing me in the women's room. I don't know why that made a difference on the set, and I don't know why Larry felt he had to apologize. I have no idea what that means. I guess the Penn of *The Sopranos* cares where he's blown. The real Penn would be happy to go into the bus station transsexual bathroom for any blow job.

When that episode of *The Sopranos* came out, I had people call me and say, "I loved your appearance on *The Sopranos*." I got more reaction to that than the many TV shows I've gotten into makeup for. I'm at my best when I don't show up. A character on *30 Rock* talked about what outfit she'd wear to watch porno in Vegas with me. For the real Penn, you can watch porno with me without any outfit at all. People called up and congratulated me for being on *30 Rock*. After *The Sopranos* blow job line, I was most shocked by the people who said, "You know, that actress, Drea de Matteo, must really dig you, or she wouldn't have said that." What? It was my buddy Lawrence who thought about sucking my cock; Ms. de Matteo had no more desire to suck my cock than James Spader desired to fuck Maggie Gyllenhaal in *Secretary*. Okay, that's a bad example, but I was surprised how many people thought that I was somehow on *The Sopranos*.

Weirder than getting my imaginary cock sucked on that show were the two Penn & Teller appearances on *The Simpsons*. It seems everyone wanted to know what that was like. What? It was like being in a recording studio in Vegas wearing headphones and reading a piece of paper on a music stand. We didn't go to Springfield. Homer didn't want to suck my cartoon dick in the cartoon women's room of the cartoon nuclear plant.

The X-Files called us in to do a script with them in the nineties. We went to L.A. for a meeting with the big cheeses on the show. They were considering having us play Penn & Teller, who discover that some bullshit wasn't bullshit. We were to play the skeptics who were proven wrong. Morally, the show is fiction and so anything is okay. My favorite movie is *Dawn of the Dead* and my twelfth favorite movie is the remake of *Dawn of the Dead* and there's nothing wrong with doing a fictional movie about zombies even when there aren't real zombies. That's okay. It was okay for us to play Penn & Teller and get killed even though we weren't killed. It was okay to have some Mafia girlfriend talk about sucking my cock. But something rubbed us the wrong way about playing skeptics who are proved wrong in *The X-Files*. It didn't feel right.

We were discussing this with the cheeses at *The X-Files* and they were being pretty snotty about it. They thought we should get off our fucking high horse and just do their big fancy TV show. They were right and they probably would have convinced us, but then one of them said something crazy. One of them said something like it was impossible to have drama without the supernatural. What? I brought up *Psycho* and all Sherlock Holmes and then they made a bigger mistake. They said something to Teller like, "I see why you don't talk much. Penn is so argumentative, you can't get a sane word in." Oh dear. When you say in real life that Teller doesn't talk because I'm too aggressive and he's dominated by me . . . well, things don't go well. Don't assume anything that Teller does isn't his own choice.

Teller spoke. Oh my glory, did Teller speak. Teller explained that he was quiet during this meeting not to stay in character or because I bullied him into silence, but rather because he couldn't figure out a way to suffer fools as well as I had. He then made a very strong case for realistic drama, quoting Aristotle and Shakespeare and using phrases such as "hacks like you." It didn't go well. They did the show without us and got a couple of other guys to transform from make-believe skeptics to make-believe believers. The guys who did the bit are friends of ours and it was a good break for them. It would have been good for us too, but we queered that deal. I think it's okay to do anything in fiction, but it's not okay to say that Teller is being quiet because I overpower him. That'll get you a new asshole ripped. Of course, their show did fine without us. It was our loss, not theirs. Sha La La La, man.

We were not the first to kill our fictional selves in a movie, but I really wanted to be the first to be the bad guy under my own name in a fictional show. I can't think of another example of that except maybe Donald Trump on *The Celebrity Apprentice*, but I'm not sure he sees himself as the villain. I wanted to be a fictional real bad guy named Penn Jillette. I asked the *CSI* guys if they'd let me play Penn Jillette on their show and turn out to be a murderer. I thought me in an orange jumpsuit with a prison ID number and the name "Jillette" on it at the end of the show would be great. But Teller and I pissed off the *CSI* guys too. I don't think there was even a story to how we pissed them off; they just plain didn't like us. We were told by our manager that they hated us. We don't know what we said or did. I guess we were just ourselves, sometimes that's all it takes.

When I was on *Numb3rs* playing myself, I asked if the fictional Penn could be friends with the lead guy, Charlie Eppes, played by the groovy David Krumholtz. I asked if I could be some sort of recurring character. I wouldn't start out as the bad Penn Jillette. I would start out as the good Penn Jillette, who was getting to be friendly with Charlie Eppes. I'd be a guy he went to for a few shows. That would be the arc of my character. And then after Charlie and the audience got used to me, there would be a case where some perp was killing showwomen or magicians or something sexy like that. Charlie would come to me to help me solve the crime, and then he'd realize that I was the bad guy and he'd lock me up as "Penn Jillette."

I've heard that people who play the bad guys in re-creations of real crimes on TV get turned in as "most wanted," but with my own name, I thought it would be even nuttier. I guess they kind of did that to me on *The Celebrity Apprentice*, but I wanted to try it with a real script and plot and not just after-the-fact editing. I think going to TV prison would be way more fun than the boardroom. The writers/producers seemed to like the idea, but the show ended before we got to do it. Or maybe they were just being nice over lunch and weren't even considering. I never know what's really going on in showbiz. I still wonder what we did to piss off *CSI*.

I've heard hard-core drinkers don't go out on New Year's Eve because it's for amateurs. I feel that way about practical jokes. Teller and I do not play practical jokes. Hardly ever. We played a real-life practical joke on an agent in Atlantic City and it didn't go well. We were too good. Way too good. It really didn't go well. I'm going to tell you a slightly watered-down version, because I'm ashamed of the real story.

Our opening act for one run in Atlantic City was Robert Wuhl doing stand-up and telling wonderful showbiz stories. The three of us decided to play a practical joke on a booking agent who we shared. We've done most of what there is to do in Atlantic City. We wanted to see what would happen if an agent had to break up a serious fight between Robert and Penn & Teller. We rehearsed with Robert, and he did a great job. We planned some special effects and rehearsed those too. With a bunch of people, including the agents, standing around backstage in the green room after the show, I started by making a small negative comment about a joke in Robert's show. He came back defensively. I came back more offensively. We escalated to screaming at each other. That led to some pushing and shoving. Teller had a pot of coffee that looked like it was boiling hot (dry ice), and he threw it at Robert and there was a lot of blood-curdling screaming, swearing and stage combat. It was wicked heavy. We convinced everyone it was real, including a few security guys who weren't in on it (though a couple were), and it really made people feel scared and awful. It was worse than what I'm writing here. No one was physically hurt, but it went on much too long and there was real panic. It was awful. The guy we did it for never believed it was fake and never forgave us. I'm on his side.

So our new rule on practical jokes is we don't do them. The one exception is if we can be sure that the "victim" enjoys the joke more than we do. I don't mean being a good sport and laughing along with us; I mean really thrilled and honored.

We've done one great practical joke in that vein. We did a thing called "LabScam" in the fall of 1989. That year will be important later. Rob Pike, super-genius, and his super-genius buddies at Bell Labs wanted to play a practical joke on their boss, Arno Penzias. Arno is a Nobel Prize smart guy, and they wanted to really blow his mind. They wanted to do a magic trick that would make him think that technology had really progressed even faster than possible. That's hard to do at Bell Labs. This is the place where the motherfucking transistor was invented. These guys wrote the book on UNIX. These are some serious cats and kitties. These are the cats and kitties who invented the future we're living in.

Another major player on our "LabScam" team was Dennis Ritchie. He was one of the most important people in computer science, and he was such a great man. He died last year and is deeply missed. On the day of "LabScam," we taught him to do some tricks with a thumb tip and he performed those tricks for the rest of his life. I have used Dennis's description of "LabScam" from the Web as the backbone of this story. He wrote up the story well, and he did a lot of the work that made it possible for me to have a Web to find it on. Yeah, he's that important to computers.

The night before the scam, Dennis sent an e-mail to Arno Penzias, vice president of Bell Labs, their big boss:

> **Subject: voice stuff**
>
> **I think rob is almost ready to invite you to look at his latest effort, which is (pretty much) voice recognition. He's able to show surprisingly good results from a fundamentally simple-minded scheme; it's worth seeing. Besides, he appears to have spent the long weekend putting some pizzazz into his demo; he claims it is like Eliza (esp. the "Doctor" program) for the multimedia age.**
>
> **Dennis**

Remember, this is the end of the eighties; quality voice recognition was still years away. This is an e-mail from a heavy cat, Dennis, about another heavy cat, rob. When these guys say they got something heavy, you best believe they got something heavy. Dennis piqued Arno's interest.

On the day, rob ushered Arno into a room and sat him in front of two terminals. There was a bright light shining in Arno's eyes, a microphone and TV camera inches from his mouth. That was just to make him uncomfortable. I never said every moment of the practical

joke had to be comfortable, did I? On one terminal, a real-time, processed image of Arno's lips appeared. On the other were printed
several words.

rob explained that he had been doing some work in speech recognition and had achieved some interesting results. The camera was
watching Arno's lips to determine when he was speaking and use the
movement of his mouth to aid in recognition. The computer would
analyze his utterances using both the audio and the video. It would
first be necessary to say each word on the second screen in sequence,
to train the program to recognize Arno's voice.

Arno said the first word, "Hello." rob typed stuff on a third terminal. rob was acting. On the terminal Arno was facing, things flick-
ered, and a graph and some numbers ("autocorrelation coefficients")
appeared. Arno said the next word, "Sanskrit." More flickering,
graphs, numbers. Arno said, "Hohokus." I had said while we were
setting the joke up, "If we can just get Arno to say 'Hohokus' into a
microphone, we will have already won!"

The words disappeared, and several sentences came up on the terminal. Arno had to pick one of the sentences, and speak it. rob re-
adjusted Arno's head to make sure his lips were centered on the TV.
There was no reason for this, but rob wanted to manhandle his boss.
Arno read, "It's a pleasure having you with us," and, after a calibrated
annoying pause, a synthesized voice said, "Please repeat." Demos are
supposed to fuck up. During this phase, the machine was supposedly
deciding which of the sentences had been spoken. Finally, it got this
right, and Arno moved on to "Kenneth, what is the frequency?" After
two tries, the machine repeated this too. It was wobbly, but rob's
demo was moving along.

Now, rob said, we can have some fun. Arno was aware of the famous Eliza program. It was a computer program that pretended to be a shrink. That demonstrates a lot about computers and/or a lot about shrinks. To bring the idea up-to-date, rob had taken a videotape of David Letterman's show, and digitized the guests' answers and the host's questions. Arno would play Letterman, on his own talk show, and ask the questions. The machine would match each question to one actually asked on a past show, and then play back the closest appropriate answer. This was serious voice recognition and artificial intelligence. First, Arno had to select which guests he would like. His choices were: The author of *Dance, Dance, Dance, She Said*, Penn and Teller, or an actress from *Dynasty*.

We were taking a gamble here, but rob and Dennis said they knew Arno liked us.

Arno chose Penn and Teller. Our little psychological force had worked. If he had picked one of the others, rob would have pretended that the system crashed and asked him to make another choice, but it would be a better trick if he chose us himself.

Arno started with a menu of questions. Arno spoke one of them: "Which is Penn and which is Teller?" On Arno's screen, after the graphs and numbers, a video image shuffled through several stills of us and finally an animated (and very lo-fi) image of P&T appeared, and my voice, scratchy but recognizable, said, "Don't you learn anything? I'm Penn Jillette, and this is my partner, Teller. Longer name, bigger person." Arno asked several more questions from this menu and got the same kinda appropriate answers.

"Does Teller ever talk?"

"No, not to you." Every answer was accompanied by the corresponding lo-fi video clip.

Now, the punch line. rob invited Arno to ask questions of his own. The theory was this would work because the computer could search for spoken words and phrases among the stored clips. This was the really amazing part. The computer would have to make it look like it understood the question and picked an answer that was closest to right. Each of Arno's questions elicited a response, though some of them were peculiar.

"How long has it been since you became partners?"

"I think it was in San Francisco, about 1981 . . . That's when Lou Reed came to the show . . ." rob acted frustrated and suggested that Arno rephrase the question.

"How long have you been partners?"

"It's been fifteen years of complete hell."

"Have you won many awards?"

"Well, Teller took the Obie, and he's going to win an Academy Award. Me, I'm holding out for a Nobel Prize!" Just our little hint for Arno that he might be being fucked with. He didn't pick up on it—just coincidence.

"What do you do with rats and cockroaches?"

"That's the way we have sex."

rob played embarrassed and asked Arno to speak more clearly, keeping his mouth in the right position, "Do you use rats and cockroaches?"

"Oh, I like that on pizza, and Teller uses it on a hot dog roll or a hamburger bun." It was kludgy but not more so than a lot of first-time demos.

rob acted flustered and suggested that Arno ask Penn & Teller to show him a trick, because rob and Dennis had loaded in a few good ones from the show, and the computer would show it.

After another peculiar reply, the computer sputtered and I finally said, "Well, we hung upside down on *Saturday Night Live*, and we dumped cockroaches right here on your show, but come with us, we have something special for you. Could the camera go handheld?"

On the video, Penn & Teller stood up and the camera followed us into corridor. It was kinda sorta like the Letterman corridor, but not quite. Arno should have found the hall a little familiar, but he was wrapped up in the new technology. I continued talking on camera, "Let's go down this hall here. We've done a lot of stuff on television, and TV is not the most conducive medium to magic. We wanted something where things would seem to go from TV into reality . . ."

On the screen in front of him, Arno watched Penn & Teller open a door and approach a man sitting in front of several terminals inside, with a bright light shining on his mouth. ". . . So we worked out this little thing where a person was watching a video screen, and we could actually come in and interact with the person—"

Then Arno turned around and was confronted with us live in the room with him.

It was pretty groovy. Arno just couldn't understand for the longest time that it was all a scam. While Arno was saying words and sentences into the microphone earlier, Dennis had been in the next room controlling what Arno saw and heard on the computer. The "video clips" were live pictures of Teller and me in the next room, digitized and turned on at appropriate times. We were just ad-libbing and monkeying with Arno. Our crew for this video shoot were some of the greatest computer minds in history. They had run the cables and were operating the cameras and mixing the sound. It was the most overqualified crew in show business history. They had high-quality video feeding to Dennis's machine and he was cheapening it and glitching it up before it was sent to Arno's monitor. I had been ad-libbing the wrong answers for verisimilitude.

Arno was shaken. It really did blow his mind. As he started to understand, he wondered if the author and the *Dynasty* star had been in other rooms with other crews. He was freaked. He told us it felt more intense than winning the Nobel Prize. I think that was something said in the heat of the moment, like saying "I love you" right before you cum, but it still thrilled us. We had learned our lesson; this is the right kind of practical joke. It was a gift to Arno from the people who worked with him and liked and respected him.

A few years later, Arno returned that thrill by an order of magnitude (that's science talk). We were at a TED conference. Teller and I were doing a mini-opera with magic about the spiritualist who tangled with Houdini. We had put together a presentation with Tod Machover and his gang at the Media Lab at MIT. It featured the "sensor chair," a new musical instrument, like a Super Theremin that I would play by moving my hands and body in space. It was pretty cool. I was there to wave my arms around in a chair and Arno Penzias was there to talk smart stuff.

During the TED conference, the whole town is filled with TED people, and during lunch at a small Chinese restaurant, I found myself at the table next to Arno's. We pulled tables together and told them all about "LabScam." We then talked about the "talks" (my arm waving) that we were giving and, just to be weird, I asked, "What joke are you opening with?" Arno laughed and moved on, but just for fun, I pushed, "You know, you really have to open your talk with a joke. You gotta break the ice."

Arno said he couldn't tell jokes. I figured if Arno could teach me superficially about the 3K of cosmic background radiation that won him the Nobel Prize, I could teach him to tell a joke. He agreed to let me try over lunch to teach him to tell a joke.

I told him my version of the "Orange Dick" joke. Here are the beats, the bare bones a comedian would build on:

A guy has an orange dick.

He goes to a doctor.

Doctor examines him, asks a lot of questions about lifestyle, work and diet, but can't figure out why the guy's penis is orange (this is the body of the joke).

Finally doctor asks him to detail his average day, and the guy does so. He describes his typical day and ends with, "I get home, open a bag of Cheetos, turn on the Playboy Channel . . ."

It's a fine joke. I told Arno those were the only beats he had to remember, but he would fill in all the details on the fly. Those were the parts of the joke that had to be all his. He needed to have the doctor ask questions about where the guy worked and his girlfriend and diet, but all of that would be done on the fly in Arno's own style. The most important part of the joke was that at the punch line his voice had to go up and trail off. His right arm should go up with his voice and hang there on the ellipsis. I don't think it matters very much for this joke whether the Playboy Channel or the Cheetos are last, as long as the audience gets to put the image together during the ellipsis. As long as the right arm and the pitch leads them to the right altitude for the punch line.

Over lunch, I had Arno tell me the joke over and over. He just kept telling it, and I kept correcting him, telling him to use more details or less and kept working on the punch line. I coached him to make sure that he had something else on the list in his mind. He had to have masturbating on the list, he just wasn't to say it, but his voice had to lead to that. The punch line is really the silence. The punch line must be the offbeat—it's gotta hit you where you ain't. Arno starting taking this joke very seriously and really working on it. He had really no experience telling jokes, but he was focused and trying.

We both knew we were kidding; he had no intention of telling any joke in his Bell Labs talk at TED. That would be inappropriate, but we both made believe he was going to and really had fun pretending the dumb guy was teaching the smart guy something. Some of what I was explaining was real information and some was just fun bullshit. It was friends playing over lunch.

We went our separate ways after lunch, and I didn't see him again until I was in the auditorium for his talk and he walked onstage. The TED audiences are heavy. I believe Steve Jobs and Bill Gates were both in the audience for Arno's talk. Jonas Salk was there in the front row. Can you imagine being onstage with Jonas Salk in the front row? I did a fake séance and waved my arms around with Jonas looking at me. He saw me at a restaurant and complimented me on all the magic and monologues he'd seen me do. I told him to shut the fuck up, in those words. He wasn't allowed to talk about stupid shit like our shows when he had fucking helped eradicate polio. He laughed and talked about some bit we did on *SNL*. "What are you doing watching fucking TV? What, have you cured all diseases already? Fuck you, shut up, get to work." I had to run and get my parents and sister on the phone and tell them I talked to Jonas Salk. I've met Lou Reed, but Jonas Salk, motherfucker. I just kept looking him in the eyes and trying to imagine what it felt like to help save that many lives. I can't imagine it. I guess Jonas could have talked about it to Norman Borlaug, but it's a short list. There's a lot of debate about the Salk vaccine, but no matter whom you give what credit to, Dr. Salk was part of it. Doing card tricks for a living is stupid no matter who you're talking to, but look Jonas Salk in the eyes, and it seems everyone else is doing stupid card tricks for a living.

Arno walked onstage with that kind of audience. I wasn't fit to eat shit off anyone's shoes in that crowd, but I was about halfway back on the aisle. I was still giggling about our goofy lunch when Arno began to speak. He started with something like, "I had lunch with Penn Jillette and he told me a great joke and tried to convince me to start my talk with it this afternoon."

Jonas Salk started heckling, something like, "Tell the joke."

Arno said that it was a great joke, and people should ask me to tell it to them during the break.

Someone else heckled him to tell the joke. Arno explained that it was an inappropriate joke and it was time for his prepared talk, which would take up all the allotted time.

Jonas Salk yelled something about not caring a bit about the same old boring Arno stuff; he wanted to hear a joke.

Arno stood onstage quietly and thought. There was a lot to weigh before the vice president of Bell Labs could tell a dirty joke onstage at TED. This was a big hairy deal. The audience was clamoring for the joke, and Arno was thinking. Salk was still heckling and being a dick about it. Jonas wanted to hear a joke.

Arno looked out at the crowd and found me. He asked from the stage, "So, Penn, can I do it?" I nodded yes and raised my right hand in the gesture of our rehearsed ellipse.

Okay.

"A guy goes into the doctor with an orange dick."

Imagine if Jimi Hendrix, John Lennon, and Elvis Presley walked out onstage together at a sold-out rock show at Madison Square Garden. The crowd went nuts. Looking back, I imagine I can hear Jonas whooping.

Arno told the joke. He got way carried away. During the section where the guy is getting his dick tested, Arno had details of the machines being used. When talking about the guy's job, Arno built an entire backstory. This was the extended play version. One of the most important parts of comedy is committing. If you hold back one bit, if you give the slightest wink that shows you're not completely in the joke, the audience leaves with you. Even if you're dying, even if the idea isn't good, you have to keep your heart in it completely. In acting, we all know the actors who let you know they're above the character. These are the actors who suck dead dog cock. We know the comedian who laughs a bit at his own joke and let's you know he's just a regular guy talking weird shit. You might laugh at the time, but those comics will never change you. They won't give you lasting beauty.

Arno committed. Like a motherfucker. Arno committed like Andy Kaufman. My mouth was bone dry. I was hyperventilating. I had tears in my eyes. At the time, I didn't have children, but I felt like my mom must have felt watching my TV appearance. I was leaning forward in my seat, moving my mouth with his. I have never wanted a joke to go better in my life. I was more nervous in that TED audience than I was on *Saturday Night Live*. Arno was going long. There was no doubt he was going way too long. He was putting in too many details. But this was an audience of scientists, and the details were killing. He knew the names of all the machines that would be used to test this guy's dick. He had the doctor in the joke do a House differential on what could have caused this perplexing orange dick.

I haven't found any recording of Arno telling this joke online, but I don't want to. I want my memory, with all its mistakes and exaggerations. My memory is that this joke went on longer than the longest Grateful Dead show. My stomach was in knots, but the audience was right with him. It wasn't too long. Penzias was killing. He got to the end of the orange dick guy's day. He got to right before the punch line, and his eyes found mine in the audience, and he went into it. He started the list, his right hand and voice rose for the ellipses and he hit the punch line on the offbeat. He nailed it. Silence for a heartbeat, and then explosion.

Remember that Madison Square Garden show with Jimi, John, and Elvis onstage? Kurt Cobain, Lenny Bruce, Dean Martin, Tiny Tim, and Jesus H. Christ joined them onstage. The crowd went nuts. In my memory (all of this is my memory, I didn't fact-check, I didn't want to), Jonas jumped to his feet. The reaction was insane.

It was a lecture hall, with a raked audience and very low stage. Arno jumped off the stage and ran up the aisle. I stood up and Arno hugged me. I was crying my eyes out. I believe if I were to win a Nobel Prize, it would be more emotional than this, but not by much. Arno was just a different person. We were all different. He finally got the crowd to calm down and went into his talk. My hands shook for the whole talk and I had butterflies in my stomach until I went to bed that night. It was an amazing moment. Payback can be a bitch, but payback can also be a super inamorata. Wow, did Arno pay me back for "LabScam." I saw scientists in a whole different way. The separate worlds in my mind joined together. The strongest moments in my life make me feel one-nation-under-a-motherfucking-groove, and I felt that when Arno talked about the guy's orange dick and Jonas laughed his genius ass off.

Several times during the next couple of days, speakers made references (some of them on graphs) to the orange dick. Arno had set up a runner for the conference.

Arno's telling of the "Orange Dick" joke in that room was the platonic ideal of a joke. Brave and true, and not the least bit mean-spirited. Rebellious and shocking at no one's expense. Uplifting and enlightening to everyone involved. Beautiful.

Think about that next April Fools' Day when you're thinking about putting Saran plastic wrap under the toilet seat. Get it?

Listening to: "I Started a Joke"—The Bee Gees

HAPPY BIRTHDAY

EXPERIMENTAL PROTOTYPE COMMUNITY OF TOMORROW was Walt Disney's idea for EPCOT Center. His idea was to have a working city of about twenty thousand people where they would test all sorts of groovy future shit, like hydroponic carrots, flying cars and apocalyptic zombies from hell. When I first read about Walt's plan, I was thrilled. I loved the idea of scientists, artists, and guys who run dry-cleaning businesses all living together and digging the future. That was before I visited some planned communities like Columbia, Maryland, and I became a libertarian. Smart city planning always seems like it's going to be inspiring and beautiful but the results are usually beige, with those "tasteful" McDonald's signs. Central planning doesn't work; give me garish Golden Arches and people being free to be stupid. Central planning is not good for us nuts. It's good for beige.

Walt Disney died and the Experimental Prototype Community of Tomorrow became EPCOT, just another Disney property. I like to think that Walt Disney would have designed his city better than Columbia, Maryland, but probably not. The problem is not who does the planning; it's the plan itself. Groovy cities have to be free and wild with lots of unexpected ugliness; they can't be planned.

The real corporate EPCOT follows the libertarian ideal of making money. Goddamn, they are good at that. Losing on *Dancing with the Stars* got me VIP treatment at all the Disney properties "forever," which turned out to be about a year. We took our children over to California and down to Florida and we were treated great. I did worry a little that my children would be spoiled by not waiting in lines, but then ObamaCare was passed and I know they'll get to wait in lines when they're sick and that'll build some real character.

I don't remember why, but my wife was at EPCOT before or after me on one trip. We often fly separately. Our schedules are very different, so she'll fly with the children the night before and I'll fly noon the next day or something. It's also good because then no one notices me flying first class while the children fly coach—hey, I'm bigger than they are, and they fit in those coach seats, right? No matter what the reason, Emily was at EPCOT for a while without me.

One of the ways EPCOT made money for a few years was by selling the little bricks that made up the walkway alongside the big white sphere known as Spaceship Earth. They called it Leave a Legacy, and instead of having to write a great novel or win a Nobel Prize, you could pay thirty-five bucks and have your picture taken or write a little message and they'd put it on a brick. Quite a deal. You got a tile with your picture or a message on it. They gave you a little map and when you come back, you could look for the message and maybe look at a few others until you be bored shitless with guys with carefully trimmed beards wearing mouse ears.

Emily Zolten Jillette is confrontational. She's a freedom fighter. Some MILFs have dress shops. Emily's fighting every time she goes through TSA and "The First Noël" at our child's fancy-ass, uniform bullshit private school. (I think my major gripe with the private school Mox goes to is that she's so happy there. How is that for a great dad? I had such a shitty education that I want her to rebel too, but she's happy and learning a lot and treated well and making wonderful friends. Maybe there is something to this good education thing. I guess it plays to my libertarian ideals. Private schools are good and Mox even loves her uniform, but Emily still keeps an eye on their "Winter Pageant," making sure Xmas doesn't sneak in even at a great school.) Freedom fighters don't take vacations, so at EPCOT she was itching for a confrontation. She decided to buy a molded piece of cement from Disney and have it signed "PEZ" (That's P for Penn, and EZ her initials and her . . . style). She wanted the message to say "No God." That's a message she wanted in modern fake rock in the Experimental Prototype Community of Tomorrow. She gave them money, and that was it. Until they told her they couldn't allow that, because the bricks couldn't mention god. Emily pointed out that the walkway was maggoty with bricks that read "God Bless." Well, they shifted, now they didn't allow offensive messages. She demonstrated offensive right in their faces at that one. She finally decided it was a private park and it's their little goatfuck, so she backed down. Emily said she'd give up and leave a legacy of "Dog On," and then our PEZ signature. There's nothing offensive about that. They took her money and that was that.

A couple weeks later they called while Emily and I were having lunch together. She walked out of the restaurant with the phone and the Disney folks explained they were sending her money back because "Dog On" was "No God" backwards and they couldn't allow that. I saw through the restaurant window that she was getting frustrated on the phone and raising her voice. I was just eating. She came inside, having given up, and said, "I told them they should talk to my husband about this." Now, you may think there's some sort of sexist, "Let the man take care of the little lady's problems here" thang going on. I assure you, there's none of that. Emily plays poker. Emily plays golf. Emily does the business in our family. Emily goes out with the guys. I'm the bath-oils-and-reading-novels gal in our family. I don't do man things. You might think she was trying to pull some celebrity card, "talk to my husband—he's a two-bit magician and that will impress Disney." Nope, she knows I lost on *Dancing with the Stars*. Emily was putting me on the phone for the reason a lot of my friends put me on the phone, "This asshole wants to be crazy; we'll show them fucking crazy. Put Penn on the phone."

"Hello, this is Penn, what's the problem?"

"We're sending your wife's money back to her for the Leave a Legacy tile she wanted to buy."

"Good, send us all the money back, we like money."

"Fine."

"But we'll still get our tile, right?"

"Well, no, that's why we're sending your money back."

"It's my wife's money. I'll never see it."

"Okay, your wife's money."

"And you're still doing the tile, right? We want that tile."

"No."

"Why not? That tile means a lot to us. You promised us that tile. You gave us your word."

"I'm sorry, but the message is inappropriate."

"Isn't the message 'Dog On'?"

"Yes, but it means 'No God.' 'Dog On' is 'No God' spelled backwards."

"Really?"

"Yes."

"Really?"

"Of course, spell it out."

"Dog . . . d-o-g . . . g-o-d . . . god. On . . . o-n . . . n-o . . . No . . . No God . . . well, I'll be fucked."

"Please, sir, watch your language."

"Right, I'm not supposed to say 'Dog On' because you find that fucking offensive, but you said it first, didn't you? Why wasn't that offensive when you said it?"

"No, the other word."

"'Fuck'?"

"Yes, don't use that language."

"But 'Dog On' is okay?"

"Yes."

"Good, then put it on the fucking legacy thing."

"Watch your language, and it is offensive because she asked for 'No God' first."

"And that's offensive?"

"Well, not like the other word you said."

"'Dog On'?"

"No."

"What other word?"

"You know."

"'Fuck'?"

"Yes, and don't say that or I will have to terminate this call."

"I see, but I can say 'Dog On' or 'No God,' right?"

"Yes, we're talking about that."

"No, we were talking about 'fuck.' You changed the subject."

"I'm going to have to hang up."

"I'm sorry. Did you know that 'Dog On' meant 'No God'?"

"Yes, because your wife asked for 'No God' and when she was told no, she just reversed it and made it 'Dog On.'"

"Really?"

"Yes."

"Let me check: Dog . . . d-o-g . . . g-o-d . . . god. On . . . o-n . . . n-o . . . No . . . No God . . . Yup, well, I'll be fu— Sorry, I almost said that other bad word that you brought into this conversation."

"Thank you. So we knew that that's what it meant, so we can't use it."

"But the people seeing this wouldn't know the backstory, so how could that be offensive? They wouldn't know the code that you broke, right? You had to have the code explained to you. It's a simple code but ingenious."

"But we know that 'Dog On' means 'No God' because she tried that first. We know what it means to her."

"So, if I tried to get a tile that said, 'Fuck you' . . . ?"

"Watch your language. I must hang up."

"Sorry, but stay with me. So I want a tile that says 'Fuck you' and you say no, it's offensive, so I say I want to change it to 'happy birthday.' Then you would now know that 'happy birthday' means 'fuck you.' Happy birthday."

"Watch your language."

"Happy birthday."

"'Happy birthday' would be okay."

"Happy birthday. But you know what it means, don't you, happy birthday? Happy birthday, you know what I mean by that. Happy birthday."

"Yes, you explained."

"Happy birthday."

"But others wouldn't know that."

"Happy birthday."

"Stop saying that, or I'm going to hang up."

"You'll hang up because I said 'happy birthday.'"

"I know what you mean."

"When is your birthday?"

"That's none of your business."

"Well, whenever it is, happy birthday, happy birthday."

"Cut it out."

"Don't send our money back, get a Leave a Legacy plaque that says 'Happy Birthday,' and then your name. You'll know what it means. Happy birthday."

"No, we're sending your money back."

"Happy birthday. Keep the money and use the plaque so the future can see 'Happy birthday' with your name. Happy birthday. My legacy to you is happy birthday, and you know that. Listen, just give us 'dog on' and be done with it. What do you care? Just tell your boss 'Happy birthday.' You remember what that means, don't you?"

"Yes."

"Happy birthday."

"Stop it and we're not going to—"

"Happy birthday."

"—we're not going to give you your Leave a Legacy plaque."

"Happy birthday."

"We'll send back the credit card receipt."

"Happy birthday."

"Stop it—you will not get a legacy plaque!"

"Because you now know what 'Dog On' means to my wife and me?"

"Yes."

"And you know what 'happy birthday' means to you and me. That's our personal private little love code: happy birthday. Happy birthday."

"We are done, sir. Your wife will get your money back."

"Happy birthday, it's her money."

"Her money."

"Happy birthday."

"I'm hanging up now, right now. I do not need to take this abuse."

"You find 'happy birthday' offensive?"

"We're supposed to hang up if there's any obscenity."

"And you think 'Happy birthday' is obscene—happy birthday."

"I know what it means. I'm hanging up now." He was yelling a little.

"*Wait*. Please don't hang up. Please. This has gotten out of hand. I'm very, very sorry I offended you. Just calm down and don't hang up. I won't say that anymore. I'm sorry. Did you hang up?"

"No."

"Have you calmed down?"

"Yes."

"Are you listening?"

"Yes."

"Fuck you."

And I hung up. A few months later, our friend went and got this plaque for us.

Happy birthday.

Listening to: "Birthday"—The Beatles

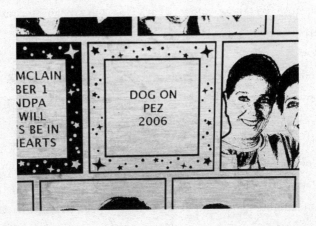

CHIQUITA BANANA WEDNESDAY

I LOVE ASH WEDNESDAY. I like the fact that Catholics run around with dirt on their head for a day. I wish they did it every day. I like people committing to things that announce who they are. I have a couple of good friends who are little people. If I were a little person, I would like the term "little person" much less than "dwarf" or "midget," but I'm not a little person so I don't get a vote. I'm fine with the term "big person," but then again I'm also fine with the term "big fat ugly motherfucker" and "Sasquatch." That's the kind of guy I am.

When I was young, I had hair that was too long and I wore eye makeup and capes and all sorts of hippy/glam garb, and I stood out, but I could change my clothes, wash my face, tuck my hair up under my hat and mix in with the farmers in my hometown. I'm tall, but not so tall that people outside rural China point, cower and laugh at me. My friends who are little people have to deal every second with a strong reaction from people, and I wonder if that's part of the reason my friends are such strong and comfortable people. My little people friends are forced to be Robin Williams and always be on. They can't be invisible. They have to face who they are, every time they go out in public. A little person ordering a fish burger at a McDonald's counter is a comedy bit for some people who live in the center of the height bell curve. My little person friends inspire me to try to be who

I am all the time and never back down. I don't want to have the choice to hide.

I like the drag-priests, and drag-nuns, and turban/beard guys, and yama yama Jews. I like that they dress so that they can't back down from that part of who they are. Some people walk around in full basketball uniforms and I like that too. I wonder why they just do it for sports and not for firemen.

I've known a lot of people, women and men, who are sexually turned on by firemen. Why wouldn't you want to fuck a hero? One Christmas a girlfriend bought me a fireman's jacket. It was just a sex aid for her. It was buying your mom a toy truck for her birthday. The jacket didn't have any insignias on it, but it was rubberized, had a reflective stripe around it and those sexy brass nautical clips to buckle it up. When I wore it in public, it was like I was a woman walking around dressed as a cheerleader, nurse or French maid. A lot of women started conversations with me when I wore that jacket. It wasn't me—it was the jacket. Once they got to know me just a little, the jacket wasn't enough to hold their interest in the face of me. I lost the girlfriend but kept the jacket. I wore it all the time, even though I live in the desert and don't hang around many hoses. I stopped wearing it on September 11, 2001—it seemed disrespectful to the real heroes.

I wear sneakers, jeans and a work shirt every day and then our P&T drag in the show, but I wish I were braver. I wish that one day I went out in one of the NASCAR jackets with all the patches, and the next day in a tux. I wouldn't want to wear a basketball uniform, but it seems like a beekeeping outfit might be cool. I love beekeeping outfits. But I never do any of that; my sneakers, jeans and work shirt announce to the world that I'm a lazy slob, and I guess that's enough. I can't back away from that.

We had a few Catholics in my high school. I guess the Catholic school in Greenfield went only through grade school, so in high school the halls were peppered with students wearing their religion on their foreheads. They were a little awkward and self-conscious, and I was envious of that specialness.

When the fatwa was laid on Salman Rushdie, my buddy and hero Al Goldstein felt left out. Al, the founder of *Screw* magazine and a nut pornographer, loved being the center of free speech attention. He went to court in Topeka for the right to send *Screw* to Kansas. Most people would have just said screw Kansas, but Al likes a fight. He's a freedom fighter. So, the ayatollah told his followers they should kill Salman, and Al put a full-page ad in *Screw* saying he'd give a million bucks to anyone who killed the ayatollah. Al is now flat busted, but at the time he had the million. He also got some attention. The death threats flew in, and the same FBI agents who had been to the *Screw* offices to bust him were now protecting him. Some of his staff members who were crazy enough to work at *Screw*, but sensible enough to not want to be around this fatwa shit, just quit. The FBI suggested Al leave his offices and go somewhere and not announce where he was going. He wanted to be the center of attention and now he was in hiding.

I was in L.A. working on some movie script that no one liked, and Al gave me a call. "Hey, Penn, I offered a million dollars to anyone who killed the ayatollah, and now there're lots of death threats and everyone is afraid to hang out with me. Wanna go to lunch and then to the Playboy Mansion with me and my son?"

"Yes."

I made the same deal with Al that I made with Ron Reagan when his father was president and Ron was our nation's most likely hostage. Ron refused Secret Service protection, and he called me to hang out one day. I told Ron I'd go to lunch with him, but I wouldn't walk to or from the car with him, and I wouldn't be in the car when he started it. Once it was running, I would go anywhere with him, but I wouldn't walk by his side in public. I don't want to get all conspiracy on your ass, but it seems there's a chance that if the son of the president is being kidnapped, the Secret Service and FBI would shoot *at* him just to remove that monster bargaining chip. I just made that up, but I'm pretty sure that both sides would shoot at the big dumb screaming Sasquatch who was pissing himself at the hostage's side just to get him out of the way so they could think.

Here's the story of me going to the Playboy Mansion with a pornographer who threatened the ayatollah: There were no women at the mansion. I saw the "grotto," in the pool where so many of the "pictorials" of my youth were shot, but there was no one there. Al's twelve-year-old son and I fed the koi fish (never saw a foldout of them), and then Hef came out with his girlfriend or wife or whatever and she said, "One of these guys threatened the ayatollah and the other one thinks it's funny to drown his partner onstage. I don't want them here." That was that. Al and his son walked to the car, started it up and drove up the block. When it was safe, I joined them and they drove me back to the hotel to work on my shitty screenplay.

Al didn't read *The Satanic Verses*. He didn't do anything to help Rushdie; he just wanted to make sure that if a billion people on the planet were going to try to kill someone, he had a piece of that attention. I got free lunch, got to feed koi fish with his son and was asked to leave the Playboy Mansion. It was a fine break from my shitty screenplay.

In high school I was envious of the Catholics on Ash Wednesday. I liked that they were declaring publicly who they were and what they believed. I love rituals and I love symbolism. Before I found a way to do an atheist baptism and an atheist first supper, I created Chiquita

Banana Wednesday. On Ash Wednesday, I would pull the Chiquita banana sticker off a banana and put it on my forehead. It's a life-affirming colorful celebratory answer to the black mourning and death cult of the capital punishment symbol made of ash. I try to do it every year, but as the years go by, I've used a Dole banana sticker. I have no brand loyalty. A bunch of my friends in high school did it too.

I was called into the principal's office.

"What's that sticker on your forehead?"

"For Chiquita Banana Wednesday."

"Take it off."

"No."

"It looks like you're ridiculing other students' religious beliefs."

"I am."

"We support freedom of religion."

"Yes, we do, but I can ridicule it. I'm not trying to stop them; I'm just making it clear I don't believe. It is wicked stupid, don't you think?" We've always liked "wicked" as an intensifier in Massachusetts.

I can't remember if the principal had ashes on his forehead. I can't even remember if I was thrown out that day for that. I obviously don't remember the exact conversation above, but I do remember that I didn't take that fucking sticker off my forehead. Fuck your burnt palm leaves hieroglyph of suffering.

If you happened into the Starbucks where Michael Goudeau, Teller and I were working last Ash Wednesday, you saw us all wearing colorful festive banana stickers (Dole) on our foreheads as we wrote our not-shitty TV show.

We want everyone to know we're atheists.

You know I'm an atheist, right?

Listening to: "I Won't Back Down"—Tom Petty

HAVE A NICE EASTER, YOU CHRISTIANS YOU

MY BUDDY MATT STONE SAID that *The Book of Mormon* (the best show I've ever seen), the musical he wrote with Trey Parker, was "a love letter to religion, written by an atheist." I'd like to add a couple X's and O's to the bottom of that love letter and sign my name. Christians have treated me fairly. When they disagree with me they represent my position fairly. I don't believe in god. I'm an atheist. I mock religion. They say that about me. They argue with me. They pray for me. They give me Bibles and have their children write me letters begging me to try to see the light. They send me tweets about how they hope I'll find god. Sometimes they say that I'm going to be punished in hell. I consider all that fair. A very small number have accused me of being a Satan worshipper, but I think that's simple ignorance. I just have to explain to them that if I were going to have faith I wouldn't pick the side that loses.

I used to date an Israeli woman. She was in this country illegally and she was thrown out of Israel, as far as I could tell, for being too pro-Jewish. She claimed that *The New York Times* was anti-Semitic. She spoke nine languages. We couldn't get in a cab in NYC without her talking to the driver in his native tongue. She was just stupid sexy and wicked smart. We hung out with her Israeli friends, and they would talk Hebrew and I would sit there wondering if they were talking about me. Her being in the country illegally was really sexy to me. At the time we were dating, Penn & Teller were regulars on *Saturday Night Live*, and I was invited to a lot of premieres and red carpet events. I would bring her as my date, and since there were photographers and she was illegal, she would cover her face as we walked in. I fancied that her hidden identity made people wonder who it was who couldn't be seen with me. I still like that thought. I hope someone is still wondering.

It's really hard to break up with someone from a different culture. Every relationship problem we had could be blamed on cultural differences and misunderstanding. "No, baby, the problem is that you didn't realize that was a reference to *The Flintstones*, it was a joke about Fred talking to Wilma, I wasn't really saying that to you personally—it's a cultural thing. By the way, do you know *The Flintstones* theme song? Let me sing it for you. . . . 'Through the courtesy of Fred's two feet' is the line there. Yeah, it's hard to understand even for an American. And you know, the chord changes in that are standard jazz changes, called 'rhythm changes,' from the chord progression of 'I Got Rhythm' and a zillion other jazz songs. . . ." How can you break up when you can fall back on that shit? I loved the cultural misunderstandings with her. I laughed harder in bed with her than I've ever laughed during sex. The first time she used the word "schmuck" for my penis, she used it like a sex word, like "cock" or something. I said, "What?"

"It means 'cock.' I thought you knew that."

"Of course I know that, but it doesn't mean 'cock' like that, it means 'cock' like 'dick.'"

"Yes."

"But it's not a sexy word, it's a comic word. This western Massachusetts goy learned it from Lenny Bruce. When Lenny was busted for using it as a dirty Yiddish word for penis, he said something like, 'Tell me how it means "penis" in this sentence: "I, like a schmuck, drove all the way to Jersey."'"

She didn't really understand, and after a little more manipulation of my schmuck, I was fine with her calling it whatever she wanted. In the Israeli army she had shot guns at people. She had pointed guns at people and pulled the trigger. I think she's the only person I've ever had sex with who has done that. She wasn't the only person I've had sex with who could kill me, but she was the only one who might have an idea what it would really feel like. I got in my head I wanted to hear the most offensive word in the world, so I asked her what she called Arabs. I wanted to hear what pure hate sounded like. I wanted to hear the word and the translation. She asked me what I meant. I told her a few of the hateful words for Jews that we have in English. She knew the words, but she couldn't understand what I was asking her for. I said, "You tried to kill Arabs. You fought them. You hate them. What's the worst word you can use for them?" She thought for a moment and said, "'Arab.' It's just the word for Arab." Wow. Of course it's just Arab.

A few years after that, there was a guy named Dave who really pissed me off. I got away from him, and in the privacy of my home I called him all sorts of names—"motherfucker," "asshole," "dickwad," "shithead," "cunt pickle"—but none of them felt right in my mouth. None of them were bad enough. All of a sudden my Israeli girlfriend's simple truth came back to me. He is Dave! What a fucking Dave. That felt right.

The worst word possible is simply "Arab," a name both sides agree on. It's deeper than an insult, it's not a line in the sand, it's an intellectual difference. It crossed over from insult and comes out the other side as respect. When Christians are showing their disapproval of me, they call me "atheist." It's the word I use for myself, and to them, it's a bad thing. "Infidel," "Heathen," "Godless"—they're all insults and they're all the truth. It's the deepest insult possible, because there's no bullshit insult—we agree on what I am, it's just they think it's wrong. There's no Yankee Doodle required. We all agree on what I am.

We atheists need to do that more. I've used the word "theist" for someone to let a fellow atheist know that this is someone who I fundamentally disagree with. That seems fair. But I try to only say about them what they've said about themselves. If they use the word "Fundamentalist," I'll use that—that's more wacky shit they believe. Same with "Evangelical," "Catholic," and "Mormon." I try not to use things that could be said about the Westboro Baptist Church to attack someone who is a Congregationalist.

So, this Easter, I would like to apologize for all the atheists who have called you true believers "racist" and "sexist," when you're not. I would like to apologize for the atheists who have called you stupid when you're not. I'll just call you "Christians," and let's leave it at that.

But fucking Dave, man, what a fucking Christian schmuck.

Listening to: "Onward Christian Soldiers"—Moron Tabernacle Choir

EASTER IS A HOLLOW WAXY CHOCOLATE RABBIT WHO SUFFERS IN AN UNSATISFYING WAY FOR YOUR SINS

WHAT THE FUCK DO CHOCOLATE RABBITS and marshmallow chicks have to do with Jesus dying on the cross? And how the fuck does god sending his son in human form (who may actually be god himself anyway), to be killed by people, wash away the sins of other people in the future—

provided, that is, that those future people give their lives to him (who already owns them anyway), in appreciation of his having been tortured by himself in order to receive that "gift"?

No one knows. It's nonsense, but I like hard-boiled eggs, and I hope that's what Easter is really about. Michael Goudeau, who is my buddy, a cohost on my *Penn's Sunday School* podcast and a *Bullshit!* writer, made a deviled ostrich egg once. It was huge, like two-dozen chicken eggs, but all together in one huge egg-shaped wiggly boat with a fluffy softball of yellow globbed inside. Scale matters with food, like those giant gummy bears. It tasted fine, but it was creepy. Funny creepy, but creepy. Not as creepy as Easter in general, but creepy.

Rabbits symbolize fucking, eggs are fertility, and Easter is really just a beautiful spring festival about glorious fucking that's made creepy by adding in grotesque torture and capital punishment caused by a supposedly loving god whose holy book is heavy on rape, genocide, infanticide, slavery, hatred of family, but pretty light on the love. Creepy creepy creepy, with no sense behind it at all, and chocolate rabbits. That's Easter.

Every year of my youth my dad and I spent Easter day, after church, driving to every drugstore in Greenfield, Massachusetts (there were three), looking for a "solid chocolate Easter rabbit." My dad and I wanted a chocolate Easter rabbit with heft to it—density, solidity, comfort and joy; that reassuring heaviness of a nice full American breast or a large expensive professional juggling ball. We didn't want a shell of crumbly, waxy chocolate in hard-to-open cellophane designed to conceal the hollow. We wanted a solid mass of chocolate goodness. A fulsome happy rabbit ear or leg with weight that Dad and I could share. We were chasing some sort of first high. I remember one big solid Easter rabbit, but I don't know from when. Maybe my dad just told me about it. Maybe we were just snipe hunting. We'd always end up with a hollow fucking chocolate rabbit, just the shell of joy, with no content. A loving Christ who died for our sins is the shell of a good idea with no content. That's why we have hollow chocolate Easter bunnies to explain the hollow empty disappointment of Easter.

I love gospel magic. Gospel *music* is a valid, inspirational form of music that comes out of Christianity. Gospel *magic* isn't a real form of magic. It's standard hack magic shop tricks presented as Christian parables. Christian music is among the best music of all time, from Bach to Ray Charles. In contrast, Christian comedy and magic aren't the best comedy and magic in the world. The tricks aren't deep foolers and the comedy is always with a *k*. The word "zany" is used a lot in the gospel magic press materials. I'm tempted to try to make the point that Christian magicians' tricks aren't that good because they feel that if Christians believe that Bible shit, how hard can it be to convince them that cupped right hand with the thumb sticking out and "flashes" between the fingers is empty and not palming a card that reads "John 3:16" in barely legible "Magic" marker? That's an unfair shot; I don't think gospel magicians do any cynical analysis at all. I think they're sincere—most of them just aren't that good. But most of all art isn't that good, so they're not special in that way either.

I love gospel magic because I don't care much about the tricks being real mysteries. I ignore comedy with a *k*. Who cares? I love the passion of gospel magic and the naïveté, but mostly I love the strained, overextended metaphors. A strained, overextended metaphor is a constantly changing labyrinth full of warm hot chocolate, where every belabored, sliding non-45-degree turn is uncertain and desperate like a waterslide crafted by a dull child on acid with a love of shapes and no knowledge of physics or architecture but a passion to not give up until everyone gets to the giant pool of marshmallow fluff at the bottom.

Let me lay on you the kind of performance you might see in gospel magic. The gospel magician takes the sports water bottle he's been sipping throughout his metaphor-packed show and starts a parable trick about how it's god's pure water that he's been drinking. He takes a big gulp and explains that the water is free of sin, the same way god created Adam and Eve, pure, fresh, and clear—even though it always seems like Eve's pussy is pure evil, but the Holy Houdini doesn't say that. He pours some of the water out of the bottle into a clear glass so the audience can appreciate the crystal virginity of sinless water that's way away from Eve's dirty woman hole, and takes another sip from the glass. Then the magic Christian (and not the cool movie *The Magic Christian,* starring Ringo Starr and Raquel Welch, who herself sported a perfect pair of totally solid chocolate bunnies) explains that sin comes along. (Writing "sin" and thinking about Raquel Welch's breasts as hefty solid chocolate bunnies is bringing a nice little solidity to the mighty fortress that is my jeans.) Mr. Christ-a-gician doesn't explain why an all-powerful god doesn't just stop sin. He doesn't want to open that can of bees. I use the metaphor "a can of bees" instead of the "can of worms" cliché because, as Goudeau has pointed out, opening a can of worms is no big deal. Can of worms—so what? But opening a can of bees—that's an unpleasant emergency. Explaining why god gave us sin only to hate us for it is a fucking can of angry wasps in an enclosed space. After not explaining why there's sin at all, magic boy brings out some brown liquid and pours that into the clear, pure water, and the whole glass of water turns yucky brown. The faithful conjurer says that when sin is added to the water, the water becomes "gross." He might use the word "gross" to show that he's down with the youngsters. "Gross" is like gangsta slang in Branson, Missouri.

Now it's time for some clever patter about how any amount of being good can't get you into heaven. This is a can of mutant immortal white-faced hornets that gospel magicians seem thrilled to open with impunity in the claustrophobic dirty-old airtight phone booth that is their gospel magic act. It's another part of Christianity that is so fucked and twisted. You need some line like "Living a good life and doing good deeds won't get you into heaven." That's a little more of the disappointing hollow chocolate rabbit full of red harvester ants that is Christianity. The Bible Blackstone explains that, nope, no amount of being good to people will get rid of the gross brown sin. The saved conjurer pours more clear sinless water into the dirty sinful Raquel Welch/Ringo Starr-in-the-trailer-between-takes water and it stays sinful. God doesn't give a fuck how good you are, you are fucked without fucking Jesus. (That's not the actual patter, but that's the idea. The real patter is probably more like "God doesn't care how good you are, he still thinks your sins are gross.")

Then the pious prestidigitator pulls out a model cross about the size of Ron Jeremy's dick and stirs up the gross sinful water in the glass that represents that glass of life that holds our dirty water, and it clears up miraculously to pure, clean, clear, no-vagina water again. That's the message of salvation. The all-powerful god makes us sinful and we can't get un-sinful no matter what, unless we pray to that all-powerful god to do what he could have done for us in the Garden of Eden without all this genocide, slavery, torture, and hate. For a guy like me, who loves overextended nonsense metaphors, this is almost as good as Raquel Welch in *The Magic Christian*. In 2012 I should be talking about jacking off to someone sexy and modern like Justin Bieber, but I was fourteen when *The Magic Christian* came out and I went to see it because it had a Beatle in it, and I stayed after the show because I couldn't stand up in public for an hour after watching Raquel Welch. She had a whip. Fuck.

To be a good magic trick and make the theological point, the Wizard of the Word needs to drink the newly pure water, but he doesn't—the trick has to end with the cross-stirring. The evangelical enchanter won't drink the clear pure water because it's not clear pure water, it's a chemical cocktail that god can't make pure any more than god can magically take our trespasses away. The presentation explains divine truth with what is admittedly a magic trick, but it's an overextended, strained metaphor that isn't even true. If god's love were real, would you have to buy a magic trick to show it? They're justifying a fairy tale with a lie, and that's why I love gospel magic. At a very deep level it really is true. They are explaining the way the universe works with an example of their god that doesn't work, just like the real world. There isn't even skill involved. There's no sleight of hand. No magic skills whatsoever are required. You just buy the chemicals, mix them up, and the trick works, except for no punch line—you can't drink the supposedly pure water. If I set it up for you right now and put your patter on a teleprompter, you could do the whole trick cold. You don't need to practice or rehearse, just don't drink the "water" at the end.

There is no good antonym for "gospel," but let's imagine this trick being done by a magician who embraces the real world and science and has the same low level of skill as a cheesy gospel magician: Me. How would I do this trick?

———————

Here's my presentation for the Atheist Magic version of the "Gross Water as Sin Trick."

"You see this pure water I've been drinking? This is tap water that I put in a sports bottle to save some plastic, some carbon, and some coin. If we left this water to god, it would be full of parasites and disease. Without filtering, and a touch of man-made chemicals, I'd be drinking dysentery or worse. God seems to want water to either be nonexistent or deadly. This water is pure not because of god, but in spite of god.

"This chemical I'm adding to the water is iodine. Iodine is processed by humans for many nutritional and medical applications. Trace amounts of iodine are needed for human health, so humans have added it to table salt in most of the world, but where humans haven't added it, god has chosen to leave about two billion people without it. This gives rise to hypothyroidism, the symptoms of which include but are not limited to: extreme fatigue, goiters, and mental retardation. If there was a god, couldn't he give some iodine to those two billion?

"I'm also sneaking in a little starch to make the water look really gross." (Atheists like komedy and use the word "gross" too.) "Iodine is an indicator for starch, so a little spray starch snuck in the water binds the iodine and really gives a strong, rich color. Hmmm, if I snuck this starch into the clear water with a bit less iodine, I could make what looked just like water turn into something that looked just like wine. Never mind, no one would ever fall for a shitty trick like that. I've got enough starch and iodine in the water so that it's not a pleasing purple like wine. I've put in enough of this cocktail that it's kind of gross, and putting in more water doesn't dilute it enough to change the color much.

"Now, I have this model of a torture and execution device that was used in ancient times. Yes, we still have capital punishment in this country and that's unforgivable. The USA is very religious, so of course we still have capital punishment. Fortunately, there is a movement to get rid of capital punishment, but god is doing nothing to help eliminate this torture and murder—like the clean water and iodine, the good for the people is done by the people.

"This cross has ascorbic acid on it, or stuck to the back, or inside it, or something, I don't know, I just bought this stupid trick at a magic shop. Ascorbic acid is vitamin C, necessary to human health and again withheld by god. God is fine with people having scurvy. If this citrus cross is used to represent Christianity, when it gets put into the sinful water, it makes the water look clear. Water has a neutral pH, and iodine is either neutral or slightly basic. The starch is also basic, so when it reacts with the iodine to produce the purple color, the resulting solution is also weakly basic. The ascorbic acid, as the name would lead you to believe, is acidic, so adding it to the solution moves the pH into the acidic range, which breaks down the starch, releasing the iodine back into the solution and 'shutting off' the purple color. It looks like clear pure water but it isn't. Christianity allows Christians to feel forgiven for the horrible things they've done, but if I were to drink this cross-purified water, it's actually still full of iodine and starch. Although the cross has made it look pure, it's still poison. You can't pray away the damage your malevolence, mistakes, and thoughtlessness have brought. The forgiving change brought about by Christianity is merely cosmetic—the sin, the hate, the poison are still there.

"Iodine is necessary for humans but this would be overdoing it. This trick requires a lot of iodine to get my water gross enough. One gulp of the not-gross-looking-but-still-toxic water probably wouldn't kill you. It would taste like rancid sin (think Eve's privates), but it probably wouldn't kill you. If you get booked in a lot of church basements doing your gospel act, you'd probably eventually hit over a gram of iodine and that could lead to burning in the mouth, throat and stomach, and/or abdominal pain, nausea, vomiting, diarrhea, weak pulse, and coma.

"Seems like a small price to pay to demonstrate god's love, so I guess I'll drink it down."

That's the version I would perform, and I would drink all the water at the end. Why not? I'm not the best sleight-of-hand artist, but I'm a passable stage magician. On a big body turn, I could certainly switch the phony, sickening Jesus-cleaned water glass for a glass of real, clean American tap water that was hanging under my suit jacket with a rubber ball in the top to keep it from spilling. A glass switch isn't that hard.

Happy Easter.

May all your chocolate rabbits be solid.

Listening to: "Gloria: In Excelsis Deo"—Patti Smith

HITCH AND TOMMY

CHRISTOPHER HITCHENS AND TOMMY ARDOLINO were my friends. I loved them both, but I should have been closer to both of them. Time doesn't just steal the future, it steals the past.

When Martin Amis and Salman Rushdie have written about something or someone, it's best for Penn Jillette to just stay away. Let geniuses write about love and truth and honor, and I'll stick to stories about dropping my cock in a blow-dryer. If you want to know what a brave and wonderful man Hitch was, go with Marty and Sally, they're playing on Hitch's level.

I've read *God Is Not Great* twice and I will go back to it again and again. I find tremendous comfort in that book. Shortly after I read it, I went into the hospital. I was sick enough to be in the hospital, but only because I'm a pussy. I felt well enough to pull the IV out of my arm every night, go to the Penn & Teller Theater at the Rio All-Suites Hotel and Casino in Las Vegas, do our show, then go back to the hospital and be put on morphine. Hospital staff told me I couldn't leave the hospital, but Nevada law says they couldn't keep me there, so I left to do the show. Nevada law also says they have to let me back in, so I commuted to and from the hospital. Someday I will be too sick to do the show, and then the show won't go on, but as long as I can pull the IVs out, I might as well do the show. What else have I got to do? If you can do a Vegas show, you're not really knock knock knockin' on heaven's door, but for someone who has suffered as little as I have, I felt pretty sick. Some would turn to the Bible for solace when watching the IV drip, but I reread *God Is Not Great* and it gave me the rage to live. Hitch's insistence on the real world makes the real world better.

I loved the too few and too brief times I spent with Hitch in person. I treasure my many e-mails from him, often signed "Insha'Allah." I started my book *God, No!* by writing about Hitch being so much smarter than me, even when he was drinking. I used the term "shit-faced" to joke about his drinking and my amazement at his intellectual ability despite the cocktails. Even though Hitch was dying, he used some of his too-precious time to read my book and sent me a kind e-mail saying he would have liked my book more if I hadn't insulted him on the first page. I was wrong to write about his drinking. What I thought was friendly ribbing was insult. So I called my editor at home in the middle of the night and begged her to let me rewrite the first two pages. She let me and I made it a little better. I sent the less insulting version to Hitch. He forgave me, but that was kind of my last real exchange with him. He was dying, he took time to read my book, and I insulted him. Fuck.

Hitch liked to drink and I've never had a drink in my life. Hitch was never "shit-faced." He was more lucid and clearheaded than anyone I have ever met. I know nothing about drinking. When Hitch thought of drinking, he thought about Winston Churchill; when I thought about drinking, I thought about my fourteen-year-old school friends throwing up on my shoes. I thought about those same children wrapping their parents' cars around telephone poles and dying young and not even leaving beautiful corpses. To Hitch, drinking meant being a grown-up. To me drinking meant never getting to be an adult and never getting out of Greenfield, Massachusetts. I never saw a respected grown-up drink until I was a grown-up. Maybe until I met Hitch.

Hitch was in town when we had a pretty fine rough cut of *The Aristocrats* and I invited him over to my house to see it with a few other friends. It was the only time Hitch ever visited my home. He arrived, I think in a cab, with a bottle of liquor in his hand. I could go to the Web and search what he drank, and write in "Johnnie Walker" and some color, but I don't really remember, and it really doesn't matter. I just know it was a bottle of alcohol.

I greeted him on the porch and I saw the bottle in his hand. I looked at the bottle, smiled apologetically and said, "I really don't like having alcohol in my house." Hitch looked at the bottle and looked at me, and said, with a sneer, "Well, I guess I should respect your religious beliefs." I was arguing, on my front porch, with the greatest debater in the world.

"It's not religious, Hitch, you know that."

"It most certainly is, and you expect me to respect that."

I didn't know what to do. I didn't mind his lit cigarette—people smoked in the Slammer all the time—but I liked that there had never been alcohol in my home. I had invited Hitch to be a guest in my home, and he had a bottle in his hand. We stood facing each other, one of the most brilliant minds of our time and me.

"I really don't want you to come into my house with that bottle."

"Are you going to stop me? Will you physically stop me from coming into your home?"

When I wrote what he said in quotation marks and read it on my computer screen, it had a swagger. It's like something from an action movie, but please try to reread it as a simple question. A question asked without any attitude at all. Just a request for information. If it were Hitch puffing out his chest and pretending to be an action hero, he'd be an asshole, but he wasn't. It was a simple request for information. I'm the asshole. There was never going to be an exchange between Hitch and Penn where Hitch doesn't win. It was asked as a simple question.

It's hard, in emotional or comedic situations, to simply ask a question the way Hitch asked if I was going to physically stop him from entering my house with a bottle in his hand. Hitch just wanted to know what I was going to do.

I looked at him, looked at the bottle, looked at my home and I thought about it. I answered as honestly as I could. There's no other way I could be around Hitch. Lying was a waste of time. He was too smart. I answered him honestly: "I don't know."

We looked at each other there on my porch. I couldn't elaborate much. "I really don't know what I'm going to do. I don't want liquor in my house and I love you. I don't know what I'm going to do. I don't know."

I sure wasn't going to hit him or wrestle him, but would I stand in front of the door to bar him, or would I just open the door for him and welcome my friend into my home with bottle in hand? Hitch looked me in the eye for a long time. Nothing macho was going on. We weren't two primates working for dominance. Just two men standing silently on my porch in the desert night. I'm always yapping and Hitch was always saying something important, but on that porch we just looked at each other. Finally, without any attitude, he set the bottle down on my porch. Not on a table, or a sill, just outside in the middle of the deck, right in the walkway. He didn't smile or hug me. He said, "Let's watch your movie" and walked toward the door. We never found out what I would have done.

He seemed to enjoy the movie. He laughed loudly and said very kind and smart things about it after. As I walked him out, he grabbed his bottle off the porch floor, said good-bye, and got into his cab.

The New York Times pulled back their front page to put Hitch's obituary on it. The Times sent out an alert that I got on my phone, breaking news—Hitch was dead. I'm old enough that my friends die, but it's not often I find out from the paper of record. I was walking out of some theater show in Vegas (yes, we *do* have theater in Vegas, thank you very much) with my wife. She had gone to the restroom and I was alone in the parking lot, so I turned on my phone to look at my messages, and Christopher Hitchens was dead. Just like that. You can read any obituary you want of Hitch, and it'll talk about his genius, his bravery, his courage. He did not go quietly into that dark night. Geniuses wrote about his genius even on his deathbed. Listen, cancer, if you're picking a fight with Hitchens, you might win, but he'll get in his licks. Everything Hitch did, including dying, was inspiring. I was lucky he came to my home with a bottle in his hand.

Tommy Ardolino, my friend, the wonderful drummer for NRBQ (New Rhythm and Blues Quartet), also got an obit in The New York Times. They didn't stop the presses, but they recorded the great rocker's death a few days after he was gone. I found out about Tommy by a tweet of condolence from someone who knows I love him. Tommy didn't die a brave and strong death. Death didn't get beat up by Tommy. Tommy didn't humiliate death. Death owned Tommy's ass way before it took him.

Tommy liked to listen to records. I like to listen to records. Some of my closest friendships with people were made in playing records for each other. I talk a lot, but I think I can tell you more about myself by sitting you down and playing the records that mean the most to me. I have bunches of goofy records that no one has heard. Really rare stuff. I have a nutty and wonderful record collection. It's hard to find rarity of any kind anymore. You can find anything on the big World Wide InnerTube. My whole collection is out there somewhere, sitting on hundreds of goofy websites. The music is there, but you won't find it. Someone has to lead you to it. Tommy led us to a lot.

Tommy spent a lot of time in record stores and finding used records wherever they could be found. He picked through Salvation Army stores and yard sales. There was a category of record that mystified him for a while. Turned out, he was finding song poem records, before anyone I knew knew what they were. Tommy led me to song poems.

Song sharks put advertisements in the back of cheesy magazines looking for songwriters. "Put your poems to music." The unknown poet would read the ad, send in a poem, and no matter what the poem was, the song shark wrote back that the fish had talent. For a bunch of monthly payments, the naïve poet would have his or her songs put to music, performed, recorded on a record and then, the scam made the fish believe, the new songwriting team could start the journey to getting the songs on the Billboard charts. The song sharks never really tried to sell the songs. Their money was made from the poet's investment. They got several hundred dollars (plus financing fees from the payment plans) to bang out a quick musical chart for whatever poem was sent in. They'd get a bunch of jaded musicians to do one take on each song and record dozens in one afternoon. They would make an album's worth of these song poems, record them, press enough for everyone whose poem was recorded, and send them off to the marks. For a few hundred dollars, you got your poem set to music and you had a professional recording of it. You also had some hopes and dreams. In some people's minds, you were also a fool. It's like that with hopes and dreams.

Some of the vinyl never made it back to the lyricists. Song sharks pressed too many, or they bounced from the address, or maybe they miscounted or got a bulk rate, I don't know, but these song-poem records were dumped into used record bins for a nickel apiece or something. Who would buy these mysterious unknown records? Tommy Ardolino. I have Tommy's collection in my home now. There are a lot of them to wade through and Tommy waded with glee. Most of the songs are about Jesus or a president, but some of them have a purity you're never going to get out of any other kind of music. The collision of the naïve and the cynical at the speed of CERN. Musicians who don't care at all performing hack music around words that are nothing but passion. Here is the poem that was turned into Tommy's favorite song-poem. I urge you to take a moment and find it on the Web and hear the music. Hear the singer struggle with the meter and the rhyme that doesn't rhyme without the writer's exact dialect ("route" and "foot"). This would never be a real song, but why not? If music is communication of the heart, this sure is that. All that's wrong with these lyrics is the juggling. The magic is perfect.

Do You Know the Difference Between Big Wood and Brush?
(Louise I. Oliver, 1974) *as recorded by Gary Roberts & The Satellites*

Do you know the difference between big wood and brush?
Do you know the difference between big wood and brush?

Some men when going through the change
Don't seem to patch things [up] at home and remain
Some men stay with their wives for many years
Keep pushin' forward, tryin' to conquer their fears

Brush sometimes seems to get into their way
Causes them to want to get out and play
Brush has a tendency to get in their way
Comes along and drives them astray

Do you know the difference between big wood and brush?
Do you know the difference between big wood and brush?

You may think this is hearsay, and I don't know what I'm talkin'
about
But hear this story about my sister, and you will soon find out
Her husband dropped her at the hospital, as he had always done
She got [up] to leave and waited for her husband to return
She went over and called home on the phone
But he did not answer, he was not at home
He had been fairly punctual in the past
Then she looked and saw him through the window glass

Do you know the difference between big wood and brush?
Do you know the difference between big wood and brush?

He said he was late 'cause he'd run over a woman's foot
This was the beginning of his search for another route
He had been accusing her of holding him back
He went out to meet that woman, he'd thought he was on the right
track
As time went on she thought that things were going along good
But he said things were bad between them as they stood
His other woman had called the house several times on the phone

But June came along, he slipped into the house, got his clothes and was
  gone

Do you know the difference between big wood and brush?
Do you know the difference between big wood and brush?

Then one year and five months later
Her life could not be any greater
He called on Thanksgiving night
Said he was coming home to get things right
Brush always seems to burn out, but big wood keeps burnin' on
That's why he turned around and came back home

Do you know the difference between big wood and brush?
Do you know the difference between big wood and brush?

I judge people by how they react when I play them Tommy's favorite song-poems. Everyone laughs, but I judge them by the quality of their laughter. Maybe it's all in my head. My analysis is probably just an extension of how I already feel about the potential new friend. The laughter is a place to project my unconscious thoughts, but it doesn't feel that way. It feels like I can hear differences. I want the laughter to be pure. Laughter about all human hearts and not at some dipshit buying his dreams in the back of the *National Enquirer*. I laugh, not because the songs are stupid, but because the songs are too true. Lady Gaga is protected by skill. She's good and good makes her bulletproof. The people who write song-poems don't have any armor at all. They are running around naked wearing antlers and we all have fully automatic weapons with laser sights.

There is something about a cynical person singing sloppy truth that makes me need to hug my children. That might make you laugh, but if you laugh the wrong way, I may not want to play you any more of my records.

Tommy's death was a tragedy, but he had a kind of charmed life. Tommy's working-class mom and dad got him a drum set as a child and he banged to his swinging records all the time. His favorite band in the world was NRBQ (he shared that with Bonnie Raitt, Elvis Costello, Paul McCartney and a bunch of other wicked famous music people). He wrote a letter to NRBQ's keyboard player, Terry Adams, and somehow, with parental consent, at fifteen years old, Terry let Tommy come on the road with the NRBQ. When their real drummer left before the encore one night, Tommy was there. He had never played drums with live musicians before. His first loose, swinging, snare explosion in front of anyone was in back of NRBQ. It was a couple years later that he was a full-time member of the Q. With Joey Spampinato on bass, Ardolino/Spampinato became NRBQ's "Ravioli Rhythm Section." Tommy bagged groceries for one day, but other than that, Tommy never had a real job. Never did a second real day's work in his too-short life. Tommy was two months older than me.

Tommy and NRBQ went along together for more than thirty years. Tommy held his left drumstick between his index and fuck-you fingers. It was neither a jazz grip nor a rock grip. It was Tommy's grip. It gave a fierce snap to the snare. Play me beats 2 and 4 from any one measure of an NRBQ record, and I'll recognize Tommy's snare pop right away. Tommy played so hard and so often (NRBQ did more than two hundred live dates every year), that he developed calluses on the inside of his fingers just a bit smaller than half Ping-Pong balls. It looked really creepy. Tommy couldn't put those two fingers together. He was forced by his altered biology to always be flashing a peace sign. Mohawk punks do body modifications in piercing parlors. Tommy did his body mod banging rhythm and blues.

Tommy played drums and he played records for people. He had long, unfashionable curly hair (look who's talking) and he was too fat for rock and roll (look who's talking). He had a smile that kept people guessing. I talked to Tommy a lot, and we loved each other, but we didn't really connect on a verbal level. I never knew what he was talking about. When I talked, he smiled and loved me, but never gave a really appropriate response. I'd compliment his performance and Tommy would meow like a cat and rub against me. Or he'd puff up his cheeks and make weird sounds like he was a little man trapped in a box. The last time I saw him he said, "Penn, what's going to happen to us?" over and over. When he sent me some song-poem records, he had written on the box, "What's going to happen to us?" I think it was one of those simple questions and Tommy was waiting for an answer.

The answer was we're all going to die. We're all going to be gone and leave behind nothing but memories and love, and Tommy left a lot of that. Tommy didn't fight like Hitch against death. He begged death to come to him.

First, throat cancer came to Terry, the Thelonious Monk/Jerry Lee Lewis/Chico Marx keyboard player of NRBQ. It looked like Terry might not survive, and the dying of their leader was enough to break up NRBQ. They all stopped working while Terry fought cancer. Big Al (I'm bigger than Big Al. I know Big Dave and I'm bigger than he; I met Big Mike, and I'm bigger than he; if I didn't have a stupid name, I would have "Big" in front of mine) had been replaced in NRBQ when he started getting songs recorded by Nashville cats. I think Joey, the bass player, started working as a house painter. Tommy got right to work on dying. He'd lost his band. His parents were dead. His wife divorced him. He lived in his parents' house in Springfield, Massachusetts (right down Route 91 from my home-town), until the house went into foreclosure. A loving friend of the band bought the house at auction and allowed Tommy to stay there. He stayed there. He did nothing but stay there. He bought food for his cats and alcohol for himself. He was offered gigs with lots of bands, real bands, good bands, but he didn't take them. He stopped taking care of himself. Maybe he'd never taken care of himself; maybe others always had. He ate only what friendly neighbors brought to him. They'd bring a big plate of pasta to last him awhile, he'd eat it all at once, and then eat nothing. When there was a big power outage in western Mass he sat in the cold dark until Terry, having beaten cancer and started another NRBQ, thought of Tommy and sent someone to check on him. Tommy went from the couch to the hospital. He was treated for all his neglect, liver problems and di-abetes for a couple months, but it was all palliative. Tommy died.

Hitch fought for life and Tommy seduced death. Hitch owned every room he walked into. Tommy wasn't much noticed without a trap set and a band around him. I loved them both and they're both dead.

I have friends, older than I, who are concerned about their lega-cies. They are thinking about how they will be remembered. They are making sure their notebooks are in order for posterity. These are friends who have brought a lot of influence and joy to a lot of peo-ple. Now they want to make sure they keep doing that after they're dead. It seems nutty to me.

I'm slowly reading *Arguably* by Hitchens. It's the last book he published during his lifetime, but unless I die wicked soon, it won't be the last Hitch book I read. I'm playing a lot of NRBQ, listening to Tommy bang those drums. I'm thinking about how much joy they both brought me and how much they changed my life. I'll be dead soon too. I don't know whether it'll be a few dozen years, a few hundred years, or thousands of years, but Hitch and Tommy will eventually be forgotten. All legacy is temporary. Nothing matters. In several generations even our bequeathed DNA will be diluted to a general human blend. None of our individual traits will be recognizable.

There is no way to cheat. Everyone and everything will be completely forgotten. That's true, but I'm a nutty optimist and I can't just leave it there. I have to add that maybe the singularity will happen and there will be a forever for at least some intents and purposes. I just got to laughing. I'm worried that something I've written here could be proven wrong and shortsighted in a hundred years. As I write about there being no legacy and Hitch and Tommy being forgotten, I'm worried about how these words will look in the future, long after I'm dead. I'm such an asshole. That's my point.

During a debate with some rabbi, Hitch was asked, "Do you believe in free will?" Hitch responded, "I believe we have no choice." I don't know how much Hitch was referencing Isaac Bashevis Singer in that quotation, and that answer is also written by Vonnegut, sung in a very high pitch by Rush, and it all builds on Sartre, though Jean-Paul wasn't the first. A while ago, I could have fired off an e-mail to Hitch and got that quotation's provenance, but now Hitch is dead. Hitch and Tommy will be forgotten, but it doesn't feel that way. Their lives feel like they mattered. Nothing but the feeling of mattering matters. That feeling is life. I can no longer get wisdom directly from Hitch. Tommy can no longer play records. The future where they are forgotten doesn't exist, and yet in our hearts' imagined futures they are remembered forever.

Listening to: "Immortal for a While"—NRBQ

Tommy and me.

MY FIRST FATHER'S DAY CARD

I WILL NEVER EXPERIENCE SENDING AND RECEIVING a Father's Day card on the same day. I don't get to feel the chain of life that allows me to look up and look down at the same time. I'll never have a day where I talk to both my father and my son. That makes me cry every time I think about it, and I think about it all the time. I cry a lot. The difference between joyous crying and sad crying is only for the young. With my parents dead and my children alive, I can never tell why I'm crying. The sadness of my parents' death is the joy of my children's lives. Those feelings are the same. That's life, motherfucker. I'm old enough to know that I'll never again really know why I'm crying.

My mom and dad never met our children. They never met my wife. Mom and Dad were dead before my children were born and before I met my wife. Worse, my parents knew exactly what they were missing, even though I didn't. They watched me piss away the shared joy of my future family. My parents knew they would never meet my children. We all knew I'd have children. They knew I'd meet someone to love and share my life with. My parents knew exactly what they were missing and they missed it. It was a hole in their hearts that's now a hole in my heart. Mom and Dad knew that I wanted to be successful professionally first and that was going to take more time then we would have together. They saw plenty of the fame. My mom and dad were at both of Penn & Teller's Broadway openings. They made the paperboy watch me on *SNL*. They were extras in the movie that Teller and I wrote and starred in. It's the Mexican restaurant scene and my dad is right behind me. I can't see him and he can't see me, but we're fiddling with our silverware in exactly the same way. Nature or nurture? Many times they mentioned gently to me that they would like to meet their grandchildren before they died, but I wanted time to go on the fucking Letterman show. What the fuck was wrong with me? My excuse now is that I hadn't met the mother of their grandchildren. That's more than an excuse; that's my real reason. I wasn't willing to settle for someone less than Emily. I wanted perfect. I wasn't looking for a wife. I was looking for Emily and she found me. Mom and Dad would have loved our family, their family, with a pure love as hot as the sun, or one of those other suns a zillion light years away that's way hotter than our little pussy sun. My parents could love. Fuck, could they love.

I'm fifty-seven years old. My parents have been dead twelve years. Emily and I have been married eight years. My daughter, Moxie, is coming up on her seventh birthday and my son, Zolten, is knocking on six. This is my first marriage and these are my only children. I started late. Way late, almost Letterman late. When Moxie is my age, I'll be 107 years old and I'm sure we all really will have flying cars, world peace, and a cooler song for twelve-year-old boys than "Stairway to Heaven." I don't know if Mox and Zz will have things to do before they let me meet my grandchildren, or if they'll even have children. I don't know jackshit. That's another reason I cry. Another reason to be joyful and sad.

It's not natural to have one's children this late in life. My body wanted to reproduce when I was fifteen. My body really, really wanted to reproduce when I was fifteen. I loved fooling my body into thinking I was reproducing with girlfriends at fifteen. It took a lot of civilization, socialization, willpower, and some emulsion polymerization technology for me not to reproduce at fifteen. When I was fifty, it took much more technology for us to get started reproducing. Moxie was a test tube baby. My wife, Emily, was thirty-nine when Moxie was born. The ticking clock was deafening, and even though trying naturally was a blast, we turned to science for Moxie. After that kick start, we conceived our son Zolten naturally. Naturally is cheaper and way more fun than IVF. But with IVF we did get to sing the Velvet Underground's "Heroin" together while I used a real hypodermic needle to give Emily her hormone shots (we both felt exactly "like Jesus' son"). It was kind of fun to see her moods change crazy fast. I'd shoot her up and she'd start crying and we'd have a good laugh together at how much our feelings are just chemicals.

We were going through IVF about the time I was on *The West Wing*. One of the actors on there (I won't say which one, because I'm not sure he ever made his IVF public) called the sample room at the IVF clinic "The Masturbatorium." I love that term and wanted to give him credit without outing his children. The masturbatorium is a little room at the clinic where you go in to whack out the baby-batter to give to the nurse so they can make the baby in the test tube. Oh dear, I just called the embryo "the baby." That's not a big deal, right? No one is going to argue over when an embryo becomes a baby. Emily had to go into stirrups while they got invasive on her ass or right near her ass; I just had to jack off. She did her part fine, and I fucked up jacking off.

I walked into the masturbatorium and there were three posters on the wall to help me get off. They were swimsuit pictures of three women—Pamela Anderson, Elle Macpherson, and Gena Lee Nolin—all of whom I had made cry in public at one time or another. I was supposed to whack off to women I had pissed off. I needed to jack to women who hated me. Some get turned on thinking about hatefucks but that never worked for me. Says a lot about the taste of our Middle Eastern fertility doctor. Pamela Anderson: made her cry over animal rights and a joke I made to her face on TV. Elle Macpherson: made fun of her hair care products and her husband's dickey (not dick, dickey, the fake turtleneck thing; I'm guessing his dick was fine) on live radio. And I professionally trash-talked Gena until she cracked on *Fear Factor*. They're all good people, and they all forgave me (maybe not Elle), but I still didn't want to whack to them. The masturbatorium had videos too, but they were way too vanilla for a Boston cream pie guy like me. The DVDs were the swimsuit edition TV special, not like latex enema nurses in bondage. The idea that there were real nurses right behind the wall to where I was jacking should have been hot, but it wasn't. I don't know why. Maybe because we were dealing with making children, which is so much less sexy than fooling my body into thinking I was making children. Emily suggested at the desk that maybe we could send in a couple hookers, and I just got embarrassed. On libertarianism, atheism and transgressive humor my wife is the hard-core one in the family. I couldn't jack off in front of pictures of women I'd made cry and if that makes me less of a man, so be it. We finally got our "sample" at home working together and then Emily drove to the doctor's like she was trying to get hot pizza home to her future family.

For Zolten, we just fucked. That's why he gets $35,000 more in his trust fund.

Lots of people are having children later in life. Everyone is living longer, and now that we have electric lights there's other stuff to do at night. A lot of older parents worry about being older parents. I hear people say, "I don't want to be too old to play baseball with my son." They worry that their kids will be embarrassed by their parents' age. I worry about that less, because I grew up with older parents. My parents were the best parents in the world, and they were old. They were older for their generation than I am for mine. My mom was forty-five years old when I was born. My dad was a couple years younger. My only sibling, my sister, was twenty-three years old when I was born. Now that I think about it, I might not have been planned. After Jack Nicholson and Bobby Darin found out that their sisters were really their moms, I thought I might have a similar surprise coming, but I've seen pre-Photoshop pictures of my mom in the maternity ward and my sister gave me her Girl Scout's honor. There were no deathbed confessions from anyone.

When my mom got pregnant, she went to the doctor. She was freaking out. She said she was too old to have another baby. She said she wouldn't live to see her baby go to kindergarten. The doctor told her that there were lots of older moms. This was 1954 and he went to his files. See? Here's a mom who was thirty-two . . . and here's one who was thirty . . . and . . . he didn't find anyone over forty. Mom was very freaked. Bud Trillin at *The New Yorker* did a big profile on Penn & Teller while we were Off-Broadway and it also showed up in a book of his. He did a lot research and went to Philly to talk to Teller's parents and teachers and went all the way to Greenfield to interview my parents. My mom was very straightforward with Bud. Bud is good, but my mom also didn't know another way to be. She confessed that she was very worried about birth defects. She worried that I might be born with Down syndrome, for which there were no tests at the time. I don't know if she would have gotten the tests if they were available, my mom may have believed that love starts at conception. I never asked her directly. She said to Bud that she heard that babies born to old mothers were either retarded or geniuses. ("Retarded" being the only word people used at the time to describe mental disabilities.) She then paused for one of those Dean Martin comedy pauses that go forever, shrugged, paused and thought some more and then said, "I guess he's a genius." She got Bud to laughing, but . . . I don't think it was as much of a joke as Bud thought. My mom knew I wasn't a genius, but I think she had decided that besides being worthy of her complete unconditional love just for being born, I might have also been okay. I could make her laugh. I could make her laugh harder than anyone in the world had ever made her laugh. You tell me, am I crying now with sadness or joy?

I grew up with parents who were just a few years younger than Moxie and Zolten's dad will be. My dad didn't play much baseball with me, but age had nothing to do with it. I was on the A&W Little League team. The other children said A&W stood for Ass Wipes, ignoring the ampersand and making me crazy. With P&T the ampersand matters. You can say P&T stands for "Pisshead & Twat" but don't you dare say it stands for Pecker Tards, that'll just piss me off. I was thrown off the Ass Wipes for not understanding why we were supposed to think that our arbitrary team was the best (the same reason I was thrown off *The Celebrity Apprentice*—jocks like Trump never change). Before I was thrown off the Ass Wipes, the best Little League team that ever existed, my mom and dad came to every game. My dad would sit in the stands, saying proudly to the other dads, "See that big boy out in the outfield daydreaming—that's my boy, he doesn't care about the game." My whole family is missing the sports gene and the military gene. During a war (they're all the same), my dad was a security guard and then a jail guard. I hope I didn't screw up the Jillette family genes by marrying a great golfer with a Navy dad. If I did, I can teach them to juggle and be medics.

The other children in grade school did ask why I spent so much time with my grandparents, and I guess that embarrassed me a little, but there was never any trauma. I just told them they were my mom and dad and they were wicked old. My parents were always proud of me and I was proud of them. It seemed that my mom and dad didn't have any problems other than mine. They loved me and they loved each other. I never heard them raise their voices except in jest or in an emergency, to each other or to me. As a very young child, I ran into the street and my mom screamed "Penn!" like Roger Daltrey screams "Yeah!" in "Won't Get Fooled Again." I never ran into the street again. I guess we also yelled as a joke, but not when we meant it. When the Jillettes mean it, the Jillettes pout.

Way back in the nineties, we did a TV show in Britain called *The Unpleasant World of Penn & Teller*. We did a lot of bits from our American show and also did most of our TV bits from *Letterman* and *SNL*. We had amazing guest hosts, like Stephen Fry and John Cleese. Stephen and John are both just a little bit smaller than me, but we're all big guys. It was the first time I met John, and during lighting and just hanging out backstage, John was chatting with me: "Penn, when you're angry, do you yell?"

"Nope. Never."

"Me neither. Did your family yell?"

"Nope, never. I can't recall my parents ever yelling at each other except when they were kidding."

"My family never did either. We sulk."

"Yes, we are pouters."

"And yet we've both discovered there's nothing funnier than a big guy yelling."

I guess that's true. For eight years on *Penn & Teller: Bullshit!* I screamed "Fuck you, asshole!" at the fucking top of my fucking lungs. In our live show, I yell several times, but not at home. I was taught if you're yelling, you're joking. That hasn't served me that well. I've had people like Lou Ferrigno scream right in my face because he couldn't understand something, and it's so hard for me to believe he was really serious. It seemed like he was going to turn green and do a cartoon show.

There must be older parents who scream at each other and at their children, but it did seem like my parents' wisdom and measured actions were related somewhat to their age. Older parents are wonderful until they croak. They both died when I was forty-five. I was with my mom and dad for about half of their lives, and vice versa. I will have to live to a hundred for Mox, Zz and I to share half our lives.

I hope I've learned something from being alive this long that will make me a better dad. I know I will be an embarrassment. I'm an embarrassment to everyone who loves and/or works with me. Moxie and Zolten have already been asked if I'm their grandfather, but that'll be the least of their embarrassments. They'll also have a dad with a stupid beard and hair down his back talking atheism at the PTA meeting and calling an almost-saint Motherfucking Teresa on TV. If they say the name of their dad's TV show in school, they'll be punished. They have a dad who lost on *Dancing with the Stars* to

Adam Carolla and lost on *The Celebrity Apprentice* to Clay Aiken. They may hang their heads in shame.

They have a dad who's a goddamn Las Vegas magician, and that's embarrassing whatever age he is.

I better buy them two ponies each.

Listening to: "I Want My Mommy"—NRBQ

Penn & Teller and Zz & Mox at the AFAN charity walk for people suffering from AIDS. My children are sometimes forced to wear pictures of their dad and his business partner on their shirts.

GRADUATION DAY—NOTHING IS FUNNY BUT PENN JILLETTE

I GOT OUT OF HIGH SCHOOL IN THE EARLY SEVENTIES. I avoid writing "graduated." I did technically graduate, but I sure lettered and not spirited. I test wicked good, and as soon as I got my stupid-high SAT scores, I went to the principal. I told him that if this gifted student didn't graduate, this gifted student would talk to the school board about how this gifted student was let down by the not-so-gifted principal. I had his gift hanging. He asked if I were threatening him. I answered I was, and I didn't go to school much after that. The threat took and he made sure I graduated at the very bottom of my class. That was his gift to the gifted student.

I had an English teacher at Greenfield High School who is still a friend, but GHS was a terrible place to learn. I lived in a dead factory town that was a half-hour drive from the University of Massachusetts in Amherst. That meant that every acid-head education major who wanted to try some *farkakte* new pedagogical system could just get a grant (it was the seventies; you could get grants to condescend to rural students) and try it at a real no-kidding school. The worst hippies didn't want to go too far from their drug dealers, so Greenfield was perfect. The college students could patronize us, use us for one paper, and be able to drive home nights to bang the tripping undergrads.

They tried "open campus," "open study," open everything but a fucking book. I had hair down my back, elephant bells, fringe jackets, and eye makeup, but I wasn't a very good hippie. I like the sex and some of the rock and roll (I could never stand the Grateful Dead), but I didn't try the drugs. I've been told by professional drug users that if I did the drugs, I would like the Dead. It seems like the most effective PSA against drugs could just play some Dead jams and say, "If you do drugs, you will like this kind of music." What other deterrent would one need? I don't understand PSAs. If we have a marketplace of ideas in this country, isn't our government just the ref? Wouldn't the marketplace of ideas allow billboards that read, "Try Heroin," and "Beat Your Spouse, Eventually He'll Dig It"? How do they justify taking tax money, received at gun point, and use it to put TV ads and billboards that tell parents to talk to their children about drugs? My mom and dad never once spoke to me about drugs or alcohol. They never even said that they didn't use them and never had. I could see that, what's to talk about? Why would the government tell us what to talk about? There was a billboard on my way to the Penn & Teller Theater at the Rio All-Suite Hotel and Casino in Las Vegas, Nevada, that read something about stopping spousal abuse. Has there ever been a person who was driving home, planning on beating the shit out of her husband, who read that billboard and thought, "No, maybe I'll go talk to my children about drugs instead?" I noticed while reading a few smart-guy books like Daniel Kahneman's wicked smart one, that the author who didn't want to use "their" incorrectly when he needed a pronoun and didn't know the sex, didn't use "he," "his," and "him" but to be modern used "she," "her" and "hers," so I decided I wanted to be like a smart-guy author and have it be an imaginary woman beating her imaginary husband reading my imaginary billboard. We don't know what sex a husband or wife is anyway, let alone the perp. Men get beaten a lot. I bet Mike Newdow, the atheist who went to the Supreme Court to try to get "under God" back out of the Pledge of Allegiance, gets beat up a lot. Re also pushes really hard to replace "he" and "she" with "re," and "his" and "hers" with "rees," and "him" and "her" with "erm." I met Mike at some atheist shindig and re really talks like that, it's rees style, it works for erm and I like it, but smart-guy books don't use it. Doing it in this book will just piss off my editor and I don't want to do that. Mike Newdow is cool about pissing off the Supreme Court so re sure doesn't give a fuck about my editors, so let erm do it.

In 1987, Bob Dylan did a tour with the Dead, and my buddy Jesse Dylan invited me to go with him to see his dad. Jesse told me we should time our arrival so we got to the stadium as his dad was hitting the stage. I thought we should go for the whole shebang. If I was going to see a little of the Dead, I should see the whole thing. I had this vision of noodling, improvised music providing the soundtrack to lots of beautiful braless women spinning and jiggling in tie-dye clothes. How bad could it be? Pretty fucking bad. I ended up backstage with Don Johnson. Crockett and I watched the show together from the wings. It would have been better if Don had been wearing a bra. Don Johnson still hates me from the episode of *Miami Vice* that I guest starred on. I was doing an awful movie, that awful TV show, and our pretty good Off-Broadway show in the same week. I went a whole week without ever once lying down to sleep. I slept in cars from one set to another, but never more than an hour a day for a week. I was sitting up in a deep sleep when I was shaken awake by Don Johnson saying, "We're rolling." I looked at him, heard "action" and started doing my lines. As luck would have it, I was playing a drug dealer, so who cares? I woke from a deep sleep to be in a scene with Don Johnson and Starsky without Hutch directing. Aren't you supposed to wake up *from* that?

My sister used to dream all the time that she was a super James Bond–type female spy. At the time she told me this, my sister was a seventy-year-old New Englander caring for her grandchild. She told me she had this theory that we dreamed the opposite of our real lives, so she was all sex and violence. She asked me what I had dreamed the night before. I told her I dreamed I was sitting comfortably reading a magazine. Magazine reading is my only recurring dream except for the dream of pulling out my own teeth, which always makes me wake up with a hard-on. This time I woke up from a relaxing dream to be in a scene with Don Johnson. He hates me and he wasn't wearing a bra backstage at the Dead and it was awkward and the music was awful and I wanted to be pulling my own teeth out, so Jesse and I ended up outside his dad's dressing room playing pinball until Bob hit the stage. Bob is always good. The Dead were not. At least not with the sexiest man in the eighties and without doing drugs.

My high school was the result of a poor community school controlled by condescending hippies. Oh boy! I didn't go to school much, but there really wasn't much of a school to go to. High school students are evolutionarily programmed to think they know more than grown-ups, but when the grown-ups are hippie student teachers, evolution wins. Fucking stoners.

The conservative community of real teachers and administrators did a little bit of push back. They'd given up any hope of teaching the students anything, but thought maybe they could give them some of the American high school experience. We had pep rallies and a yearbook. The graduating class ahead of us was all hip and had voted to not have class personalities. Those are the people who are "Most Likely to Succeed," "Class Clown," "Class Flirt," and so on.

Our class also had a vote on whether to have class personalities and we also voted it down. We were hip and modern too. The yearbook committee and administrators decided to ignore our vote and have the personalities anyway. The same people who had voted against "class personalities" also had to vote for the "class personalities." I thought maybe I could exploit that.

I knew the majority of my fellow students didn't want "class personalities" and I knew when they were planning the vote for the student personalities. This was worth going to school for. We had a fairly small class, a few hundred students. If I was systematic, I would be able to reach every one of them personally before the vote, but I also did some group speeches. If we were in a class before a teacher came in, or there was any gathering of students, I stood up in front of them and gave a little speech like this: "In a few days, we're going to be asked to vote for school personalities, you know, 'Class Clown' and 'Most Likely to Succeed' and all that shit. If you sincerely want to vote for these things, please write in the name you want, use your votes how you want. But if you're thinking of writing in 'Abbie Hoffman' or 'Mickey Mouse' or 'Mike Hunt' or just writing 'Fuck you' and throwing the paper away, please just take the time to write in me, Penn Jillette, for everything. I promise you, if you do that, it'll be more fun. Write me in for every category for both sexes. Class Flirts should be 'Boy—Penn Jillette,' 'Girl—Penn Jillette,' 'Class Clown—

Penn Jillette,' 'Best Athlete—Penn Jillette.' Please remember, they will try to bust us on technicalities so write it perfectly, 'P-E-N-N J-I-L-L-E-T-T-E' and make it legible. Please block print it, two N's, two L's, two T's—if you're disgusted with the school or just making a joke, write in my name. If we work together, we can make this funny. Please, nothing is funny but Penn Jillette."

The day of the vote, I used the school copy machine to print out and cut up many little slips of paper that said, "Vote Penn Jillette for everything—Nothing is funny but Penn Jillette." I tried to give the slips out to everyone, so they would have the spelling in front of them. I put full-page versions of my message on every public bulletin board—"Nothing is funny but Penn Jillette!"

I went to class to vote. There were a lot of categories and they were doubled with a choice for each gender. I took the page and I wrote my name in every space.

I hung around until the end of the day and then headed to the administration office where I figured the yearbook committee would be tallying the votes. I walked in to see the head of the yearbook committee crying. Good sign. The principal was standing over her, very angry. Even better sign. I walked in with a big smile, like the class clown, and I said, "Which do you think is funnier, taking a different picture of every category, some of them in drag, or is it funnier to take one picture and just repeat it dozens of times. I'm kind of leaning toward the one picture over and over. That's also a lot less work."

The principal said, "Get out of here, Penn. We won't be having class personalities."

"But you wanted a vote and you had a vote. You can't ignore it. You went against the wishes of the people, and the people won. You must do this. It's only fair." I said that like somebody "Most Likely to Succeed."

"Don't push it. Get out of here now."

"How much did I win by?"

"Get out of here."

"What percentage did I get? Did I win by a lot?" He started walking toward me, and like the "Class Coward" I was, I ran away.

If they keep giving us two evils from two identical parties from which to "choose" our president of the United States, couldn't we just do "Nothing is funny but Penn Jillette"?

Listening to: "High School"—MC5

Clown College

Penn Jillette, son of Mr. and Mrs. Sam Jillette of 48 Place Terrace, has been accepted at Ringling Bros. Clown College of Venice, Fla. where he will major in entertainment.

Jillette is a 1973 Greenfield High School graduate where he was a member of the band and participated in two senior plays. He received the National Merit Award and was active in community talent shows and the First Congregational Youth Group.

Unibikes, Yet!

Doing their unusual act, juggling balls while riding unibikes, are (l to r) Mike Moschen, 14, Penn Jillette, 14, and Colin Moschen, 15. They take their act to nursing homes, churches and to the jail. Sunday, they rode the bikes 15 miles to Lake Wyola and back to Place Terrace, Greenfield, where they live — just to sharpen their coordination, they said. Their benefit shows are put on free of charge. —Recorder Photo by Blake.

"VISSI D'ARTE" EVEN ON *THE* CELEBRITY APPRENTICE

I FIRST SAW THE WHO ON TV. I was watching with my parents, and when Pete, Roger, and Keith started smashing their instruments, we were appalled. We were just barely middle class. My dad was a jail guard and we lived in a nice, neat little house that my parents had built with their own hands. I loved music and I had a newspaper route, and I mowed lawns. I took drum lessons using a practice pad and was saving all my money to buy a used drum set so I could join a rock-and-roll band. At my rate of earning, it would have taken me decades to afford Keith Moon's drum set and I didn't understand how he could destroy it on TV. How could Keith do that? How could he have such little respect for music, for the TV show he was fortunate enough to be on, and for me and my family? My parents didn't like the music or the act, but they still tried to console me. These rich rock stars just didn't understand what money meant to us common folk. Then in a flash everything changed. I started to cry. Right then something happened and I understood The Who. I understood that passion and art could be more important than money. I went from sad and disgusted to exuberant. It was the first time I had ever understood real beauty. I loved The Who. I loved rock and roll. I loved life. It was at that moment I became an artist.

I use Teller's broad definition of art: "Whatever we do after the chores are done." There's one show business and Bach, Dylan, Ron Jeremy, and the guy at the mall in the Santa suit are all in it. By that definition *The Celebrity Apprentice* is art, and for my sins, I was on it.

I've done a lot of TV, but one of my proudest moments in my career was shown on *The Celebrity Apprentice*. I didn't watch it, I don't know how it was edited, but I was there and it was beautiful. *The Celebrity Apprentice* is all about watching people argue and lie while they covet money and success. Those are the artistic ideas. Donald Trump scowls and passes judgment and we all suck up and rat out to win more time on TV and get money for our charities. The theme song is the O'Jays' "For the Love of Money," used as awkwardly as "Born in the U.S.A." at a political rally.

Some of the "tasks" on the show are measured by money, so if you convince a rich famous person to buy a sandwich for ten grand, you have a better chance of winning. I've been a fan of and friends with Blue Man Group since we were all working in NYC. They make my heart soar. They make me proud to work in the arts. They are the best of us. They've also got some money, so I called them, told them I was doing this TV show and did they want to donate some money to charity? They said yes before finding out what charity or how much I wanted because Blue Man Group is like that. They do charity all the time. They really deeply care about people and they do a lot for many charities. *TCA* is not the most likely show to have something beautiful happen, but the Blue Man Group can make beautiful anywhere. They are the best of us.

BMG asked if I wanted them to show up and do something. Oh yes, please. After weeks of sitting on boardroom sets pretending to do business, I really wanted something beautiful.

"Can you deliver the money in a fun way?" I asked them.

That was the problem. In the Blue Man Group world, money doesn't exist. To the Blue Man Group, money means nothing. The ideals that they've established in their art don't include avarice. The Blue Man Group donates tons of money out of the blue makeup, but in it, well, they're not above money, but they're beside it. It doesn't exist. They asked me to give them some time to think of something beautiful. A couple days later they sent me a video of them filling a balloon with thousands of ten-dollar bills and blowing it up with a leaf blower. It was beautiful and it delivered money, without the Blue Man Group having to respect it. It was so beautiful.

I really wanted to save their appearance and money for "my task" and my charity (Opportunity Village, for people with intellectual disabilities, a charity that BMG helps a lot), but I was on Dee Snider's team and he asked me to help raise more money on his watch. I ran the idea by all our team members, the production company, and NBC. Everyone signed off. Blue Man Group would march up, with a loud parade and giant puppets and they would blow up a balloon full of money with leaf blowers and fill the air with ten-dollar bills that the Blue Men wouldn't care about. Whatever our team could gather out of the wind, we would have to score for our team. Teller would join BMG and add thirty grand of his own money, not blown around, but handed politely to our cashier, American Idol Clay Aiken. Clay took *The Celebrity Apprentice* very seriously and played the game for all it was worth.

We were outside selling our bullshit little jive guidebooks (the sandwich of the week). I gave the signal, and from blocks away we could hear the parade. BMG with their giant drums and confetti cannons were changing traffic patterns in NYC. They arrived at the park where we were set up to sell our guidebooks. My business partner for my entire adult life, Teller, was in the parade, firing streamers into the air and dancing. Teller had the eyes of Keith Moon in The Who. I had been sequestered on *The Celebrity Apprentice* with all the complaining, backstabbing and phony heart-to-heart talks, and down the street came joy. Pure joy. Honest human joy personified by Teller and Blue Man Group. I started to cry.

They got to our stand, they exploded the balloon full of cash, and suddenly the air across from Madison Square Park in New York City was filled with money. Blue Man Group stayed in character and just enjoyed blowing the money around. Their joy was more important than the money or us winning our game. They were there for art and to help the cause, in that order. We all scrambled to pick up as much money as we could. Paul Sr., the reality star from *Orange County Choppers*, and Lou Ferrigno held people back, while Dee, Arsenio, Clay, and I tried to grab all we could. Everyone had been prepared for the money balloon exploding, but for some reason Clay was surprised and disgusted by the chaos. I was still crying with joy, and Clay was crying with pure hate and anger toward me and my blue buddies.

Some of the camerapeople, the producers, the sound people and crew ran up after the Blue Men had gone and said they had never been prouder of anything they worked on. Some of them were crying with me with joy. It made them remember why they had gotten into the arts. It was like being just a few feet from The Who while they smashed their instruments for America. They proved that art meant more than money. I'm pretty proud of Penn & Teller—we've done some pretty groovy stuff—but I was exploding with pride at the beauty of Blue Man Group.

When we had the first break from the cameras, Clay was gathering evidence to take me down for this in the boardroom. He was angry and detailing the humiliation and the injuries he endured in all the beautiful chaos. He was very vague about the injuries. When I asked him if he needed medical attention, he made sure the cameras weren't on and screamed, "I need you to shut the fuck up!" It was so easy to shut the fuck up right then. Teller and Blue Man Group work without words and they had said more than I could ever say in defense of art. I drifted away in the NBC van, to my childhood and the moment with The Who when I understood that I needed my life to mean more than "Money, Money, Money, Money."

The "boardroom" didn't matter. Clay lowballed the amount of money we were able to gather, but I didn't argue. Clay said that the Blue Man Group's money that Clay wanted to go to our TV charity had ended up going to some homeless people. Trump joined him, disgusted by the idea that some of the Blue Man Group's money might have gone to people who needed it instead of the people Donald Trump would get credit for giving it to who needed it. Trying to explain to Donald Trump that beauty and art can be more important than money is like trying to explain to Donald Trump that beauty and art can be more important than money. The "contest" was revealed to be very close (in terms of money, beauty wasn't discussed) and Donald Trump tried to make me say that I regretted what the Blue Man Group had done. Clay tried to get me to say that I should have gotten the Blue Man Group to be more responsible, and by that he meant, give us more money so he could win his game.

It was during this episode that Donald Trump understood that he didn't understand me, and feeling misunderstood by Donald Trump and Clay Aiken is its own kind of joy.

I thought about some family at home in a small town watching

THE FOURTH OF JULY

ALL THEATER, MOVIES, LITERATURE, AND ART can be broken down into any number of plots you want. Pick an integer and someone has broken all basic plots down to that number. You can even do that Joseph Campbell monomyth jive: "A hero ventures forth from the world of common day into a region of supernatural wonder: fabulous forces are there encountered and a decisive victory is won: the hero comes back from this mysterious adventure with the power to bestow boons on his fellow man." That thinking gave us the New Testament and Star Wars, and a few good things too. Plots are either infinite, with every tiny detail changing the whole thing, or it all breaks down to one plot, and that one plot is always "Things happen." I watched the Joseph Campbell interviews and read *The Hero with a Thousand Faces* and all I could think of was the Bob Dylan line "At dawn my lover comes to me and tells me of her dreams, with no attempt to shovel the glimpse into the ditch of what each one means." Campbell spends all this time abstracting plots to meet his taxonomy, and then never gives us a hint of what it tells us about being human. He's really just saying, "things happen" and then labeling them anyway he wants.

Even the 1964 black-and-white silent movie *Empire* by Andy Warhol has things happen. It's just a single shot of the Empire State Building. They shot slightly over six hours of raw footage, then slowed down the film so it ran more than eight hours. The camera doesn't move, nothing really happens. Empire State Building window lights do go off and on, and during the three reel changes you can see Andy's reflection and the cinematographer's before they turn the lights out in the room they're shooting in. It breaks the fourth wall of, in this case, the Time-Life Building where the camera was set up. I loved Andy. His last on-camera appearance was in our Showtime movie *Invisible Thread*. The plot of our movie was that aliens came to earth and were going to destroy all humanity unless we could prove we were unique in the universe. Andy and a bunch of others were gathered to make the case for humanity, and P&T were brought in to entertain them while they waited. After everyone else failed, we, in our cheesy way, tried to snow the aliens with a trick claiming we were using "invisible thread," and that was unique. The aliens realized that nowhere in the universe were there creatures who would lie about something that stupid, so Penn & Teller saved the world. I sat in our greenroom area while Amazing Randi told Andy that he shouldn't trust crystals but should go to a real doctor. I thought Randi was pushing pretty hard against an eccentric genius on an issue that didn't really matter. If Randi had pushed harder and if the rest of us had supported Randi, if we hadn't respected Andy's nutty ideas so much, would Andy have lived longer? No way of knowing.

Andy was certainly a hero and had several faces of his own, most of them wig-wearing ones. He certainly ventured forth from Pittsburgh, the world of common day, into a region of supernatural wonder, Manhattan in the sixties. Fabulous forces were certainly encountered and Andy won many a decisive victory—producing the Velvet Underground's record against record company wishes to name one stunning peripheral one. He came back from this mysterious adventure to have the Andy Warhol Museum built after his death (should we have pushed with Randi more?), in Pittsburgh and that sure is a boon to his fellow men and women. Joseph Campbell's jive is an example of this: if something explains everything, it explains nothing. If a disease has too many mysterious symptoms, it's probably not a real disease.

Stage magic is the idiot little brother of real theater, and there is also one mono-plot in stage magic: A loser without friends in the world of common day discovers there is no supernatural wonder, but he's willing to lie about that. Mundane forces, like needing to get a job, are encountered and he grows out of it. If our loser sticks with magic past adolescence, the loser stays in his little dream world, playing shitty gigs and annoying women.

That's the one plot, but there are a few basic effects actions in stage magic:

Animation—inanimate object moving, or a person levitating

Production—making something appear

Vanish—guess

Transformation—something turns into something else

Penetration—something goes into something else, sexy by definition

Teleportation—moving an object to impossible location

Escape—get out of something

Prediction—you'll figure it out

Restoration—you fuck something up and magically fix it

A transformation is really just a vanish and an appearance of something else. A penetration is just a half vanish, followed by a half appearance. An escape is a vanish, and an appearance outside gimmicked chains and a box with a trapdoor. If you want to be a real asshole about it, and I always do, a vanish is just an appearance of empty space where something was. Everything is a production, but the list is still useful in organizing magic shows. We open our Penn & Teller show with an object in an impossible location: We borrow a cell phone from an audience member, vanish it, and it appears again inside a dead fish. Then we produce a lot of metal objects and a live person out of nowhere while adhering to the TSA red tape. Teller animates a ball; we transform one person into another; and we perform our "Bullet Catch": signed bullets appear in impossible locations— each other's mouths.

We have done a few restorations. We cut a live snake in half on *Saturday Night Live* and restored it. Lorne Michaels said we got more complaints then they had gotten on anything else ever. Some people wrote that they knew cutting a snake was a trick, but it "might give sick people ideas." Wow. Jamy Ian Swiss, a wonderful magician who's worked with us now and again, gave us an idea. He said that the burned and destroyed handkerchief trick was a fine technical trick, but didn't mean anything. He said he thought that if we did it with an American flag, it would mean something. Jamy gave sick people an idea.

At the turn of this century, Teller and I had just come back from doing a series of shows where we explored street magic in Egypt, China and India. The idea for the show, which came from our Canadian producers, was that we'd see "real magicians" in these countries—magicians who performed for locals and not the posers who performed for tourists. This put us in Sally Struthers hell. We weren't living the hell. We were fine. Although we got sick and miserable, we were in five-star hotels eating canned food. We brought tuna fish, crackers and bottled water with us, and that's all we ate. We had no complaints for ourselves, but we had a picture window on hell.

Magicians in India can be part of the "untouchable" caste, the Dalit, and we went, in our gray suits, to meet them in their slums in Shadipur. These slums were worse by far than those depicted in *Slumdog Millionaire*, and in contrast we were slumdog zillionaires. Holy fuck: polio, flies, raw sewage, tortured animals, leprosy, and we were asking to see the "Cups and Balls." The images in that day will live in my nightmares forever. Among the wretched magicians were also wretched puppet people, jugglers and animal trainers.

The animal trainers had fallen on hard times, so they had animals that they couldn't afford to tend to properly (if they ever could). There were emaciated monkeys and bears running around. The bears were the worst. I'm not a pet guy. Maybe I care too much *about* animals to be a pet guy, I don't know, but I don't like to have them sucking up to me. I like them at a distance. I have a lot of empathy and compassion for animals, but I don't like them being put above people. I hate when the dog is okay in a disaster movie and everyone cheers. Who cares about dogs during a disaster? But the bears in Shadipur still suffer in my nightmares. The bears were starving; you could see their bear ribs. They wore collars, or maybe rings through their noses. I didn't want to look closely enough and I don't really want to remember. They were chained to the ground, on a short chain that didn't allow them to stand up. It wasn't that they couldn't stand up on their rear legs like stuffed bears frozen in attack mode at a natural history museum or circus bears wearing hats; they couldn't even stand up on all fours. They couldn't straighten their legs or their necks. They were perpetually bent over. It's hard to read that, but imagine seeing it live, all around. We couldn't complain to the owners, because the owners were starving, so who cares about the fucking bears? My nightmares do.

My old friend Wheeler is a geologist. Geologists are always the first to die in fifties and sixties monster movies. In movies, it's a very dangerous profession. In reality, the biggest danger to geologists is bears. Wheeler put himself through college as a male stripper. I named him "Mark St. Helens" after the volcano that was active at that time and he made a lot of money adding cock value to a can of whipped cream. One summer Wheels kept his clothes on, took a pay cut, and worked for the U.S. Geological Survey. He was assigned to Alaska. A bunch of college students walking around in the wilderness of Alaska have to be ready for bears. They all carried .44 Magnums. Wheeler sent me a copy of the booklet he'd gotten on how to avoid being eaten by a bear. They were instructed to keep making noise, taking turns talking and singing. Wheeler is from New Jersey, so he sang Springsteen. They were told that bears didn't want to attack people, but that bears were very nearsighted so they would run at a person to find out what they were. The tasty ex-stripper college students were told to point the .44 Magnums right at the bear's heart, stand straight up facing the bear and to talk loudly, so the bear could identify them as people and not rivals. The pamphlet said that when people are attacked by a bear while they're shitting themselves, they often can't think of anything to say, so everyone was advised to memorize something and practice saying it while holding the gun out. When the real bear situation showed up, you'd have your routine all rehearsed. Since I had given Wheeler his stripper name, he figured I was his word man and could write him something. Let's see: You're holding a .44 Magnum pointed at a bear and you have to talk. I bet you guessed what I suggested:

"I know what you're thinking, bear. 'Did he fire six shots or only five?' Well, to tell you the truth, bear, in all this excitement I kind of lost track myself. But being as this is a .44 Magnum, the most power-ful handgun in the world, and would blow a bear's head clean off, you've got to ask yourself one question: Do I feel lucky? Well, do ya, bear?"

The untouchable bears of Shadipur were no physical threat to me, but they did damage to my heart. There Penn & Teller were, wearing our matching gray suits—flies covering our faces, our boots in sewage, suffering children and tortured bears at our feet, pouring bottles of Purell on our hands more like Lady Macbeths of shit— doing a Canadian comedy show. Teller thought some of the magic in India was okay, he was happy seeing some mango tree thing and some diving duck, but I can't remember one pleasant moment. The TV show came out okay—and you think *The Celebrity Apprentice* has fanciful editing. At the time we were there, they were still throwing widows on their husbands' funeral pyres, and it was the bears that freaked me.

Egypt was no better. The women dress like Batman, and the air was so dirty I felt like I was chain-smoking Camel Straights. I felt like a fucking bear. We went to see the pyramids. The Pizza Hut right near the Sphinx disgusted the Canadian crew, but the pizza smelled like freedom to me. When we went to see the thousands-of-years-old wall paintings of the "Cups and Balls" in a cave, we were escorted by soldiers with machine guns. This is comedy.

In China we were a couple hundred klicks out of Beijing. We vis-ited a village where our translator told us we were the first Ameri-cans they'd ever seen. At 6'7" and 3 bucks, I'm big in the USA, but in China I was supernatural. They screamed when they saw me. They asked if I was Michael Jordan. It was freezing cold. We went to a magic and circus school. It was like an old Albert Brooks routine of people learning comedy spit takes. They were all being taught the exact same linking rings routine. The big artistic cultural difference was how they dealt with originality. Any magician who had come up with some little change or wrinkle to a classic routine would pretend that the wrinkle went back centuries. He would lie and say he was just doing what his teachers had taught him. We're American magicians and we want to take individual credit for everything. If Teller and I could convince you that we invented the idea of playing cards, we would.

Near Wuqiao there was a magic theme park, but it was all gray and cold. It was housed in a huge stadium-like building, with no color and no heat. It was the middle of the winter, and even indoors, in these big, cavernous rooms, we could see our breath. There were freezing performing area caves and no patrons. No one was there but our crew carrying in video equipment and the Chinese performers, in skimpy costumes huddled together for warmth in broom closets. These caves were theme rooms, like cheesy honeymoon suites for honeymoon couples being punished for capital offenses. The performers would come in, in spandex and top hats, play "Puttin' on the Ritz" on a tiny boom box and do back-palming card productions and vanishes with frozen fingers in the cold dark in front of a painted skyline of New York City. Those Indian bears didn't have it that bad. It felt like the result of some sort of central planning that hadn't quite planned for nobody wanting to see back-palming in the dark, in the winter, in the geographical center of nowhere. What the fuck were we doing?

Because of China's centrally planned one-child policy, infant girls were being abandoned and the ones who won the lottery were being delivered into American families. So our fancy-ass hotel was full of

American couples waiting for an adopted daughter for their family. Lots of strollers and diaper bags. The unwanted infant girls might be raised as Christians or yuppies, but it was better than being left to die in China. With the Indian women on the funeral pyres, the Egyptian women dressed like Batman, and the poor little Chinese girls, Teller and I were cracking. We just couldn't get over how wrong all of this was. We would rant about it in our warm, comfortable bus to our female Canadian boss. And these particular Canadians, these kinda PBS Canadians, dismissed us by saying we were "typical Americans." We didn't understand cultural differences. The same women who would rant about the sexism of *Baywatch* were telling us to try to understand why abandoning infant girls was okay. They put a Canadian flag up in the windows of our bus so that the locals wouldn't think we were Americans. We weren't ashamed of being Americans, but they were ashamed of us being Americans.

Our young translator had lived his life equally in Beijing and Toronto. We had a lot of time to talk on the bus. He explained that the word they were using for Caucasians was a pejorative, kind of a translation of "white devils." I said, "So, they're that racist?" He explained that it wasn't racism, that it was racial pride. So, the KKK has racial pride? Nope, that was different, and an American couldn't understand what it was like to be proud of your race without being racist. I said, "Yeah, we're racist in the USA, there's no doubt about that, but we're working on it. We really are." I proposed an experiment. I suggested that he get twenty randomly selected Caucasian Americans together and invite them all out to supper with me at a T.G.I. Friday's, or someplace that the world thinks is just too American. I said that I would tell a story about—let's make it really awful— driving, and I would say that a "chink" cut me off in traffic. I was willing to bet him a large amount of money, and a larger amount of pride, that someone in our randomly selected group of Americans would either take issue with that racist word right there, or would take me aside later and say they didn't appreciate it. They'd make it a teachable moment. They would bust my ass.

I wanted to make sure that the bet included people talking to me in private later. Sacha Baron Cohen, a brilliant comedian and an amazing actor, claimed in a rare interview as himself that his Borat character illuminated the anti-Semitism of Americans because those who weren't plants (or as some TV magicians call them, "friendlies") didn't bust his foreign character on his outrageous attacks. I don't believe it proved any such thing. I think it proved how far human beings from anywhere would bend over and spread them to make someone from another country seem a little less awkward. Penn & Teller would fall for any of Sacha's gags. Once, a couple of young Japanese women came to Vegas because, we were told, they were big Penn & Teller fans. High school–aged Japanese women are not our usual demographic, but they had a camera crew and they claimed they had won a contest or something. They interviewed us backstage and had us do a little trick for them. They gave us ornate fans and hats and said stuff that just confused the fuck out of us. We played along with everything. If they had had us say that Jesus was our lord (and they might have, I was just repeating Japanese words that we didn't understand), we would have gone along with it, just to make it a little more comfortable. We weren't thinking about what we were saying; we were trying to make them feel comfortable in our country. That's all *Borat* documented, but it sure was funny.

So at the T.G.I. Friday's, when the test "chink" was thrown out, I'd want our subjects to be able to take me aside in private afterward to express their concerns. Our translator agreed that Americans would bust one another. I then asked if twenty Chinese people chosen at random to go to . . . Panda Express (see, that's a joke about Americans not knowing anything about China, it's not a racist joke) and hearing "white devil" would object in public or private. He said no way. It was racial pride. But Americans were racist even though they were trying not to be. I was sitting next to my friend Sarah Silverman when she used the word "chink" on Conan's show. It was a joke, and the joke, considering Sarah's character, was not racist at all, but everyone still ripped another asshole into her very attractive ass. Our Canadian producers would probably think that that comment on Sarah's ass is sexist, but the abandoning of infant girls in China was a cultural difference that typical Americans didn't understand. I've got your cultural differences hanging ready to knock you out with my American thighs.

The trips to Egypt, China and India each took a little over two weeks. Teller and I were so uncomfortable. I'm embarrassed by us eating canned food and washing our hands every ten minutes. We were so scared of these foreign countries. The people we were working with weren't. They had done documentaries on Ebola and had gone into hot zones to shoot. They said Penn & Teller were more of a pain in the ass than Ebola. I tried to get some women to dance topless for us in China, and I ended up uncovering some sort of Chinese-Russian prostitution slavery ring that the Canadians did their next documentary on. If there was something about other countries to not be understood, I think I'm the man to not understand it. It was an awful time for me. While I was watching all this misery, my mom was dying back home and I felt alone and cut loose in the world. I was not at my best. I was confused enough that maybe if there really was a difference between racial pride and racism, I couldn't understand it. I couldn't learn to say even one sentence in Mandarin and I tried.

We came back from overseas in time for my mom to die. What a treat. World travel was supposed to broaden us, give us more understanding of the world, but it didn't feel that way. I couldn't stop thinking about the hotel full of Americans adopting baby girls, the women dressed like Batman, the stinking poverty, and those fucking tortured bears. It felt like our country of stupid fucking situation comedies and Dunkin' Donuts was a paradise island floating in a nightmare world.

That's when we decided to burn the American flag. We wrote a bit for the live show in Vegas that we call "Flag" or "Flag Burning." The idea was that we'd take the American flag down from a flagpole fold it properly, wrap it in the Bill of Rights and then burn it. Then we'd restore it. Then we'd show how the trick was done. We'd do the trick again with what we call the Chinese Bill of Rights (clear acetate with nothing on it). We'd show how the flag was switched out and it was flash paper that was burned. We'd end with vanishing the flag in another burst of fire while I recited a verse from "The Star-Spangled Banner." We'd end with the flag magically appearing back on the flagpole. We found the only verse of "The Star-Spangled Banner" that didn't mention god, and even though it was pretty pro-war, we used that.

When we were working on the flag burning, our crew became pretty freaked out. They had not signed up to be part of a show that burned the flag. I told them that the patter was all about the Bill of Rights and freedom, and it was going to be patriotic. I was on G. Gordon Liddy's radio show and I told Gordon that we were going to burn a flag and he was going to cheer. He attended our show and he did cheer the flag. I'm not sure that Liddy is our best example of a patriot, but at least he thinks he is. Our crew was proud.

Then the terrorist attacks happened on September 11, 2001, and all of a sudden our burning of the flag got much *too* patriotic for our taste. The burning of the flag was ignored and all of a sudden the trick was just waving the flag. This bit that was supposed to be about our complicated reaction to being American overseas became this rah-rah-rah pro-American thing. It was getting the biggest reaction in our show, but it wasn't the right reaction. There was too much applause and cheering. We were afraid maybe they weren't cheering for our ideas; maybe they were just cheering for the flag. What had we become? We cut it from our show for a while.

Things calmed down and we put "Flag Burning" back in. At the time, Lawrence O'Donnell was writing for that liberal-porn show *The West Wing*. He loved our flag burning and asked to use it as the B story on an episode. We did it. We played our real selves and did the trick in their fake White House. The story was about some controversy around the president burning the flag, and we gave some of my lines from the bit to Martin Sheen, the pornographically liberal president. People seemed to love it, and then they started saying it was nice of *The West Wing* writers to let us use that bit in our live show. That's socialism, I guess.

We've been doing the "Flag Burning" since the end of the last century. We've settled into it. People don't just cheer for the flag anymore, and they gasp a little when we first burn the flag. Our audience seems to understand it. But I don't know if I really understand it anymore.

It celebrates the First Amendment. It's about the enjoyment and privilege of living in a country where we can burn the flag in protest. I get that part. Part of my patter while we perform the trick includes me saying that Teller and I consider ourselves patriotic. When we wrote that, it was true, but I don't know if it is anymore.

One of the things I love about the USA is that it's built on an idea.

Other countries were built on everyone having the same heritage, the same ancestry, but this country was built by neophiles who wanted to get away. Wanted to live an idea. No matter how long you live in Italy, you're not really Italian, but once you become a U.S. citizen, you're an American. I've talked a lot about how the USA was the first country built on technology. The idea of freedom of the press is based on the printing press, freedom of speech and freedom of and from religion. All that is groovy, but . . .

Every Fourth of July I worry. I worry that we're just a sports team. I worry that I'm American not because I love the ideas, but because of an accident of birth. I hate clubs. I'm not a joiner. I've played on the same team with Teller for my entire adult life, but I'm not a team player. I never wanted to be part of a team; I wanted to work with Teller. There's a difference. Just like I never wanted to do a Broadway show or a Vegas show—I wanted to do our show. Venue never matters to me.

I can sit and tell you all the things I love about this country. I carry the Bill of Rights with me. It's called the "Security Edition" and it's the Bill of Rights printed on a piece of metal. We give them out at our show. They are designed to set off metal detectors. It turns anyone who has a "Security Edition" into a freedom-fighting performance artist. It sets off the metal detector and then you look the TSA person in the eye and say, "Here, take my rights" and hand them the metal Bill of Rights. I've had a lot taken away from me, but I always replace it so I have those words with me. But I didn't move here because I believed in the ideals of this country. I didn't move here at all. I was born down in this dead man's town; I was born in the USA. Born in the USA. When the real patriots broke from England, there were real philosophical reasons, but would I agree with them now? If England had won our revolutionary war, would they have freed all the slaves? We won a war that was, among many other things, a war to keep slavery. I believe in the free market, but there's no free market here. We have government entitlements on one side and crony capitalism on the other; it's all just using the government to move money around. We wouldn't know a real free market if the lowest bidder bit us in our ass. There's no real separation of church and state. Obama brags that he prays about the decisions he makes in the White House. We have bloody wars against common nouns—drugs, poverty and terrorism.

I imagine two asshole Indian magicians coming to the USA to see the magic done for locals. I imagine them staying in five-star hotels and going to our worst slums, looking for the "Cups and Balls" in Appalachia. I don't even know where the worst poverty in the USA is, but it's certainly in every city. I just don't go there. I think about some smart-ass who can't pronounce the word "hello" after a week of practice in his bus, freaking out that we still have the death penalty and kill people who kill. I think about the culture shock of walking into a casino where we do our shows and seeing people pissing in their pants while waiting for the slot machine to pay off and get them back to even. I think about our Indian Penn & Teller pouring sanitizer over their hands and eating canned curry (I know that's an English invention, and just makes my point even stronger). I go back and read what I wrote about Egypt, China and India, and it sure seems like it was written by an asshole. Maybe the Canadian producers were right about Americans not understanding. Maybe there is a difference between racial pride and racism, which I just can't see. Maybe I am a white devil.

Richard Dawkins makes the argument that if religion were true, it wouldn't be geographically determined. People tend to follow the religion they were born into. That's not true of scientific theories.

There never really were speed-of-light pockets. I hear Christians make arguments for how Christianity is true, but it's hard not to just hear them saying that they believe it because they were born into it.

When we do our bit that turns flag burning into flag waving, what are we really celebrating? When I take my children to eat hot dogs and hamburgers and watch the fireworks, what do I teach them about the country of their birth? Is it just their birthplace, or did they just happen to be born into a really good idea.

I don't know.

Maybe we're just celebrating that we don't have those fucking bears.

Listening to: "Born in the U.S.A."—Bruce Springsteen

MY SON'S MORALITY DOES NOT COME FROM GOD

THERE WAS A BIG ATHEIST SHINDIG IN WASHINGTON, D.C., IN 2011. There were about 20,000 people on the mall getting together in the rain to be recognized as atheists. I wanted to be there, but I was contracted to do a magic show in Vegas that day. I couldn't get there, but I sent a video and made a few jokes.

Atheists will not have their Stonewall riots. Unfortunately, gays needed to riot. There were draconian laws preventing them from just living their lives. They were attacked and beaten. They were killed. They are still oppressed by the government. Obama "evolved" to the point that he thinks he feels okay about people loving one another, but not okay enough to help them get the freedom to do that. There are comparisons between gays in the sixties and atheists today, but we have to be careful not to exaggerate those comparisons. Yes, gays and atheists are pitied, shunned and insulted. There are some awful stories of atheists being beaten up in the USA, but I think many fewer than gays. Twentieth-century atheist pioneer Madalyn Murray

O'Hair was put on the cover of *Life* magazine as "The Most Hated Woman in America." Ms. O'Hair's family was beaten and some very bad things happened to her directly as a result of her lack of belief. It's possible the worst things that happened to Madalyn (kidnapping and murder) had nothing to do with her atheism, but she might have gotten more help if she had been a believer. Atheists lose jobs and too often lose the love of their whole families when they come out of that huge benighted closet.

I'm afraid that the main reason I'm proud to be an American is that I was born here. That's the way that our tribal shit is wired, and it's hard to fight. But there are things I like about the USA apart from the built-in patriotism. I love "Yankee Doodle." I love that the British made up a song to make fun of the American rubes with their bad wigs and bumpkin ways, and the asshole Americans adopted it as their fight song and sang it while kicking ass. One of the most successful businesses in my hometown area of Massachusetts is Yankee Candle, and there are books of Yankee wisdom in all the gift shops. "Yankee" began as an insult for all Americans and ended up an insult for New Englanders, but we all use it with pride.

I'm a little bummed by the word "gay" for gay. If I had been in charge of the gay movement they would have done it more "Yankee Doodle" style. Of course if I were in charge of the gay movement, we'd be listening to Sun Ra instead of Lady Gaga and we'd have way worse haircuts.

If I had my way, we would be using "queer" (not "fag" because it excludes women) or even "homo." I love when those words are used with pride. Let them name you with hate, and come back with love. I'd be a homosexual infidel before I'd be a gay bright. I gave a very small amount of jingle to the "brights." They were trying to find a term to make atheists a more marketable brand. "Bright" seems as good as "gay," but it didn't catch on. You can argue that "gay" doesn't really work either. "Gay" is now used as a negative term that doesn't quite mean "homosexual" but is close enough to be creepy and bum my shit. "Atheist" is like "homosexual" and I like that more. It's the term I like the most. I way don't like any of the "humanist" names for atheists; it's like if gays tried to pretend that sex wasn't really part of who they are. We atheists don't only love humans, we also don't want religion. I would love to adopt "heathen" or "infidel" and say them with pride. I'd love to call myself a "Yankee Heathen," more than an "American Bright." But "heathen" and "infidel" in this country are a little too goofy.

Madalyn Murray O'Hair went with "American Atheist," so I'll go with her. O'Hair sure was nutty, but I'm okay with her as our leader. Atheists have always been a little ahead of the curve on feminism. In a list of the superstars of modern atheism, you have Ayn Rand, Madalyn Murray O'Hair, and Ayaan Hirsi Ali right at the top. So much of the oppression of women comes from religion, so that shouldn't be a surprise, but it's still something we godless heathen infidels can be proud of.

My son was born May 22, 2006. Since the birth of my Moxie and Zz, it takes all my willpower to write and talk about anything other than my children. Every word they speak, everything they do, seems to cry out to be recorded and shared, but I try to leave my camera and my notes in another room. An unexamined life is not worth living, but an electronically recorded life is not lived at all.

Zolten Penn Jillette took his first steps walking toward the porn star Nina Hartley. She was visiting our home and Zz was just under a year old. His standing was still wobbly, but as Nina and I sat talking on the couch, Zz pulled himself up and toddled over to her arms. When Moxie was one, Bob Dylan let her bang on his keyboard and lick his guitar. Our children have privileged lives.

When Zz was about two, he was playing by himself one day as I sat on the other side of the room, reading or something. I don't know where Mox was. Because our children are eleven months apart and best friends (for now), they're always together, but for some reason Mox and Emily were out of the room. At least that's the way I remember it now. It's possible I wasn't even there and my wife witnessed it and told me about it, but when I hear a great story, my memory often puts me in the middle of the scene.

The way I remember it, Zz was playing quietly by himself and I was reading on the other side of the room. He was oblivious to me. He tried to grab something with his teeth and instead must have bitten his own arm. There are coordination issues at that age. Zz's bite hurt him a little. He made a distress sound, which got my attention and then he said to himself, "No biting. Time-out." He put down the toys, stopped playing and walked across the room. He stood, sadly and quietly, in the corner for a couple of minutes and then said, "Okay," walked back to the center of the room, got happy, picked up his toys and went back to playing.

My son was perpetrator, victim, witness, police, prosecutor, jury, judge, jailer, parole board, and rehabilitated citizen. He had learned the lesson of not biting. He didn't need me, and he certainly didn't need any god. Zolten's morality gets more sophisticated every day, but it doesn't need to. He was pretty much there at two years old. He had the basic principles in place. Don't cause pain.

I'd like to say this story is evidence that my son is a moral genius, but I don't believe that. I believe he's a normal child (yeah, most children take their first steps into the arms of a porn star), and all normal children understand the moral code at an early age. Children are cruel, children are violent, children have no patience, children are moody, and children can't seem to understand that sneaking under Daddy's desk when he's lost in thought while writing his book and grabbing his feet is going to scare the living shit out of him. Maybe they do understand that last one. Children have a lot of work to do on impulse control, but morality takes its place early on. There are studies about normal children knowing the moral difference between a teacher saying it's okay to stand up during circle time and a teacher saying it's okay to lie and hit. They know the teacher can't turn something that is morally wrong into something right by just saying it. They understand that right and wrong are separate from authority.

Years ago, I brought a date to hear an atheist speaker (I knew how to pitch the old woo, huh?), and during the Q&A a stranger sitting next to us stood up with a question, "If there's no god, what's stopping us from just raping and killing all we want?" Before the speaker onstage could give his answer, my date raised her hand, stood up and asked, "Quick question: may I change my seat please?" She got a huge laugh and had made the philosophic argument perfectly. If you rape and kill, people will move away from you. That's all.

I do rape and kill all I want. The amount I want to rape and kill is zero. I completely condone murder fantasies—there are no thought police—but I don't have those thoughts myself. "Didn't you want to punch Clay Aiken in the face?" Nope. Not once. I just wanted to get back to my real business partner, Teller, and back to my real team, my family. When I'm pissed off at people, I have no desire to kill them or even hurt them. I don't even want to yell at them. I don't want to talk to them. I just want to get away from them. Whether rape is a crime of hate or a crime of sex, it doesn't ever cross my mind. I don't want to fuck when I'm angry, and there's nothing sexy to me about someone who is not attracted to me. I take it as sexual rejection if my wife pauses for a moment to pull back her hair before she kisses me. We have sickening evidence that not everyone feels the same way about rape and murder, but I believe my lack of desire for violence is typical. Many religious people seem to think that it's nothing but faith that stops them from committing three-state killing sprees with a side of forced sodomy.

It's not fair to say all Christians are murdering rapists being held back by fear of hell, or desire for heaven, but as unfair as it is, it's bothersome how many Christians lead with it. The argument that the only reason you're not killing and raping me is that your magic book teaches you not to is not reassuring, and I don't think it's even true. Christians defend the insanity of the Bible by saying how good, kind and peaceful Jesus was in the New Testament, even though he negates none of the Old Testament's horrors. What do they mean by "good" about Jesus anyway? If all morality comes from god, isn't all of the Old Testament's genocide, slavery, rape, incest, torture, and ignorance good by definition? If all morality comes from god, what does it mean to believe "god is good"? Wouldn't that be a tautology? If Satan were to win the final battle (the spoiler says he doesn't), defeat god, and become the most powerful force in the universe, wouldn't he be our god? We'd meet the new boss, and he'd be the same as the old boss—good, by definition. Would we just replace the cross with heavy metal horns and start fucking our sisters' assholes on beds of goats' blood in the name of all that is unholy, while listening to Slayer? Wouldn't that be community service?

That's beyond flippant, but anyone who says god is good has made the argument that morality exists outside religion. Either that or they're saying "X = X" and there are quicker ways to say that. You can say that clearly by just shutting the fuck up.

If Zolten refrains from hitting Moxie when I'm watching, I don't consider that morality. Maybe he's hoping that I'll reward him if he doesn't and worried that I'll punish him if he does. He's right—if he hits his sister, he gets a time-out, except for that one time when she was being a real douche and Daddy turned a blind eye. (I'm a peacenik, but she was being such an asshole.) That's not morality. Morality is when they aren't being supervised and they get along without hitting. It's morality when Zz controls his temper from the inside because it's the right thing to do. That's morality outside god, and if there's morality without god, we don't need god for morality.

Richard Dawkins writes about morality in animals other than humans. Many religions say that only humans have a soul, and in claiming that, they can't attribute any non-human moral action to god. If monkeys are good and god is good, good means something other than god. Oh boy, the beginning of that sentence is so close to:

Monkeys = good
Good = god
Therefore:
Monkeys = god
And by the commutative property:
God = monkey
God is a monkey!

I came so fucking close to convincing myself to be a priest.

When I have just my 140 Twitter characters or a sound bite on Bill Maher, I've said things like, "Only atheists can be moral. If you're doing it for reward or to avoid punishment, it's not morality." That's 100 characters on the nose, which leaves you room for "@Penn Jillette" and the appositive "SexyBeast" and you still have room for a hashtag. Those 100 characters are provocative, but not completely fair. It's not only that atheists can have morality, it's that morality *is* atheist. We judge religion with our morality. We judge god with a morality that's outside god. Every person who talks about what a good man/teacher/god/superhero Jesus was is saying they know good outside Jesus. Here I'm talking about real morality, the not killing, not raping, not stealing morality. Some of the rules religion adds in, like kill gays and atheists, wear magic underwear, and don't eat certain stuff on certain days, is not morality. It's just nutty cult rules—like wearing peach and black to a Prince concert. Morality is outside religion. Morality is above religion. You must first have morality to say that god is good.

I didn't have to teach my son that hurting people is bad any more than I had to teach him to walk toward Nina Hartley. Those are just part of being human.

Listening to: "Beautiful Boy"—John Lennon

IT'S TODAY AND YOU'RE ALIVE— CELEBRATE!

THANKS

It might have been a mistake to tell my wife, Emily, that I felt that my editor, Sarah Hochman, understood me better than anyone in the world. I meant, you know, outside of my family. You know, professionally. I've made that clear now. It was Sarah's idea for this book— thanks, Sarah, and to all the Blue Rider and Penguin people. Thanks to my agent, Steve Fisher, for doing the wheeling and dealing. I would have written the book for free.

Robbie Libbon has been my dear friend for my entire adult life. He makes sure the Penn & Teller show goes up every night and he read this book over and over, gave a zillion suggestions and helped Sarah figure out what the fuck I was trying to write about and shared the burden of taking out all those commas. I think someone told me sometime that "but" was supposed to always have a comma after it. Fuck public schools.

Lana Strong is a buddy who's read all my other books a little too carefully, so I could send her each of these hunks and ask her if I'd written any of the stuff already in another book. I often can't tell what I think and say from what I write—she can.

I love Spicoli, but it's our co-manager, Peter Golden, who really has my heart.

Glenn Alai runs everything that Penn & Teller and/or Penn and/or Teller do. If he only had good-looking clients, he'd make Colonel Parker look like a slacker. Glenn can do anything. He could have written this book, but he was busy with other things.

I want to thank everyone who is mentioned in this book. Thanks for letting me in your lives. When that whole weird Chick-fil-A gay thang happened (remember that?), I called Clay Aiken and asked him if we could make out together at a Chick-fil-A near him. He laughed. That would have been a real photo op. Yup, I make fun of Clay, but you know . . . I like him. Same with Donald Trump. Well, not the same with Donald Trump. Nope, not exactly the same with Donald Trump—for the love of fuck, get rid of that birther shit—but keep the hair. I love stupid hair.

Teller—you all know, and he knows better.

I can sum up this whole book with three short names—EZ, Mox, and Zz. My family gives me the love and joy to make every day an atheist holiday. They taught me what it means to cry with happiness. I never understood that before these guys.

Bob sang, "It frightens me the awful truth of how sweet life can be."

EZ

Mox

Zz

They made me feel that. Love minus zero, no limit.